Northern Irish Writing
After the Troubles

New Horizons in Contemporary Writing

In the wake of unprecedented technological and social change, contemporary literature has evolved a dazzling array of new forms that traditional modes and terms of literary criticism have struggled to keep up with. *New Horizons in Contemporary Writing* presents cutting-edge research scholarship that provides new insights into this unique period of creative and critical transformation.

Series Editors:
Martin Eve and Bryan Cheyette

Editorial Board: Siân Adiseshiah (University of Lincoln, UK), Sara Blair (University of Michigan, USA), Peter Boxall (University of Sussex, UK), Robert Eaglestone (Royal Holloway, University of London, UK), Rita Felski (University of Virginia, USA), Rachael Gilmour (Queen Mary, University of London, UK), Caroline Levine (University of Wisconsin–Madison, USA), Roger Luckhurst (Birkbeck, University of London, UK), Adam Kelly (York University, UK), Antony Rowland (Manchester Metropolitan University, UK), John Schad (Lancaster University, UK), Pamela Thurschwell (University of Sussex, UK), Ted Underwood (University of Illinois at Urbana-Champaign, USA).

Volumes in the series:
Transatlantic Fictions of 9/11 and the War on Terror, Susana Araújo
Life Lines: Writing Transcultural Adoption, John McLeod
South African Literature's Russian Soul, Jeanne-Marie Jackson
The Politics of Jewishness in Contemporary World Literature, Isabelle Hesse
Writing After Postcolonialism: Francophone North African Literature in Transition, Jane Hiddleston
David Mitchell's Post-Secular World, Rose Harris-Birtill
New Media and the Transformation of Postmodern American Literature, Casey Michael Henry
Postcolonialism After World Literature, Lorna Burns
Jonathan Lethem and the Galaxy of Writing, Joseph Brooker
The Contemporary Post-Apocalyptic Novel, Diletta De Cristofaro
David Foster Wallace's Toxic Sexuality, Edward Jackson
Jeanette Winterson's Narratives of Desire, Shareena Z. Hamzah-Osbourne

Forthcoming volumes:
Thomas Pynchon and the Digital Humanities, Erik Ketzam
Music, Religion, and Society in the Writings of Ian McEwan: Creaturely Forms in Contemporary Literature, Dominic O'Key
Encyclopaedism and Totality in Contemporary Fiction, Kiron Ward

Northern Irish Writing After the Troubles

Intimacies, Affects, Pleasures

Caroline Magennis

BLOOMSBURY ACADEMIC
LONDON • NEW YORK • OXFORD • NEW DELHI • SYDNEY

BLOOMSBURY ACADEMIC
Bloomsbury Publishing Plc
50 Bedford Square, London, WC1B 3DP, UK
1385 Broadway, New York, NY 10018, USA
29 Earlsfort Terrace, Dublin 2, Ireland

BLOOMSBURY, BLOOMSBURY ACADEMIC and the Diana logo are trademarks of
Bloomsbury Publishing Plc

First published in Great Britain 2021

For legal purposes the Acknowledgements on pp. viii–x constitute an extension
of this copyright page.

Cover design by Eleanor Rose and Namkwan Cho
Cover images © Shutterstock

A catalogue record for this book is available from the British Library.

A catalog record for this book is available from the Library of Congress.

ISBN: HB: 978-1-3500-7472-9
ePDF: 978-1-3500-7473-6
eBook: 978-1-3500-7474-3

Series: New Horizons in Contemporary Writing

Typeset by Newgen KnowledgeWorks Pvt. Ltd., Chennai, India

To find out more about our authors and books visit www.bloomsbury.com
and sign up for our newsletters.

For all my wild women,
shameless hallions
and bad articles

Contents

Acknowledgements

It might be a cliché, but there truly is no such thing as a single-authored book. I am so grateful for the kindness and generosity of the people I have named below and also for anyone who has asked an interested question or offered their opinion in my classes or after a talk, over a pint or via social media. These brief exchanges have been my own 'small worlds of sustenance' when I thought no one really gave a damn about Northern Irish fiction.

During the course of writing this, I have worked with a fantastic group of colleagues and students at the University of Salford, and a lot of this book was written on a generously awarded sabbatical from the School of Arts and Media. My students, especially those who've taken Alternative Ulster, Modernism, or Theory, Text, Writing, have endlessly inspired me with their willingness to try new things and learn more about Irish writing. I'm also exceptionally grateful for conversations with my PhD students Amjad Al-Shalan, Sophie Anders and Katie Barnes, and to all the magnificent undergraduate and MA dissertation students that I have supervised. Your commitment and curiosity has been inspiring and helped me keep the faith in 2020.

Thanks to Martin Bull, Tracy Crossley, Karl Dayson, Iván García, Kirsty Fairclough, Tim France, Frances Piper, Maggie Scott, Scott Thurston and Allan Walker for supporting this research at Salford. A particularly special thanks must also go to my English at Salford brothers and sisters, particularly Jane Kilby, Jade Munslow Ong, Carson Bergstrom, Glyn White and Ursula Hurley for reading chunks of this manuscript during a pandemic. To Jade and Jane, especially, thanks for your endless encouragement when I was finishing up and only able to communicate in anxious emoji. Two biscuits or a swift half in the New Oxford is on me, if allowed when this book comes out.

I'd like to thank the event organizers and audiences who allowed me to test out my ideas – in particular, the organizers of Irish Seminars at Oxford, Cambridge, Queen's Belfast and Senate House and also the John Hewitt Society and Eastside Arts. Also, thanks to the Moore Institute at Galway for hosting me as a visiting fellow, organizing invaluable opportunities to share this work and to Dan Carey and my Fellow Fellows for the camaraderie. I am grateful to the editors of *Études Irlandaises* for allowing me to reprint a small portion of an article as the introduction to Chapter 2.

I've benefitted hugely from the kindness of academics in scholarly associations and organizations which have provided much needed solidarity and intellectual stimulation. Thank you to my colleagues on the executive bodies of the British Association for Irish Studies, the British Association for Contemporary Literary Studies, the European Federation of Associations and Centres of Irish Studies and the Higher Education Committee of the English Association, as well as the team at English Shared Futures.

I'd like to thank everyone at Bloomsbury: David Avital, Ben Doyle, Lucy Brown and Laura Cope at the publisher and the peer reviewers for their extremely helpful comments. Thanks to Martin Eve and Bryan Cheyette for their editorship of this series and encouragement of this project from the outset.

To the writers in this study – I've been stunned by your generosity towards me and this project, as I know academics can sometimes be an awful dose. Thanks to those who sent me unpublished material and to Lucy Caldwell, Jan Carson, Billy Cowan, Susannah Dickey, Wendy Erskine, Phil Harrison, Michael Hughes, Rosemary Jenkinson, Bernie McGill, Roisín O'Donnell, David Park and Glenn Patterson for their contributions to the appendix of this book. Thanks to Martin Doyle of the *Irish Times* and Damian Smyth of the Arts Council of Northern Ireland for their endless support in my mission to bring this writing to wider public attention. I cannot thank David Torrens and his team at No Alibis enough for filling my luggage with books on every trip home and their support of the writing community in Belfast.

To the following people who manage to balance rigour and kindness, I am forever in your debt for your encouragement of this project – Kate Adams, Éadaoin Agnew, Timothy Baker, Veronica Barnsley, Alex Beaumont, Stephanie Boland, Edward Bujak, Matthew Campbell, Sarah Campbell, Claire Connolly, Linda Connolly, Jennifer Cooke, Hillary Copeland, Eli Davies, Caroline Edwards, Deirdre Flynn, Alison Garden, Clare Gill, Adam Hanna, Thomas Hennessey, Seán Hewitt, Eamonn Hughes, Judy Kendall, Simon Kövesi, George Legg, Stefanie Lehner, Dan Lomas, Ali Matthews, Paul Maddern, Katie Markham, Fiona McCann, Shaun McDaid, Gerardine Meaney, Anne Mulhall, Lucia Nigri, Maureen O'Connor, Stephen O'Neill, Emilie Pine, Aida Rosende-Pérez, Katharina Rennhak, Sara Martín Ruiz, Charlotte Riley, Jo Scott, Derval Tubridy, Tom Walker, Aimée Walsh, Jack Wilson and Mark Yates.

I couldn't do a thing without a special quartet of friends who never fail to cheer me up or set me right: Claire Lynch, Sarah Roddy, Maggie Scull and Chris Vardy. Between reading drafts, offering advice and your endless kindness, you've gone above and beyond. I also have to wish all my love to Katie Lowe, my best woman, for providing a rare kind of kinship that enhances my life every day.

Thank you to my wonderful family, Catherine and Nicholas Bell, for their many and varied kindnesses. To know that I can always come home to you means more than I can say. I am also grateful to the Barnes/Ryan family for treating me like one of their own, especially Di for taking such a sustained interest in my work.

And, finally, all my appreciation and love to Edward Ryan for everything, every day. Always a pleasure, never a chore.

Intimacies, affects, pleasures: An introduction

This book is preoccupied with a central question – what does it mean to pay attention to the representation of the body, intimacy and pleasure in Northern Irish writing? It is a question that I have been interested in for many years, for intertwining personal and political reasons. I am the owner-occupier of a Northern Irish body and will not claim to be anything other than heavily invested in these depictions on a personal and political level. To deepen the understanding of this topic, this book will explore the critical mass of literature that has emerged in recent years which foregrounds issues that many of us feel are vitally important to the way that we construct our identities and live in the world. To write about your own body and its pleasures and discomforts is to break away from taboo, shame and stigma, and to fictionalize an assortment of bodily sensations is to offer the reader a powerful sense that they are not alone in their smallest, most vulnerable moments. This is, unashamedly, a feminist book that celebrates feminist scholarship on affect, intimacy and pleasure. It draws not just on feminist thought but also on feminist conversations in academic and non-academic spaces. These conversations, often centred around intimacy and vulnerability, build a kinship and a community which has been vital in opening up new ways of thinking about these representations. While not all the texts I will consider in this book are written by women, those written by men showcase an alternative viewpoint on relationships with others and with the self than are traditionally portrayed in Northern Irish writing. This book is deeply invested in small moments within the novels and short stories that follow as they offers us flashes of revelation about ourselves and others. They may not be scenes that you have experienced, but to really think through them, to hold them, is an imaginative act on behalf of writer and reader.

There has been a remarkable flourishing of Northern Irish[1] prose writing in the twenty-first century, particularly those works of fiction which deal with themes of intimacy, bodies and pleasure. The texts in this study engage with what it means to have a Northern Irish body, how that body is depicted in relation to others and how we might reconsider pleasure in this context. The years 2016–20 have seen an unprecedented volume of Northern Irish novels and short stories. This has featured outputs from some of the largest publishing houses (Faber, Bloomsbury, Penguin) as well as innovative work published by smaller independent presses, such as No Alibis Press, Doire Press and Stinging Fly. To engage with fiction at such a time is exciting and a formidable challenge – the critic of contemporary fiction is regularly left feeling overwhelmed by the variety and quality of new fiction coming out of the North. This study features authors who were born or raised in Northern Ireland and who return to it in their fiction. Some of them have moved elsewhere, particularly to London, but many have also settled in and around Belfast where they contribute to the local arts scene. The novelists and short story writers range in age from late twenties to late sixties, so broadly they were born from the 1950s through to the 1990s. As a result, their proximity to the 'past' of the Troubles is different, ranging from those who saw the outbreak of violence during their youth through to those who primarily experienced it through the memories of others. In addition, these authors have a very different relationship to concepts of intimacy, as you can clearly see from the short pieces that form the appendix to this book. Several of these texts are set in and around contemporary Belfast (Erskine, Caldwell, Park, Jenkinson, Cowan) and some delve backwards into the recent history of the Troubles for their setting (Burns, Hughes). Many of them, particularly in the short fiction, place Northern Irish characters in unfamiliar settings. This book does not seek to be a complete account of Northern Irish writing: the scope of inquiry relates specifically to texts which closely engage with the language of intimacy, pleasure and the body and offer new ways of relating to private life. Northern Irish fiction is moving at such an unprecedented pace as we enter the 2020s that one hopes in the coming years critical attention will move towards more stratified appreciation of its diversity in form and genre and attend to crime writing, speculative fiction, romance, historical fiction and writing for young people. The texts in this project have been chosen because they speak to the central concerns of the monograph: how small moments of intimacy can be transformative. They begin to rewrite and reshape the representation of intimate life in Northern Ireland. It is not my intention to claim that a new relationship to intimacy was invented in the 2010s: each generation wishes to believe they have created the world anew. For decades, Northern Irish fiction has been invested in depicting relationships and domestic configurations, most prominently in the fiction of Mary Beckett, Maurice Leitch, Deirdre Madden, Brian Moore and Janet McNeill. But in the writing in this study there is a change in emphasis: there is a greater variety of intimate relationships, bodies and pleasures shown in texts. The intimacy that formed the backbone of social life in Northern Ireland is now foregrounded.

'And yet we must live in these times':[2] Towards some sort of a context

The novels and short stories under consideration were written in a specific moment – around twenty years after the signing of the Good Friday Agreement, between 2015 and 2020. While this could be considered to be a thoroughly 'post-conflict' context, sporadic violence marks this 'peace' as uneasy. In particular, the creative community was rocked by the murder of journalist and author Lyra McKee in 2019. This unease is palpable throughout several of the texts, particularly in the work of Jan Carson and Rosemary Jenkinson. I hope that this book will be read in the future, then, as a snapshot of literary responses from a specific time – after the effects of the Good Friday Agreement have been tentatively established but before the further consequences of the Brexit Referendum and the Covid-19 pandemic. It was written during a time of political upheaval (2017–20) when I regularly had to shift my focus from watching the situation unfold on rolling news and Twitter to return to the fictional world. During this period, the Northern Ireland Assembly was suspended for over three years and then reinstated, just in time to work remotely. The Democratic Unionist Party (DUP) shifted the balance of power in a hung parliament in 2017 in Westminster but then were no longer kingmakers due to the Conservative majority in the 2019 election. The year 2020 also saw a major political shift in the Republic of Ireland as Sinn Fein topped the poll ahead of Fianna Fáil and Fine Gael. I did the final proofread in the weeks following the election of Joseph Biden to president of the United States. At the time of writing, the most significant news story is the second wave of the Covid-19 pandemic and what it will change not only in politics and society but also in a reconsideration of work, home, family and sexuality.

While the novels and short stories in this study obviously cannot fully represent the most recent developments in the ongoing uncertainty over the ramifications of Brexit, Trumpism and the Covid-19 crisis, they do explore some of the debates which informed these events and establish some of the concerns which preoccupy writers then and now. Fiction is conceived of, written and published in the years before it's publication date, so a simple tracking of historical influences would be futile. For example, the effects of Brexit uncertainty are not quite fully realized within text but a concern over the border is evident in Michael Hughes's *Country* (2018), and Glenn Patterson published a non-fiction collection of essays in 2019, *Backstop Land* (2019), which engaged directly with some of these constitutional questions. However, in a turn typical of the analysis that follows, I am more invested in the intimate relationships in Hughes's novel or the depiction of adolescent sexuality in Patterson's fiction. Questions of the relationship between Northern Ireland, Britain and Europe are examined in Rosemary Jenkinson's *Aphrodite's Kiss* (2016), which emphasizes mobility and the sexual attractiveness of Europeans, but these wider questions of identity are filtered through an erotic lens. With all this flux, an over-deterministic reading based on an author's religion and perceived stance on the National Question feels reductive. Authors privately report an ambivalence at being repeatedly invited to talk about the border, Brexit, the DUP, rather than their fiction. Very few of these texts respond directly to specific historical events but rather turn towards small, intimate moments which have a more complex relationship with the political, social and economic context than this framing allows. This book seeks to offer a redress to hegemonic accounts of Northern Ireland by reconsidering elements which are marginalized in accounts of Northern Irish social and political life. While a broad political reading of this prose is reductive, in the last ten years there have been social and legal changes that have informed the depiction of intimate life in Northern Ireland. The move towards a more liberal society away from moral conservatism[3] has been a complex process in Northern Ireland, particularly on issues of intimacy.[4] At the time of writing, regulations on same-sex marriage and abortion are in effect that were passed by the Westminster Parliament during the Stormont hiatus in 2019. These amendments, brought by Labour MPs Conor McGinn and Stella Creasy, seek to bring Northern Ireland's laws into line with the rest of the UK. In the fictions that follow, there is a celebration of a variety of intimate configurations that reflect these changing social attitudes to gender and sexuality in the North.

Writing about intimacy

In addition to these social and legal changes, critical writing is also beginning to attend to the complexities of Northern Irish intimate life. Academic books regularly claim kudos for novelty, but none of us work in isolation. I want to claim solidarity and kinship with writing on Northern Ireland that attends to intimate configurations and also to pay tribute to the next generation of scholars who seek to reenvisage what intimate life might look like in 'post'-conflict Northern Ireland. In recent years, academic scholarship which revisits the past and considers the future in innovative, challenging ways is reshaping the critical landscape. This writing orientates us away from the traditional narratives that surround academic work on Northern Ireland which prioritizes the violent act and the violent actor. The work of Leanne Calvert,[5] Sean Brady,[6] Fiona McCann,[7] Stefanie Lehner,[8] Alison Garden,[9] Eli Davies[10] and a new generation of PhD scholars is galvanizing in their reconsideration of intimacy in a variety of cultural and historical settings. I am indebted to the generation of feminist thinkers who bravely opened up new ways of relating to Irish writing. In conversations with my students at Salford, I learn from fresh eyes how powerful these texts can be as my students challenge my thinking and offer valuable, nuanced interpretations of their own. Interesting conversations about Northern Ireland happen in a variety of places, within and without the traditional gatekeepers of journal publishing and privileged access to the conference room. Sara Ahmed reminds us that 'feminist theory is something we do at home.'[11] I learn more about Northern Irish family life from a conversation with my mother as I do from reading some academic monographs that elide women's voices. This is not to say that I am 'done with experts' as the value of reading, thinking and teaching in a scholarly community is still vitally important and generative. But rather, it is to say that when I started turning towards the body, intimacy and pleasure for this project I began to appreciate other forms of understanding away from the voices I had been academically 'raised' with. I was galvanized by an article from 2020, where Anne Mulhall blends the knowledge she gained from activism and academia to rethink Irish studies and whiteness.[12] I am fortunate to have access to a variety of kinds of knowledges – and while this book might not tick every box of a Jesuitical citational culture it comes from a dissatisfaction with the ways I have seen Northern Ireland represented in literary criticism.

My research is also profoundly influenced by thinkers from outside of Northern Ireland, such as Sara Ahmed, Lauren Berlant, Judith Butler, bell hooks and Audre Lorde. In particular, the rich tradition of Black feminist writing offers up such generative ways of thinking from writers who took profitable risks, particularly the use of autobiography in the works of hooks[13] and Lorde, but also, in particular, Lorde's emphasis on the erotic as a political force.[14] To follow Sara Ahmed on the work of theory:

> Within the academy, the word theory has a lot of capital. I have always been interested in how the word theory itself is distributed; how some materials are understood as theory and not others ... Some work becomes theory because it refers to other work that is known as theory. A citational chain is created around theory: you become a theorist by citing other theorists that cite other theorists.[15]

There is a powerful citational chain around the study of Northern Ireland which is profoundly hierarchical. I have, at times, been an active participant in academic cultures which have produced and recycled debates around Northern Irish writing that have made me feel ill at ease. To be frank, I wanted a criticism that would be as attentive to the experiences of my late grandmother, who raised six girls and a boy in Portadown during the Troubles, as it would be to the experiences of a combatant. That would consider teenage girls deciding the risk was worth it to go to a nightclub in Mid-Ulster in the 1990s a kind of political act. I thought about the Northern Ireland I knew, that my friends knew, and started to see this variety of experiences represented in texts but not academic criticism. I feared that the smallness of these precious moments would be elided by critics hungry for what a novel might say about the politics of the Troubles. I wanted to refuse, for myself and the authors in this book, the status of fetish.

I have heard innovative, thoughtful, rigorous engagements with Northern Irish literature, culture and society, but sometimes I listen to academic papers that are delivered as if the people I knew and loved were fodder for a case study and felt profoundly alienated from my chosen course of study. But, these over-deterministic readings by some scholars, which prize the overarching political context above all else, are not exclusive to academics from outside Northern Ireland. Indeed, I have actively participated in events and publications where the prioritization of violent acts and actors was the focus. I performed the version of Northern Ireland that audiences seemed to want to hear. But, slowly, I began to pay attention to when what I was hearing and saying *felt* wrong. Some of this work has added invaluable scholarly insight but some of it did not sit right. When blithe points were made about 'the Republican community of the Garvaghy Road', all I could think about was my family who still lived there and their diverse relationship to their perceived political allegiance. Continuing to write as if these things were not personally important has begun to feel like an act of bad faith. Those feelings, that intuition, that gut, make the representations this book considers *feel* vitally important to me, and as we will see in the discussion of *Milkman*, feeling is a powerful force in Northern Irish writing when it is attended to. I started to consider the relationship of these feelings to the afterlife of the conflict in the body when I spoke to friends and family – when you hear of an attack in Derry and your stomach falls through the floor or read about a bomb scare near your family home and your body becomes rigid. At the same time, I feel more at ease in Belfast than anywhere else, galvanized by the potential of a wild night out in the city. Belfast *feels* different. These feelings did not square with being regularly depicted as being part of a haunted, traumatized population. The expectation of writers to speak profoundly of their relationship to nation states at festivals instead of their literary influences did not *feel* right. As I read more and more of this 'post'-conflict writing, I started to see the complicated world I knew emerge. There was laughter, wild imagination and the tenderest moments mixed in with a consideration of history and memory. These two influences came together for me – the move away from traditional theory and the emergence of a body of writing that thrilled me. The kitchen table could be a place to theorize, a night out could be profound, terrible and magical things could be imagined. Crucially, the texts I read became sites to think about not only history and memory but also sensuality and the physical body, they are vitally important spaces to do and undo theory-work.

Coming back to the body in 2020

This book was conceived of in 2017 as a way to draw together some initial thoughts I had about what I considered to be a new wave of Northern Irish writing. Since then, an even greater variety of fiction have been published that speak to the central themes of this book – intimacy, pleasure and the body. But this writing does now feel boundaried by the epoch-changing events of 2020 and the way in which they will reorientate the way that we relate to each other in terms of intimacy, pleasure and the body. It was developed and written during a time of political and social upheaval (2017–20) and most of the fiction featured were published in the period around the calling of the Brexit referendum (2016) and the mooted exit date (2020). The final manuscript was finished in what is known as the transition period – as if British and Irish relations were not in a continual state of change – and edited during the Covid-19 pandemic in 2020. The majority of the writing was conducted long before the pandemic, but what follows was edited in my home in Manchester during the lockdown in spring and summer, with final proofing done during the American election and the second wave of the pandemic. As I send this off to Bloomsbury, I do not know what kind of world it will be launched into and whether, indeed, it will be launched. Revisiting this writing initially seemed perverse – much like watching a television programme where people are being so reckless as to have a drink in a packed bar or go home with a stranger. All of a sudden, our circles of intimacy have become radically smaller, many of us think more critically about the vulnerability of our bodies and reorientate our pleasures. Revisiting this work during the current moment was a strange experience for me and reading about these representations of intimacy may also be a strange experience for you. It may feel like this writing came from another time, and perhaps it did. It is impossible to know from our vantage point how the Covid-19 will change the way in which we relate to intimacy. To attend to fictions of intimacy at any time has a simultaneous familiarity and strangeness, but negotiating these proximities is currently heightened. Many of us remember what it was like to be cavalier with our displays of affection, although this was not a privilege open to all. Writing in a wide-ranging essay on the potential social and political consequences of the pandemic, Judith Butler notes that

> vulnerability is not just the condition of being potentially harmed by another. It names the porous and interdependent character of our bodily and social lives. We are given over from the start to a world of others we never chose in order to become more or less singular beings ... Humans share the air with one another and with animals; they share the surfaces of the world. They touch what others have touched and they touch one another. These reciprocal and material modes of sharing describe a crucial dimension of our vulnerability, intertwinements and interdependence of our embodied social life.[16]

This book attends to some pivotal vulnerabilities, particularly skin contact, and in thinking through why these are so necessary and pleasurable, begins to offer a rationale for why the current moment can be so acutely painful. Intimacy involves a continuous negotiation between proximity and distance which will inevitably be altered by the question of social distancing. The body has become something which is agent of and vulnerable to the deleterious effects of the virus[17] and also the economic precarity that it engenders. At times in this book, I will read the body and its component parts, especially the skin, as signifiers of a 'post'-conflict reorientation with an awareness that what the body 'means' will be reinscribed in the coming years. I want to turn more towards the experience of rereading Northern Irish literature during a global health crisis with ideas of intimacies, bodies and pleasures in mind. For example, Chapter 1 discusses the representation of the domestic space within Northern Irish literature. When I've spoken to family members during 2020, they have noted that it has raised the familiar sensation of feeling trapped indoors with uncertainty beyond the front door that they felt during the Troubles. Of course, home is not always the sanctuary that we need it to be, then or now. The enforced return to the domestic has made me return to some familiar Troubles texts – Mary Beckett's bread making in *Give Them Stones* (1987) and the novels of Deirdre Madden and the earlier fiction of Glenn Patterson. I've returned to this writing that shaped me for a social media public engagement project and was shocked to find how vivid and relevant the concerns of these novels still are. What it means to be at home is a theme that is not unique to either our current moment or these Troubles texts. It is a constantly evolving question involving the negotiation of politics, identity and economics.[18] Particularly in our current political climate, the after-effects of the Conservative government's policies on home and family can be felt in the fabric of the home – from the bedroom tax through to the effects of Universal Credit. These questions of domestic confinement were once seen as the preserve of people with disabilities, refugees, migrants, the economically powerless, the abused and others for whom home is a vexed question. They have come into sharper focus for more people as their world narrowed in 2020 and to return to complex fictions of intimate life helps us think through the value and dangers of intimacy.

Reading Northern Irish books in 2020

To turn to fictions produced in and about Northern Ireland in the 2010s is to contend with several contexts that inform how we view ourselves in this renegotiation of home and family – the legacy of the home in Northern Ireland and the social and economic forces which shape how and what we view as home. Attending to these fictions in the current moment is to remember not only what we value about our home but also the dangers within those four walls. The first chapter of this book examines a variety of novels and short stories which speak directly to these concerns. In Wendy Erskine's collection *Sweet Home* (2018), a house can be a place where women find self-esteem through DIY or create a home from home for other women in the form of a beauty salon. It can also be a location which hosts estrangement and resentments. Home is also a vexed question in Jan Carson's *The Firestarters* (2019), which showcases the dangers and possibilities of the domestic, which is both a target of violence and a site of unrest. These texts foreground the complexity of our relationship with the domestic. Michael Hughes's *Country* reminds us of the restrictions placed on intimate life during the Troubles but also finds some ways out of the representational dead ends that haunted older Troubles fiction. This is a necessary counterpoint to the 'post'-conflict fictions in the study and their attendant negotiation of intimacy. A different kind of relationship to sex and violence is shown in Phil Harrison's novel *The First Day* (2017), which explores the legacy of familial conflict and the power of the word in the representation of intimacy. Reading Lucy Caldwell's *Intimacies* (2021) during lockdown is a particularly heightened experience as it engages directly with the problems of digital communication for maintaining intimate bonds. Whereas Caldwell mainly discusses this in the lives of Irish women in London, the situations she details have become the mainstay of our everyday lives – the politics of the family WhatsApp group and frantic internet searches feature among her foregrounding of the digital intimate.

The second chapter of this book focuses on skin and touch in a Northern Irish context and rereading it in 2020 felt like viewing a remnant from the 'Before Times'.[19] The emphasis in the early days of 2020 was on handwashing and avoiding skin contact, despite the Prime Minister Boris Johnson stating after visiting a hospital with confirmed coronavirus patients that 'I shook hands with everybody, you will be pleased to know, and I continue to shake hands'.[20] Hands became a focal point of National Health Service (NHS) campaigns, and touch was discouraged among all but your household. People were encouraged to not touch their own face by the World Health Organization.[21] Businesses which rely on close physical contact, particularly the beauty industry, faced steeper challenges to adapt to the crisis. Medical professionals proposed more sanitary alternatives to the handshake or cheek kiss. The after-effects of this will not be felt for some time, even if our touch relations return to 'normal'. As a result, the encounters in this chapter reveal something meaningful about our relationship to touch, how fundamental it is to human connection and point to what has been lost. I think of the encounters in this chapter as part of a network of skin encounters that opened up a powerful meeting place in 'post'-conflict Northern Irish culture. The desire for skin contact is evidenced in David Park's *Gods and Angels* (2016), which strains with people yearning to touch each other and the outstretched hand. Rosemary Jenkinson's *Aphrodite's Kiss* and Bernie McGill's *Sleepwalkers* (2013) present skin in relation with other bodies and examine cultural transmission through touch. Roisin O'Donnell's *Wild Quiet*

(2016) presents skin as something fantastic and other-worldly. Perhaps, in the writing to come, skin and touch will come to be prioritized as vital transmitters of comfort and knowledge, or perhaps further fetishized, or stigmatized. These skin fictions offer a way to think about how powerful haptic contact is to healing and recovery.

The third chapter engages with the way in which we might examine moments of pleasure within a text. It considers how pleasure after conflict might have a very particular politics. It asks what it means to experience genuine joy at a time when horrific suffering is taking place. The suggestion was made by Ben Voyer at the London School of Economics that, during the coronavirus pandemic, Britons went from a 'pleasure-seeking' to a 'pain-avoiding' mentality.[22] The texts in this study engage with the idea of what pleasure in literature might mean, socially and politically, against a climate where the prevailing mood is one of trauma. During the worst moments of social crisis, there have still been moments of joy. However, to discuss these is taboo as to announce one's pleasures when another is suffering is fraught. But to attend only to trauma is to not offer a full picture of the very complex ways that people *live*. Anecdotally, in spring 2020, I've seen a lot of people on social media reading adrienne marie brown's *Pleasure Activism: The Politics of Feeling Good* (2019), which engages with the complex politics of healing and happiness while doing social justice work.[23] The collected essays draw on the tradition of Black feminist thought to offer something with transformative power: it is possible to be ethical and attend to challenges in society while still caring for the self and engaging erotically with others. In this third chapter, then, the first three texts showcase sensual encounters during the Troubles: Billy Cowan's *Still Ill* (2014), Glenn Patterson's *The Rest Just Follows* (2014) and Lucy Caldwell's 'Here We Are' from *Multitudes* (2016). These authors represent different facets of the interaction of trauma and sensuality. Cowan offers a queer erotic influenced by the legacy of the conflict but also the repressive regime of homophobia in Northern Ireland. Patterson's novel takes the long view of intimate life and also exposes moments of sheer joy alongside a detailed discussion of the path to the Good Friday Agreement. Both Cowan and Patterson showcase the influence of pop culture on the ways that we learn our erotic scripts, orientating the focus away from the traditional representation of sensual life in Troubles fiction as intertwined with political violence. Caldwell's short story offers a brief glimpse into the moments of joy that comprise two teenage girls' relationship, with romantic walks across Belfast. Here, pleasure is transformative to the individual and the way that they relate to the world around them. Most of this chapter, however, is dedicated to the short stories of Rosemary Jenkinson, who might be dubbed Belfast's pleasure laureate. Many of her short stories in *Catholic Boy* (2018) and *Lifestyle Choice 10mg* (2020) read like a catalogue of the most heightened moments of pleasure from a pre-Covid world. They are full of busy, noisy pubs and wild parties. They are stories of unpredictable nights out that often end in skin contact with a brand new acquaintance. There is a wild abandon to them that feels, from this vantage point, a relic from another time. But, the will to live and to enjoy yourself despite a traumatic rupture pulses through the pages. I found rereading these short stories oddly hopeful as these bodies yearn towards the sensual and orientate us towards a future of connection.

The final chapter examines the most critically and commercially successful Northern Irish novel in the study, Anna Burns' *Milkman* (2018). This is a break from the thematic structure of the previous three chapters due to the monumental literary achievement of Burns's novel and the way in which her work offers a singularly nuanced, complex depiction of intimacy and the body. This chapter will examine how Burns creates an atmosphere of feeling, how this is mediated through the body and the mechanisms for releasing the cumulative tension of prolonged trauma. In particular, this novel has a preoccupation with the limitations of the domestic and the ways in which confinement troubles our bodies to their core. The novel foregrounds not only this tension but also the ways in which a reclamation of bodily autonomy can be a vital calmative during difficult times. Finally, I want to gesture towards the future of Northern Irish fiction with a short reading of Susannah Dickey's *Tennis Lessons* (2020) and the awareness that the current crisis will shape our understanding of intimacies, bodies and pleasures in ways we cannot yet fully comprehend. The book closes with a series of pieces from writers featured in the study, who were simply given the prompt from me via email to 'write a short thing about intimacy'. Some of these have been used in the chapters that follow to deepen the readings of the texts under consideration, but they are presented here in their entirety in the hope that they will encourage future readers and scholars to examine the powerful influence of the intimate on these writers' lives and practices.

In this fiction under consideration in this study, the same imperatives persist as our currently shaping our world – the desire for connection, the balm of touch, the yearning for pleasure. While a newer generation of Northern Irish writers will most likely further push against the taboos around intimacy and the representation of the body, the current social, political and intimate challenges will reshape the way that we relate to each other and the bodies in relation that we see in fiction. The body is our tool for understanding our social world, and the texts in this study not only foreground the complex ways in which our bodies come into contact with others and are 'read' but also help us interpret the situations in which we find ourselves. Returning to them has been a reminder that, in the midst of terrible times, the impulse to be with and for each other is undimmed.

1

Intimacy

While intimate life has provided a source of inspiration for writers from the North of Ireland for centuries, the decades since the signing of the Good Friday Agreement have seen a marked interest in this theme as a central object of creative inquiry. This chapter will argue that recent novels and short stories demonstrate the richness of intimacy as a way to re-examine the experiences of Northern Irish people in the twenty-first century. The introduction to this book set out the changing social context for these representations, and subsequent chapters will examine two facets of this turn towards intimacy in more detail: pleasure and touch. This chapter will examine five texts that examine intimate relationships in very different ways. Michael Hughes's *Country* explores paramilitarism during the mid-1990s. Because the novel involves a retelling of the *Iliad*, its depiction of intimacy is informed by both this source text and also the ways in which decades of conflict take their toll on romantic, filial and familial life. This novel also involves a reworking of some of the tropes of Troubles fiction and so acts as a point of comparison with the more contemporary-focused writing which follows in this chapter. Wendy Erskine's *Sweet Home*, a collection of short stories, examines domestic life in East Belfast, and while the conflict does not loom as large as in Hughes's work, she subtly explores domestic mores and what goes on behind closed doors. Returning to East Belfast, Jan Carson's *The Firestarters* considers faith and family in her signature variant of magic realism, offering an inventive perspective on intimacy and domesticity in an East Belfast terraced house. Phil Harrison's *The First Day* shows an interplay between sexuality and violence that is distinct from the way this trope is used in fictions of the Troubles as the author is heavily influenced by the language of philosophy, literature and faith. Lucy Caldwell's *Intimacies*, from the title onwards, meditates on the complex ways in which our public and private lives intersect. All of these novels and short story collections demonstrate the complexity of representing intimacy.

All of them are influenced by the legacy of a long violent conflict and the dictates of an uneasy peace. Taken in total, they create a compelling exploration of the different ways in which they engage with intimate life demonstrates the plurality of experiences that make up contemporary Northern Irish experience.

Intimacy is not a concern specific to Northern Irish literature. In recent years, approaches to contemporary fiction have traced the affective economies of what Jennifer Cooke calls 'intimate reading encounters'.[1] I want to – drawing on the work of Cooke, Lauren Berlant and others – first to consider the concept in a more general sense, and then to ask how we might position Northern Irish intimacy. The term 'intimacy' is used for a variety of acts, practices and orientations. It can function as a euphemism to cover a range of ambiguous, usually sexual, acts: essentially, it can be way of talking about that which is hidden or behind closed doors. This imperative is particularly keen in fiction grappling with the representation of relationships in a 'post'-conflict society. Within the prose fiction under consideration, truths unspoken feature heavily, and the inability to fully articulate desire, apathy and disgust plays a role in several. Equally important, an intimate is a term used to refer to a confidant, with whom you make sense of your personal life by setting it out into a narrative, and this process is both mirrored in, and complicated by, the act of writing fiction. To intimate to someone can also mean to tell them part of a possibly sensitive story: intimate as a verb is often followed by a 'might' or a 'should', indicating a state of affairs that is not quite ready to be fully shown. This ambivalence is also a strong characteristic of these texts and an aspect that I want to draw out – intimacy can be both a sense-making narrative and a hidden world.

Within the Northern Irish context, a turn to the intimate could be read as fundamentally apolitical, as a deliberate orientation away from the sectarian violence of Troubles, but this elides the complex relationship of the personal to the political. The 'public' politics of sectarian conflict and the 'private' politics of intimacy is a binary that is easily collapsed by examining the lives depicted in the fiction that follows. In intimacy, we find the interaction of the public knowledge of telling or writing and the private realm of our own hidden knowledge, as Lucy Caldwell notes '*To intimate* means to imply, to communicate something urgent or delicate or otherwise impossible to articulate with the most sparing of signs'.[2] Intimacy is a way of knowing that can only occur through an exchange. Most obviously, we learn the culturally appropriate behaviours for our intimate encounters through what we have seen and read, but accordingly, as Cooke points out, the 'ways we write and the forms in which we choose to write about our most intimate states – such as love or mourning – are capable of altering our conceptions of them'.[3] When we write intimacy into being, whether as authors or critics, we are engaged in a process of reinscribing and renegotiating our part in this process.

Intimacy in literature, then, lives at the intersection between our private and social worlds – it does not just represent a sanctuary from the external world. Berlant articulates the complex way in which the intimate functions:

> This view of 'a life' that unfolds intact within the intimate sphere represses, of course, another fact about it: the unavoidable Troubles, the distractions and disruptions that make things turn out in unpredicted scenarios … moral dramas of estrangement and betrayal, along with terrible spectacles of neglect and violence even where desire, perhaps, endures.[4]

Indeed, we often find disappointment due to discordance between scripts of intimacy, for example, with a partner who does not perform their affection in the manner that we want. Intimacy can be a disruptive force on a continuum, from the smaller ruptures of awkward lovemaking to the larger problems of abuse and violence meted out by a trusted partner or family member. The spectre of what is called intimate partner violence hangs over any idealization of home and hearth. In the texts under consideration, we will see unwanted sexual encounters and difficult decisions, but domestic violence and sexual abuse is not quite the narrative catalyst so often seen in earlier Northern Irish fiction: these texts often feature women taking control of their living spaces and intimate lives, especially in the work of Caldwell and Erskine.

The consideration of the intimate could be seen as offering a reverse exceptionalism when considering Northern Irish culture. Bodies are not necessarily encoded with the legacy of violent civil conflict when a lover runs their fingertips up your back or a grandparent hugs you with happy tears in their eyes: acts of intimacy that occur throughout the world occur in Northern Ireland (with all the complications that Berlant outlines above). But, as these acts are framed within narratives set in a 'post'-conflict society, the representational legacy of violence does influence the context in which they are encountered and read. Readers often expect political engagement from texts which are set in countries with a recent history of violent conflict, so when these authors turn to the intimate, critical readers often seek to extrapolate historical meaning. This is understandable because the private and the public have been tied to each other in complex, ambiguous ways in Northern Irish culture. Such readings, as we will discuss in Chapter 2, seek to homogenize the experiences of writers who relate to the conflict in markedly different ways while exploring a variety of intimate acts. Two of the texts in this chapter (Carson and Harrison) directly address faith as a prism through which to see relationships, both between people and between God and the faithful. Some of Erskine's and Caldwell's characters also have faith-based upbringings that influence their relationships in direct and indirect ways. Faith often relies, as does intimacy, on that which is not fully revealed. I do not intend to paint a crude picture of Northern Irish intimate life as something solely influenced and constrained by the dictates of religious institutions, it is clear that it is a factor in the way we understand the development and representation of the moments that follow.

In this fiction, intimacy is regularly examined in a domestic setting. Indeed, two of the texts (Erskine and Carson) explicitly focus on the home while the other three (Caldwell, Hughes and Harrison) regularly feature interior spaces. Of course, intimacy does not only happen in the home: public displays of affection and 'sex in public',[5] to borrow Berlant and Warner's phrase, demonstrate the vibrancy of that intimate life outside the confines of the domestic. But the house also is the primary staging post for much of our intimate lives. The fictions considered here were all published in the late 2010s and in 2020, over twenty years since the signing of the Good Friday Agreement. Only one of them (Hughes) is set explicitly during the Troubles. To that end, most of these dwellings are 'post'-conflict houses, but each writer demonstrates an awareness of the representational history of the Northern Irish house, especially East Belfast terraces of Erskine's and Carson's writing. Critics have drawn our attention to the ways in which the supposedly private space of the home was co-opted and given meaning during the conflict. Bryony Reid asserts that 'because of the intimate nature of the Troubles, houses have been on the frontline of violent struggle'.[6] Adam Hanna argues that the house, coded as private, appropriates a remarkably public role in the work of poets from the North[7] and Eli Davies[8] shows us the ways in which, traditionally, the home has been used by writers pre-1998 'as an escape from the conflict'.[9] The home here acts as a sanctuary, but, as Davies notes elsewhere in her essay, this often elides the radical possibility of home as a space to renegotiate memory and the public/private dichotomy. This chapter seeks to build on this Troubles-era analysis to explore the post-conflict domestic and ask to what extent the novelists under consideration rewrite the terraced house of the Troubles and the sorts of lives with which they choose to fill these homes. In the negotiations of intimate life that follow, we will find authors keen to imagine new domestic configurations, new ways of writing and new intimacies.

'Nothing political, nothing sectarian, just a small personal matter':[10] The legacy of Troubles intimacy in Michael Hughes's *Country*

Michael Hughes's second novel *Country*, published on the twentieth anniversary of the Good Friday Agreement in 2018, examines the political changes of the mid-nineties era through an Irish Republican Army (IRA) Active Service Unit. Stationed on the border, while these men are bound together by duty, they display an intense personal animosity towards each other. For not the last time in this study, it is a novel that focuses on men and masculinity. While Hughes wrote the novel in the period leading up to the Brexit referendum, the political concerns of the novel gained a particular currency afterwards: 'I was sharply aware of militant ideas of nationalism resurfacing. But the Irish border wasn't seen as particularly significant at that stage of the referendum – that realisation came much later for a lot of people. So I'd accidentally written a rather topical book.'[11] Accordingly, this chapter will examine some of the political resonances in the novel, it will focus particularly on how these public concerns shape and are shaped by intimate encounters. Hughes's depiction of intimacy is also filtered through a very particular narrative style, as Eoin McNamee noted:

> The register is coarse, furious. Hughes has an ear for his own tongue, brings into it a gnawed-at vernacular of fear and savagery. It needs to be tonally on the money and it is. But underneath it and through it you hear Homer's cadences, the long lines of chant in dactylic hexameter. He mixes Border idiom with Greek formalism.[12]

This lyrical style assumes a sense of intimacy with the reader by engaging with the storytelling traditions of both the Greek oral poem and Irish seanchaí culture. A repeated refrain in the text is 'Wait now till you hear the rest.'[13] This address, common in Northern Irish vernacular ('Wait til you hear') serves to create a sense of intimacy with the reader, as does the tragic familiarity of the source text. Hughes notes that it 'was very important to me the book presented the intimacy of person-to-person close-quarter violence, as the *Iliad* so graphically does.'[14] The plot of the novel is roughly based on the *Iliad* (Henry for Hector, Achill for Achilles, Nellie for Helen and so forth) but remains inescapably a Northern Irish novel in subject and vernacular. Hughes said of the novel, 'Leaning on an existing story and an existing structure gave me permission to write in an imaginative fictional way: I'm simply setting a story that's been around for a few thousand years within the dynamics of the last days of the Northern Ireland conflict.[15] Classical references are frequently used in twentieth-century Northern Irish poetry and Michael Longley's poems in *The Ghost Orchid*, especially 'Ceasefire', have ingrained the association between Homer's epic and the uncertain period of the 1990s. Florence Impens details when, in August 1994, Longley heard rumours of an IRA ceasefire and began to write the poem, which was published soon after.[16] Although Hughes notes that Longley's work was not uppermost in his mind as he wrote the novel,[17] the wealth of critical material on both Longley and the *Iliad* allow us some way into how the representation of intimacy in *Country* both chimes with and deviates from these other sources. Impens emphasizes the intimacy of the source text for Longley: 'In Longley, Hector, Achilles, and Priam are not defined by their belonging to either one of two antagonistic communities – Trojans or Achaeans – but by their family ties: they are fathers, husbands, and sons.'[18] Indeed, we might argue that any rewriting of the *Iliad* must take into account some of the central tensions of the epic: the interplay between intimate life and public duty. Nikolopoulou draws our attention to the variety of moments within the text that examine the theme of intimacy: 'More specifically, the tragic eventualities of the Iliad are precipitated by various kinds of intimate exchanges involving both persons and things.'[19] This chapter examines how Hughes renders these intimate moments and transposes the tragic significance of them from the epic to 1990s Northern Ireland.

This novel, along with *Milkman*, thus acts as a useful point of comparison with the writing of Park, Erskine, Caldwell and Carson as it is set not just in the past but firmly engages with the paramilitary world. Any representation of intimacy in *Country*, then, must be inflected by this hyper-masculine setting. Sexual intimacy, in particular, is depicted as a transactional event rather than the tender encounters that are displayed in other writing. As Eoin McNamee states in his glowing review of the novel, 'the sex is brutish and brutishly rendered'.[20] It is a world of carnivalesque grotesque: from the sense of tragic fatalism that belies the *Iliad* through to the overwrought masculine posturing and misogyny, where paramilitaries fantasize about 'Provie sluts'[21] who 'cream their knickers every time a Brit gets plugged'.[22] The novel emphasizes the role of women in the home alongside their depiction as interchangeable sex objects: 'She was shacked up now at his place, doing his washing, cooking his dinner. Whatever else.'[23] Young girls are typically represented as currency to be traded by men who seek to establish their dominance: 'She's hardly fourteen, the light of my life. Please don't touch her, big man. Not yet a while. Give her a couple more years to be a wee girl.'[24] The novel does not represent these encounters in an eroticized way – but a matter-of-fact exploration of the dominant cultural codes of male sexuality in a hyper-masculinized society during wartime.

Country features the Troubles' literary and cultural trope of the honeytrap,[25] but reinvents it to examine the critical failure of intimacy in a society in conflict. Moments of tenderness spring up in the most unusual places in the novel, such as between Achill and Theresa, a suspected police informer and sex worker: 'But then the Brits got hold of her, so the story went, and the word went round she was working for them too, a honeytrapper, getting the gossip off horny Ra men.'[26] She becomes a fantasy object comprising the archetypes of sexual availability and maternal comfort: 'After, she sat up and he lay down with his head in her lap, the usual. She stroked his hair and said he was her own little boy. He had a quiet wee cry and whispered about his mammy.'[27] Traditionally, literary portrayals of women during the Troubles tended to fall into one of two categories, either 'angels of the home, their political involvement confined to … providing shelter for the fugitive' or sexualized *femme fatales*, beautiful but deadly.[28] Nellie provides one of the few female characters on which the novel focuses at length, but she is mostly viewed through her relationships with men, particularly her lover Brian/Dog and her British Intelligence handler. Similar to Helen, her beauty is emphasized: 'She was the best-looking in her year. Maybe in the whole school.'[29] Sex acts in the novel are depicted for Nellie as 'fucking disgusting,'[30] but she is also keen to perform compliance and enjoyment to appease her partner: 'She hoped she hadn't ruined it. Her and her smart fucking mouth.'[31]

Nellie spends the novel seeking intimacy but the scripts afforded to her by the Troubles frustrate her efforts. She finds herself interested instead with the subcultures in an attempt to imagine a life outside of the conflict: 'Nellie started hanging around with a few of the goths and the indie kids. Reading Hot Press and the NME, and watching Network. Listening to different music. She went up Belfast every month just to buy The Face, and see what she could pick up in Fresh Garbage or the market.'[32] Alternative pop culture provides a link to different kinds of possible intimacies through music and fashion. Nellie seeks a different kind of identity, and finds it in the drug culture of 1990s Belfast: 'It was round the time everybody started doing E.'[33] Hughes shifts to the second person and a more flowing narrative style to describe the experience of taking ecstasy: 'You knew the best thing the only thing was to be close to someone anyone that person right there and you knew they felt the same and they all felt the same. She'd never felt closer to anybody in her life.'[34] Ecstasy is part of a group of psychoactive drugs known as empathogens or entactogens[35] as they promote feelings of togetherness and connection. This 'synthetic intimacy' serves to highlight the paucity of positive relationships within the text and how 'closeness' is elusive for many of the characters due to their proximity to paramilitary conflict.

However, this feeling of intimacy, of oneness, is temporary as the conflict intrudes with the British Security Service exploiting Nellie's need for an abortion to bribe her to become an informer. By including this detail, Hughes exposes the unequal class access to abortion in Northern Ireland, which was criminalized at the time the novel is set. Working-class women resort to dangerous backstreet procedures but middle-class women can afford to travel: 'You see, I know people who could organise you to have the thing dealt with over here, very simple and very quick. Done properly, a real doctor.'[36] Hughes emphasizes here the destructive impact that intimate relationships can have on Northern Irish women's lives. For women in the novel, their relationships seem more for survival than for affection: 'Nellie used to wonder did she love Brian. She wasn't too sure how she was supposed to know. Which meant the answer was probably no. He never said it in so many words, so she didn't either.'[37] There is an absence of pleasure, and in particular female sexual pleasure, within the novel. For Brian/Dog, his experience of love is ultimately linked to an experience of proprietorships: 'You're everything to me. I would die if you left me. I would kill any man who laid a finger on you. I would track him down, and I would take off the side of his house with a JCB, and I would nail him to the fucking wall.'[38] Violence and love remain intimately intertwined in the minds of Hughes's combatants and their paramours, a common trope in Troubles fiction. However, the IRA men are not the only characters in the novel who are unable to perform certain kinds of intimacy. The life of the security forces in the novel is different: as they are not on the run, it is easier to maintain the veneer of acceptable heterosexual stability, if not the levels of intimacy required by their partners. Henry's relationship with his wife is strained, and he needs to perform intimacy with his son to satisfy her: 'He lifted the boy back from her. Held him high. She needed a display of affection. He gritted his teeth behind his own smile. Couldn't risk cracking the shell. Not today. Keep all that out.'[39] Children and their welfare barely feature within the narrative, the absence of which emphasizes the way in which warfare distorts established norms of home and family life. But rather than the different kinds of kinship that other fiction engage with, there are rarely alternative to these structures.

The most vivid rendering of intimacy in the novel is the depiction of Pat, a close friend of Achill, and their closeness stands in for the ambiguous relationship between Patroclus and Achilles in the *Iliad*, which is often taken by critics to be queer.[40] Some of the greatest physical tenderness in the novel is shown between Achill and Pat, with the former roaring 'out his grief'[41] at the sight of the latter's body. Achill laments that 'I might as well be dead, for I couldn't protect that gentle boy'.[42] Indeed, multiple characters emphasize the kindness and gentle qualities of Pat, who offers them a glimpse of home while they were displaced from home comforts during their paramilitary activity. Pat is depicted in the domestic domain, looking after the sustenance of the men and offering comfort to their partners ('fussing and footering at your wee biscuits and buns, and making sure I had enough in my tummy before I'd go out on a job').[43] In addition to this domestic work, he is also depicted as doing the emotional labour that typically associated with women: 'You'd have some wee remark would make it all seem okay. God forgive me bringing you anywhere near it all. I'd happily offer up my own life to bring your smiling face back.'[44]

Where the novel depicts male/female relationships as either brief and transactional or arduously domestic, the complexities of emotional intimacy are between men, in keeping with the novel's source text. To return to Longley's poetry, the scene of 'Ceasefire' is carefully restaged by Hughes, where Achilles/Achill and Priam/Bernard discuss the burial of Hector/Henry. The scene is described by Longley as 'I get down on my knees and do what must be done/And kiss Achilles' hand, the killer of my son'.[45] Hughes renders it as 'He took Achill's hand in his own. He touched his lips to the knuckles.'[46] In a novel marked by transactional intimacy, this encounter superficially seems to echo this: Bernard needs to persuade Achill to give him Henry's body through a performance of grief. His approach is to plead with him and to try to evoke empathy through reminding Achill of his own family:

> Please. I can't do any more. I don't think a British officer has ever before kissed the hand of the man who killed his best soldier. Please. Think of your own father, and the great joy it brings him to hear you're alive. Please. This man was like a son to me … The men standing around. But nobody said a thing. Just like as if it wasn't happening. See nothing, hear nothing. Say nothing.[47]

This moment in the novel is pivotal, as it was for Longley and in the original text. It is a rare glimpse of masculine vulnerability in texts that deal with male violence. The pleading is on an intimate level, emphasizing familial love. Nikolopoulou discusses the afterlife of the Homeric text: 'The Iliad continues to forge communities of reading that restage, in some way or another, its deeply intimate moment of shared disinheritance.'[48] We can therefore begin to think of Hughes's novel, with its mix of brutality and tenderness, as a way to restage the intimacy of this moment. This moment is in dialogue with other iterations of intimacy in Northern Ireland and beyond. The text is a complex discussion of the intimacy between men during times of war and the way in which conflict has the power to radically reshape intimate relations of all kinds. As we shall see in this chapter, writers who focus on the contemporary engage with changed intimate landscapes, but Hughes's work asks us to meditate on what was lost during the darkest days.

'Weird little box of a place but she liked it': Rewriting domesticity and intimacy in the short stories of Wendy Erskine

Wendy Erskine's debut short story collection, *Sweet Home*, was published by Stinging Fly Press in 2018 and then by Picador in 2019 following the success of the collection in Ireland. The stories focus on one small area in East Belfast, but it is a location that the reader would have to know intimately to place. In 'Arab States: Mind and Narrative', when the main characters joke about the Middle East, one proclaims it is 'somewhere in between Ballyhackamore and Cregagh Estate'.[49] Erskine said of her geographical focus, 'I knew I was working on, in some respects, a small palette. Within a couple of streets, really.'[50] She has also stated that 'I'm a real urbanite – I love concrete. I'm not one for going for walks in forests. I've always loved Belfast, too.'[51] While the stories in *Sweet Home* could be defined as city stories, they have a clear focus throughout on representation of the home, from the title through to the careful detailing of sofas, duvets and serving trays kept for best. In two different interviews, Erskine stated her aims when writing the stories. To the *Irish Independent* she said, 'I want to write about people who are on the point of collapse. I want to write about people who've faced major trauma or people who can't articulate how they feel, or are excluded.'[52] To the *Irish News* she said, 'I want to write about people living their everyday lives, going to their jobs and doing their dishes or whatever but dealing with quite complex and profound sorts of issues. That's what I'm trying to get across.'[53] These two ideas encapsulate what lies at the core of Erskine's representation of intimacy – the representation of people who have been excluded from society and the profoundness of everyday acts of intimacy.

In these fictions, character's homes often mirror their mental state. Stoic loner Barry in 'The soul has no skin' inhabits a place that mirrors his insularity: 'Alright, the flat's pretty spartan, can't deny it.'[54] In 'Observation' the glamorous mother is depicted as always surrounded by objects, but distant from people: 'Kim Cassells was on the sofa with a glass of wine and a magazine.'[55] The story consistently emphasizes her consumption of fashion and meticulous self-maintenance, and this is further examined through the depiction of the domestic: 'The house was full of stuff and they all bathed in it.'[56] In 'Inakeen', Jean's loneliness and desire for connection is expressed through her curtain twitching and obsession with the precise domestic moments of the family across the road. In 'Arab States: Mind and Narrative', Paula's distance from her husband is set against a picture of untidiness and lack of care: 'A handful of bills and a takeaway menu on the mat, a solitary black banana in the bowl, but no Jimmy.'[57] This detachment extends to her lack of interest in her daughter's intimate life. In 'Last Supper', Jester's coffee shop is run through a charity and takes on the function of a home from home for patrons and staff alike. The modern cafe seeks to mimic home comforts, from the sofas to the soft lighting. By comparison, 'JD shares, with an assortment of people, a once grand and elegant house on the other side of town, long subdivided into little cold rooms.'[58] As the staff are recovering from issues, such as alcoholism, there are moments of camaraderie in this story which feel domestic, offering alternative kinds of spaces for intimacy.

This collection features not only traditional homes, but also places that function as a second home when the actual home is a fraught space to occupy: cafes, salons and community centres. The first in the collection, 'To All Their Dues', is a beautifully crafted short story that focuses on the lives of three protagonists: beauty salon owner Mo, 'hard-man' Kyle and his girlfriend Grace. Mo eschews her career options of phone sex operator or psychic, both of which involve kinds of faked emotional closeness, to offer a different kind of intimacy in her treatments. Beauty therapists offer what Paula Black calls the 'intimate routines of body maintenance.'[59] Black also draws our attention to the fact that more attention has been paid to the 'social spaces and intimate worlds open to men'[60] rather than those traditionally open to women, such as the beauty salon, the hairdressers and the laundrette. The most overt sign that the salon is an intimate space is the necessity of undressing for many of the treatments. Mo muses on the stories that the bodies in front of her tell: 'Oh there were questions you could ask if you wanted to, bodies that begged for someone to ask why, what's that all about … Those arms like a box of After Eights, slit slit slit, why you doing that, you with your lovely crooked smile, why you doing that?'[61] Treatments can involve complete or partial nudity and skin-to-skin contact, such as massages. Also, *intimate* waxing refers to hair removal in the pubic region. Beauty is intimate work, often between people who identify as femme, nearly always behind closed doors. Salons are often women-owned, and their clientele is mostly women. The business trades on intimacy (the cup of tea, the light chat) but can also be a radical space for women to express their desires. For the therapist, this is emotional as well as physical labour: in Black's study, all of the therapists she interviewed 'claimed that one of their functions was to offer counselling in their relationships to clients'.[62] The beauty therapist is often party to confidences from their clients and also the unexpressed hopes that these treatments provide: 'People looking at their faces, seeing a crumpled version staring back at them, hoping that the dermabrasion was going to make them feel like the time when they were thirty and told that funny story at their sister's party and everybody laughed.'[63] A beauty therapist gains access to bodies and the narratives they produce, and Mo presents an atmosphere of comfort where these vulnerabilities can be exposed. Erskine stated that 'I am often drawn to locales – real and fictional – where intimacy between relative strangers is legitimised, such as the beauty salon. Within minutes of meeting, one woman can be tenderly touching the skin of another, skin rarely seen, private skin.'[64] In her stories, Erskine carefully reveals the intimacy of showing this 'private skin' to another.

Into this haven Mo has created for others, then, comes a flying projectile in the form of a snooker ball through the window and barely veiled threats from Kyle, who appears to be a paramilitary enforcer. While Kyle attempts to improve his life through hypnotherapy, this is doomed to failure as he cannot articulate why he is attending this treatment, and without a specific ailment to focus on, the practitioner is unable to offer him any sort of targeted help. Significantly, he does not have access to the scripts of intimacy he would need to benefit from the therapeutic exchange. He chafes against vulnerability and therefore cannot participate in the dialogue needed to create intimacy. Healing requires an admission, not of fault, but of need. Then, a brief moment of pause in the treatment room allows him to remember a pivotal moment from this childhood: 'Kyle is in the old front room where their dad is lying half on, half off the rug and the blood from his mouth is pooling on the floor.'[65] He thinks about his brother's death and the domestic violence that the two young boys were subjected to. Here, intimate violence between men is shown to have damaging, lasting consequences. The narrative of the Troubles and domesticity interact to reiterate the dual-sided nature of the home as both sanctuary and danger zone.

Kyle and his girlfriend Grace meet at a restaurant which is depicted as the epitome of East Belfast gentrification: 'There were now white tiles and pictures from local artists. Every table had a couple of tea lights and a posy in a jam jar.'[66] While Grace is initially depicted as acquiescent and detached, she has possibly the richest backstory of the three as she has an evangelical background but has also had a pivotal experience of same-sex attraction in her adolescence. Her family's faith sets her apart from her classmates: 'The girls in her class used tampons. Grace's mother thought tampons tantamount to rape.'[67] She is tasked with befriending a local foster girl, Kerri, who has an untidy room. The intimate space of the bedroom is further complicated by Kerri showing Grace pornography featuring a woman who was 'not totally naked, she had on gold platform heels'.[68] When Grace recoils, she entreats her, 'Look at it again. Look at this one. They're all at it.'[69] Kerri then attacks Grace and they have a scrap on the bedroom floor. This is a pivotal moment in Grace's sexual development that haunts her as she fantasizes about Mo: 'That ponytail, you could wrap it round and round your first, pull it tight.'[70] Her sexuality is never clearly defined in the story: we do not know if she is sexually attracted to her partner Kyle, and she never describes herself as lesbian or bisexual. These unexpressed feelings cause a loss of faith in Grace:

> There was pain and there was passion and there was no God. Some people had to wait a lifetime to find out that kind of thing, had to study and read books, gaze up at the stars. But it has been made apparent to her when she was young, it had come all in a rush when someone was whacking her with a porno mag. You might never experience that intensity of revelation ever, ever again.[71]

Here, intimacy acts as a point of revelation that allows Grace to express something fundamental about her home, family and faith. This is a painful but necessary rupture. The comfort, then, comes in the hands of another woman. In Mo's intimate, feminine space Grace finds solace, not knowing that her own male partner has threatened her haven. She describes the feelings engendered by visiting the salon: 'The woman was just starting out. Weird little box of a place but she liked it. It was always warm, and it smelled of coconut.'[72] The intimate work of beauty, then, emerges from both the therapist and client's perspectives in this story – Erskine allows us a peek into this vital, private space to show the variety of stories that are revealed on the folding table of a salon, or go unspoken. She depicts a word where the intimate world of women can be shattered in a moment.

'Locksmiths' focuses on a young woman who inherits a house following her grandmother's death. Her mother has been imprisoned for beating a man to death, possibly with a poker, and her release exposes the rift between the two. The introduction to the story establishes the house as a contested territory, as it discusses the aftermath of the Spanish financial crash, where workers were ordered to lock people out of their homes. Following a spate of suicides, Erskine notes, 'The guys, the locksmiths, masters of cylinders and springs, had never anticipated that their work would run to this kind of thing.'[73] This idea of the power of a front door lock runs through the story. Her mother's intrusion into her domestic space is one that is described reluctantly, and the spartan items she buys reflects her lack of enthusiasm for this perceived interloper: 'I bought a cheap bedside light and a single quilt cover, cotton, the sort that could take a boil wash.'[74] Her presence is read as fundamentally destabilizing the affective climate of the house: 'The air was pounding with so little.'[75] In particular, the unnamed narrator, finds comfort and confidence in her ownership of the house and its attendant DIY projects: 'Back when I first got the house I was in here all the time. It was a fairly exciting place. Home improvement, by its nature optimistic … My tool kit grew. I began with a few cheap screwdrivers and moved on to a DeWalt drill, secondhand.'[76] Here she ventures not just into the stereotypically feminine pursuits of interior décor but is also unintimidated by power tools. Her confidence grows as she expands her repertoire of domestic expertise, claiming ownership over the maintenance of her domestic space. When her mother defames her home as 'Welcome to the shithole', the narrator responds with 'My shithole though, I said quietly.'[77] Here, mother devalues her daughter's handiwork and living space, which becomes one of the final straws in their tenuous relationship. The full breakdown of this is rendered through the daughter's new found capability for domestic control: 'In the cupboard under the stairs I had my tool kit and I knew I was nothing like the Spanish guys who wouldn't change the locks. The DIY superstore had that whole aisle of mortices and sashes and it opened in less than an hour's time.'[78] Here, then, domestic intimacy can be reclaimed by women for their own autonomy through manual tasks traditionally reserved for men. If you can change your locks, you can change your intimate configurations.

In 'Sweet Home', there are multiple attempts at cultivating a sense of home, none of which prove fully successful. The central couple, Gavin and Susan, are defined by their relationship to it: he works from their domestic space while she, as an architect, designs other people's homes. Their marital house, by contrast, is an unhappy place following the death of their daughter and, subsequently, an accident involving Gavin and the child of one of their garden labourers. Bucky and Emma bring their little boy to Gavin and Susan's home, and Gavin forges a bond with him – this changes his relationship to the home that he usually find unbearable. He wanders through Belfast in search of warmth and human intimacy: 'If sitting in the new house all the time had little to recommend it then it was fortunate that in the streets nearby Gavin could look in the windows of bakeries and second hand shops. He went to the same old café where he always left a generous tip. They always looked pleased to see him.'[79] In this story, it is not that the house is unfit for purpose or uncomfortable, it retains long, negative associations with the failure of his personal life. Home is a fluid concept in the narrative.

Despite the couple settling in their domestic environment, it is referred to throughout as the 'new house'. This is also despite the house having a distinct history: 'The rooms in the new house were high-ceilinged with rococo cornicing. Although the grates were empty, most of the rooms had ornate fireplaces. An old house, it creaked.'[80] This house stands as a monument to a changing Belfast, with the architecture landscape of the city forever changed by the post-conflict march of 'progress', especially in the East. This old and new heritage meet in the extensions and modifications placed on the house: 'Gav continued for a while in the new house, sitting in the glass box in the mornings, waiting for the day to turn right.'[81] The home from home that endures in the narrative, however, is the community centre, which eventually becomes part of the landscape. It is called a People's Centre as the 'name usually given to this type of building – community centre – was rejected since it was through to be pejorative in its suggestion of entrenched cultural and political ideologies'.[82] In this story, Erskine demonstrates that the home can be the least homely place, and that a home from home can offer more profound intimacy and solidarity.

In 'NOTES FOR THE ATTENTION OF THOSE WORKING IN THE XANADU NIGHTCLUB, THE HENNESSY COURT HOTEL, BELFAST, 1983, found in the pocket of an old handbag when clearing a roof space, 2018', Wendy Erskine explores different kinds of intimacy within another closed space that becomes a home from home: an after-hours drinking spot in Belfast. The patrons largely fade into the background of the story as the focus falls on the 'Ooh La La' girls who serve in the club and on the careful ways in which they are instructed to feign intimacy and perform glamour. Erskine does not spare detail of the labour that goes into producing a body that is both acceptable and desirable. Her narrator discusses gusset placement and difficulties with intimate hygiene. The women's dressing room serves as a space for difficult discussions and also unexpected intimacy: 'Be wondering the next day why my knickers were tight and I'd realise it was because they were somebody else's.'[83] Their conduct and their standards of personal grooming are expected to be exact, with instructions from their management inserted into the text in italics, like an insistent interdiction to get the performance correct. Erskine references 'the pitiless gaze of other women'[84] as the Ooh La La girls size each other up, from the shape of their legs to the coif of their hair. Erskine offers the reader glimpses into the social lives of the men who frequent the club, who are often foreign correspondents, military personnel or international businessmen. They are instructed, '*It is imperative that you are highly discreet in your dealings with guests, many of whom may be involved in activities deemed "sensitive".*'[85] Erskine makes it clear that the women's own pleasure is rarely discussed, except on the rare occasions where there are parties in the adjoining hotel rooms: 'There were nights when Belfast was the most exciting place on Earth, a ripped, blasted adrenalin high.'[86] This scene represents an aspect of Troubles-era Belfast that is rarely discussed: pleasure enhanced by the hedonistic air of danger. While our narrator details some pleasurable encounters, she also features Rhonda, who has been violently sexually assaulted. For Erskine, then, sexual intimacy is something that exists on multiple levels. It can be feigned, enjoyed and is also a source of danger. In Erskine's stories, then, we have a complex engagement with the way in which space relates to intimacy in contemporary Northern Irish culture. She allows us to view houses that are not homes, and other places which allow the deepest intimate secrets to be revealed. In her diverse stories of contemporary East Belfast, we find new ways of looking at the city and what happens behind closed doors.

'I'm just watching my wee house':[87] Intimacy, domesticity and faith in Jan Carson's *The Fire Starters*

Jan Carson's *The Fire Starters* was published in 2019 by Doubleday. She has described the novel as 'a magic realist romp through East Belfast during bonfire season.'[88] It features the parallel narratives of two Belfast fathers, Jonathan Murray and Sammy Agnew, who both live in fear of their offsprings' potential. Set in contemporary East Belfast, most of the narrative takes place in the interior spaces of the home or the doctor's waiting room. Against this private, domestic world stand two exterior forces: the 'Summer of the Tall

Fires'[89] and the Unfortunate Children, of whom more later. Carson depicts the 'Tall Fires' as a phenomenon across Belfast but particularly concentrated in the East: an epidemic of arson focused on the destruction of homes and public buildings. The novel muses on the role of fire in Northern Irish culture: 'In the East, people are torn. It is part of their culture to burn things, yet they cannot possibly condone burning without order.'[90] Colin Graham, writing about the photographs of John Duncan, states that 'bonfires are the remnants of a rural tradition have survived disingenuously in the life of a city … they are an out-of-sorts relic of a Troubles mentality.'[91]

These two historical contexts are important for Carson's novel: the city on fire and the use of bonfires in 'post'-peace process Northern Ireland. The author depicts an uneasy city, an uneasy country, an uneasy peace. At the time of the writing of the novel, violence was ongoing and also the 'Promise of Peace' was not distributed equally.[92] She represents the moment in which she writes, ostensibly in peace time but with ongoing acts of violence, as an era that retains a physical presence despite a sense of an ending: 'The Troubles are over now. They've told us so in the newspapers and on television … We did not believe it in our bones. After so many years of sitting one way, our spines had set. We will take centuries to unfold.'[93] What Carson illuminates here shows what is left out of straightforward narratives of peacebuilding. Accordingly, she is careful to set the conflict in Northern Ireland against violence across the world, which justifiably now pulls the focus of the international news media: 'The world is not waiting for us. There are louder voices around the table now. African. Russian. Refugee.'[94] Part of the issue with contemporary Belfast that she identifies is the lack of language to describe a 'post'-conflict situation which is subject to sporadic outbreaks of violence. In the novel, Belfast is not only a bustling, busy city but also, critically, a city full of talk. Speech is everywhere in the novel but language often seems inadequate to the current moment: there is no lexicon available for a city between peace and violence that merely needs a teenager on social media to start a conflagration. It is a novel about the problem of communication and miscommunication, and about the tension between old and new ways of making yourself understood. This has clear consequences for the representation of intimacy. Carson discusses her intention to foreground these issues in her novel:

> The more I talk about *The Fire Starters*, the more I realise it's also a book about language … Language is an ambiguous thing in Northern Ireland. I open the first section of the book with the line, 'This is Belfast. This is not Belfast.' There are always two sides to everything here. When you consider Jonathan's

relationship with Sophie, it's about trying to restrict the potential problems with her use of language. For Sammy, it's already too late: his son is using language in a negative way. I am quite fascinated with rhetoric and how words can be used as weapons.[95]

Indeed, chapter 1, 'This is Belfast', unravels the ambiguities and inadequacies of language to describe our current moment. Carson's novel is specifically of East Belfast, an area which also features prominently in the work of Wendy Erskine and Lucy Caldwell. Carson's novel does not homogenize the experience of living in the East, and Sammy and Jonathan's parallel narratives emphasize the class divisions in Northern Ireland. Jonathan's cold, remote parents are bound by their middle-class social conventions and give little away about their intimate lives ('They did not move in the kind of circles where babies could be given away'[96]). Belfast is described thusly: 'This is a city like a word that was once bad and needs redeeming, "queer" being the first that comes to mind.'[97] The word is especially carefully chosen, given not only queer activism's reclamation of this term but also how queer theory uses language and the performative utterance to re-examine the speech act.[98]

Carson notes that, while writing the novel, she carefully observed the area, in which she has lived and worked for many years: 'When writing *The Fire Starters* I carried the idea of the book – it's characters and plotlines – in my head for many months, allowing the novel to gestate whilst I paced the boundaries of what would become its written landscape.'[99] Indeed, the novel clearly maps out the external and internal topography of the East Belfast house. Therefore, intimacy can refer not just to what happens behind closed doors but also to the experience of intimacy realized in a community: 'Ah, now, if there's one thing the people of the East are good at, it's holding a secret close. All them wee houses jammed together arse to elbow, you can't so much as turn in bed for letting your neighbours know.'[100] Carson has detailed that these close-knit quarters informed her writing process:

> There is no such thing as absolute privacy when the city encroaches so heavily upon your personal space. There is no such thing as perfect silence either … With space so limited personal boundaries are often blurred. In my tiny, terraced home it is impossible to fully divorce myself from my neighbours' lived experience … The line between outside and inside often feels equally fluid.[101]

She collapses any idea of the house being a clear, discrete dividing line. Sounds, sights and smells easily breach the domain of a terraced house. In *The Fire*

Starters one is not merely intimate with one's own family, but with the whole community. Carson refers to this as 'forced intimacy' as she notes,

> [There] is something about the forced intimacy of the architecture, (both physical and social), in this part of the city which seems to be exactly the kind of creative constraint I like to push against and challenge. I'm increasingly fascinated by small, enclosed spaces, (I've lost track of how many stories I've recently written which are set in cars, caravans and buses), and how they throw people together, exposing both the best and worst of their personalities.[102]

As Carson states here, enclosed spaces are powerful spaces for an imaginative reconsideration of intimate life, and she has a commitment to representing the positive and negative aspects of these interactions.

The language of the novel, and its attendant relationship to intimacy, is influenced by religion. Carson discussed her relationship to her Presbyterian upbringing ('Old Testament stories, the King James Bible and hymns are definitely at work, and I'm more aware of it now') with an interviewer who offered the comment, '*The Fire Starters* is written in what Carson describes as her "primary language", that of her Presbyterian upbringing.'[103] When the *Irish News* asked Carson 'Is there a God?' she answered, 'Yes, I think there is but I'm pretty sure I'll be wrestling with this question and its implications for the rest of my life.'[104] I want to be wary about extrapolating too much from this background and over-deterministically proclaiming Carson a 'Presbyterian' or 'Evangelical' writer because the novel retains an ambiguity about the role of religion in its characters' lives. This is certainly not an evangelical novel, and the important word in Carson's statement is 'wrestling': the novel demonstrates several acts of faith and belief but this is never uncomplicated. While faith is sometimes understood as offering its adherents a kind of comfort, in this novel it can lead to painful revelations. Religion and intimacy are also complex bedfellows: the major faith traditions in Northern Ireland share moral conservatism around homosexuality, premarital sex and abortion. Carson's writing focuses on destabilizing the authority of the patriarch of the house in Northern Ireland, and this questioning of patriarchal authority underscores Carson's complex attitude towards religion. In the novel, one father inadvertently sacrifices his own son after trying to sacrifice himself, and another one cannot bear to mutilate his own daughter. It becomes, then, about the tenderness of fatherly love. Both are understood using biblical metaphors, despite neither man's faith being discussed at length. We presume both have had a Protestant upbringing, but the exact nature and depth of belief is unclear. Despite this, Christian imagery runs throughout the novel and is set against the magic realist elements of the narrative. Against this, however, is the mythological systems that are at play and also additional imaginative elements devised by Carson. This multilayered textuality leads to a hybrid approach of making sense of contemporary Belfast and will inform the consideration of the novel's relationship to scripts of intimacy.

This novel is written in what might be termed a 'magic realist' style although this term has been debated and 'magical realism' and 'marvellous realism' offered as alternatives. Nonetheless, Carson describes her writing as 'magic realism', and she cites the influence of writers such as Borges, Allende and Rushdie.[105] Tellingly, the stories of the 'Unfortunate Children' are set out from the narrative, in short vignettes that are marked out from the main Sammy/Jonathan plot by italics. These stories become less set apart as the plot progresses and the Unfortunate Children feature in Jonathan's story. This collapsing of binaries further adds to the effect of magic realism as a textual and narrative strategy. Carson has stated that, for her, the 'realism comes before the magic'.[106] Dawn Sherratt-Bado, discussing the relationship of magical realism to the aftermath of the Troubles, argues that 'Northern Irish magical realist fiction also undermines these assumptions because it disrupts the order of dominant cultural narratives'.[107] While this point on the disruption of narrative is well taken, Sherratt-Bado puts an over-deterministic focus on 'trauma' as an agent in the lives of Northern Irish writers. I want instead to foreground the representation of intimacy rather than just trauma in the novel and examine the narrative frames that Carson's characters use to try and make sense of their personal lives. Jonathan, for example, seeks to make sense of his lover and child through literature and popular culture, as his medical training is not helpful in deciphering the mystical or magical. He begins with medical textbooks and googling 'other human beings capable of flourishing on nothing but liquids, for adult men and women with skin as flawless as that of newborn children'.[108] He watches *The X-Files* ('The truth might still be out there'[109]) but turns away when there is potential for harm towards the creatures: 'The other is always the enemy, and I don't think I can stomach watching a Siren killed or kept in a laboratory for experiments'.[110] In a self-satirizing moment from a magic realist writer, Carson has Jonathan find his parents' copy of Borges's *Book of Imaginary Beings* but prefers instead the succinct summary of myth on Wikipedia. This choice speaks to broader questions of the tools that we have to make sense of the world around us but, most critically, how we make sense of domestic and intimate challenges through existing representations in literature and popular culture. Jonathan imagines his former paramour as something malevolent that could unsettle the uneasy peace: 'Everything seemed fine and healing, until she came floating up the Lagan. ... Now the city is like a raw wound, gaping ... The old trouble could kick up its heels and go in for another round.'[111] She is described throughout as a Siren, a figure perhaps most famously explored by Ovid and Homer. Their singing was said to lure sailors to their deaths. The painter John William Waterhouse depicted them as lithe young women, and their representation is often linked to the perceived dangers of female sexuality. Here, mythology offers a way to make sense of the disruptive forces of intimate life – both pleasure and trauma.

It is significant, therefore, that Carson fashions a distinctly East Belfast magic realism. Protestant folklorists such as Lady Gregory and Douglas Hyde had strong nationalist convictions, but the community generally does not feature heavily in accounts of Irish folklore.[112] However, a recent academic project has rediscovered a rich vein of supernatural writings among Northern Irish Protestants. Andrew Sneddon and John Privilege's *The Supernatural in Ulster Scots Folklore and Literature Reader* 'demonstrates that in Ulster Scots culture, both rural and urban, there was a range of sincerely held, supernatural beliefs, similar in many ways to those held elsewhere in Ireland ... This includes witchcraft, fairies, the evil-eye, magical practitioners, ghosts, and the general supernatural (including banshees, omens and fortune-telling).'[113] Carson exploits the tension, then, between the taboo of expressing a belief in the supernatural and the centuries long presence of these beliefs in a traditionally Protestant culture. These beliefs prove particularly potent when channelled towards an understanding of intimate life. Carson represents the Protestant people of East Belfast as remarkably laissez-faire about the presence of the supernatural in their midst: 'There's plenty of people in the East believe in your so-called supernatural crap: ghosts and God and weans with powers nobody really understands.'[114] This novel begins to reinsert some light touches of magic to a community bound together by religious belief. Former mission halls become spaces where the parents of magical children can meet. The terraces of the East hold other-worldly beings. Carson represents the domestic and the fantastic as everyday bedfellows: two forces that were marginalized during the realist heyday of the Northern Irish novel.

Into this other-worldly narrative, Carson embeds particular focus on the role of the child. In the novel, she explores two forces that are brought to bear on the figure of the child – the Northern Irish context and how this figure has been shaped by the language of faith and mythology. The tropes of both self-sacrifice and child sacrifice have been ascribed to various religions and civilizations: both constitute intimate kinds of sacrifice. Scholars have recently confirmed that children were sacrificed in fire pits in pre-Christian Carthage.[115] The language of child sacrifice run through the Old Testament although there is theological disagreement over whether Jephthah burned or banished his daughter.[116] Potentially the most germane context for this novel, though, is Abraham who, in Genesis, was prepared to murder his son on God's command. Abraham is thought of as the founding father of Judaism, Christianity and Islam, so, in representing the father as infanticidal, Carson is further exposing the patriarchal violence at the heart of established traditions. Similar to Abraham with Isaac, Sammy is stopped in the act of sacrificing his son: 'Abraham then he will be, or maybe God, offering his son up as a sacrifice.'[117] In addition to the patriarchal codes of Abrahamic faiths, Carson also takes aim at the traditional role of the father in Northern Irish society and culture.[118] This is influenced by religious tropes but is also inflected with the legacy of a conflict that prized certain codes of masculinity above all else. Typically, the father assumes the role of a protector of the home in Northern Irish culture.[119] While this might be a prevailing norm in Western patriarchal societies, in conflict zones it has a more literal meaning, where the father might have to be prepared to use physical force to defend the domestic realm. Despite the end of the conflict, such tropes endure in the minds of both Jonathan and Sammy: both of them spend large portions of the novel considering on acts of violence that they believe to be protective. In this novel, then, the potential for domestic violence and tenderness sit side by side. Both fathers exhibit feelings of God-like arrogance/delusion throughout the novel but ultimately choose sacrifice instead. Significantly, Sammy attempts to sacrifice himself but fails, and one might argue that Jonathan's final actions are also a kind of sacrifice. This novel represents men who have had initial failures of intimacy, then over-identify with their role as father, seek to destroy their potentially volatile children, but ultimately love prevents them from sacrificing their children. Intimacy as sacrifice requires not just small everyday moments of compromise but also, potentially, larger acts of faith.

The child operates as a powerful symbolic figure within Northern Irish culture and revered in culture. Christopher Vardy notes that, for critics, the child as '*figure* does political and ideological work … the ongoing function of the figure of the child in structuring discourses of social and political futurity is difficult to dispute'.[120] Accordingly, there are two powerful tropes that are regularly used to represent young people in Northern Ireland: the blameless child caught in the crossfire and the potent figure in Northern Irish culture of the 'rioting youth'.[121] The former type functions in discourse as emblematic of the worst consequences of the Troubles and illuminates the edict that children must be protected at all costs. Often, the most dangerous place for a child is the family home. The rioting child, in contrast, is often manifested in visual imagery, particularly Clive Limpkin's iconic photographs of children during the Battle of the Bogside.[122] In an interview following Lyra McKee's death in 2019, her partner Sara Canning said that group such as the 'New IRA' were 'no better than paedophiles' in their 'grooming' of children for violence.[123] As well, Liam Kennedy notes the level of paramilitary retribution towards their younger members: 'The victims are mainly young men from working-class areas, and not even children are immune.'[124] This figure of child as violent aggressor manipulated by paramilitaries endures beyond the end of the Troubles because each summer brings televised footage of young people rioting.

What Carson does in this novel is to complicate this narrative of the Northern Irish child as victim or groomed aggressor. She describes children as 'unfortunate heirs of someone else's spite'.[125] The young people who are committing the acts of arson belong to the generation Lyra McKee described as 'Ceasefire Babies':

> The Ceasefire Babies was what they called us. Those too young to remember the worst of the terror because we were either in nappies or just out of them when the Provisional IRA ceasefire was called … We were the Good Friday Agreement generation, destined to never witness the horrors of war but to reap the spoils of peace. The spoils just never seemed to reach us.[126]

Carson presents a rootless generation who have not reaped these 'spoils of peace' and who prefer nihilism over the ideology of their parents' generation. This representation is more destabilizing than the figure of the rioting child as, at least, they can be ascribed a particular political viewpoint. The arsonists are indiscriminate in their targets, beginning with homes and moving on to large targets of libraries and government buildings. The violence begins in this most intimate of arenas. This generation would not have been witness to house burnings of the 1960s, but their choice of target is telling: the home here acts as a symbol of their relationship with their parents and a certain kind of past. In the novel, we see young men unable or unwilling to move out but still unhappy with their living conditions. The relationships between Sammy and Mark acts as a microcosm of the Northern Irish post-conflict domestic: the Ceasefire Baby and the former paramilitary under one roof.

In Sammy's narrative, home is a deeply troubling place. Sammy articulates fantasies of a simple domestic life, which revolves around a peaceful family

Christmas, snacks from Marks and Spencer and watching films. Indeed, throughout the narrative he regularly considers the pleasures of the familial domestic such as Chinese takeaway and the comfort of watching television on the sofa. Despite these fantasies, home is not a place of safety or sanctuary, but rather disturbed and uneasy: 'If Sammy's honest, it hasn't felt like home for years. The house seems smaller every time he walks through the door, as if the walls are inching inwards and the ceiling will soon be brushing against his head.'[127] His son is as a kind of madman in the attic because his presence functions as an uncanny reminder of the consequences of decades-long violence. The fact that he chooses to focus on house-burning is significant. Adam Hanna notes that the 'house-burnings of August 1969 were the latest incident in several years of escalating violence that had begun in the mid-1960s'.[128] Throughout his study, Hanna discusses the symbolic importance of the burned-out house to Heaney and Longley's work. In particular, he notes that, in Longley's work 'the sight of burnt-out houses is, like a murder, something which one cannot see and yet remain indifferent to'.[129] This iconic figure of the Troubles, then, is repurposed by Carson, to destabilize the intimacy of 'post'-conflict domestic life.

These houses offer a false barrier in *The Fire Starters*: the domestic area is not contained, or the home a safe haven, rather, its solidity can be easy disrupted through arson or flooding. The cliche of 'safe as houses' does not hold in this novel due to the ability of forces of the elements, water and fire, to breach the domain. The novel oscillates between war and peace, also has clear opposition at its core: Sophie is a child of water and Mark is a child of fire. Both of these elements have obvious biblical references. Fire is used throughout the Old and New Testament, often as the instrument of wrath of a vengeful God. It is also used as a point of revelation, which reveals something fundamental, such as with Moses and the burning bush in Exodus. Significantly, it is also regularly linked with the speech act, as in Acts, where the Holy Spirit descends as tongues of fire. In James 3:6, speech through the tongue corrupts the whole body: 'The tongue also is a fire, a world of evil among the parts of the body. It corrupts the whole body, sets the whole course of one's life on fire, and is itself set on fire by hell.' In contrast, the representation of water is a hugely important symbol in Christianity, particularly around the ritual of baptism. Other than communion, it is the only sacrament celebrated by the Presbyterian Church. Of Sophie, we are told, 'Now, here she is, a little mermaid baby, riding high and happy on the surface of a flood.'[130] Water offers rebirth, cleanliness and the promise of new life. Indeed, after the Summer of Fire, rain acts to dampen the ardour of the arsonists: 'What a relief the rain is. What a way to start again.'[131] This relief is experienced in an almost religious sense because all the denizens of Belfast experience the 'same sudden baptism'.[132] These elemental forces, with the force of biblical association, then, have the ability to permeate the boundaries of the home and family and expose the fragility of intimacy.

Sammy, a former combatant, is used to raise vital questions of men, mental health and medicalization during the Troubles. He represents the men who, having been part of a sustained campaign of violence, now take on caring roles within the home. Although Sammy is a perpetrator rather than a victim of violence, he is anxious that his son does not follow in his footsteps: 'He needs to tell his son that violence is a passed-down thing, like heart disease or cancer. It's a kind of disease.'[133] However, Carson shows that Sammy can only see his son's malevolence as nature rather than nurture. In one brief moment, the reader discovers that Mark has been violently abused by his father: 'Sammy looks at Mark and he cannot see a bad man, only a little boy lost and broken, only a thing he had lifted his fists to and ruined.'[134] Against the two competing discourses of childhood discussed earlier ('Children of the Crossfire' versus the 'Rioting Youth'), Carson sets another figure: the spectre of the abused child. While Jonathan stops short of mutilating his own child, it is implied that Sammy has been a domestic abuser to at least one of his family members. Here, intimate is presented as a potentially toxic, dangerous place where corrosive shame harms everyone.

While Sammy has issues connecting emotionally with his family, Jonathan is depicted as a man starved of intimacy. His conception was an unhappy accident, and he suffered the weight of his parents' indifference throughout his life. He tries to form bonds with his medical student friends but remains distinctly neutral in his interactions with them: 'I didn't really like them or enjoy their company, but perhaps friendship required something more than ease.'[135] He uses television as a substitute for intimacy, and, as a result, develops a deeply skewed idea of what relationships entail. He finds the imperfection of real-life intimacy a poor substitute for the idealization that he has seen on screen. As he confesses, romantic relationships pose a particular problem for him: 'I had never once been in love with anyone. I couldn't imagine myself loose enough.'[136] All of his interactions, except with his daughter, have a particular kind of detachment. He has no one with whom to voice his fears with, both his loneliness and then his mounting fear that his daughter is a force for destruction. He states, 'I was a forgotten kind of person.'[137] Elsewhere in the novel, Carson examines the problems and possibilities of intimacy, we see bodies used to produce feeling in others through international tourism: 'We dance for them and their foreign money. We are also prepared to cry if this is expected.'[138] This is a performance of a certain kind of Northern Irishness that is palatable for an international audience. In particular, the performance of a certain kind of bonhomie or pathos is feigned intimacy. This is acutely rendered in Jonathan volunteering for a tourist initiative. His vulnerability and desperate desire for connection lead him to volunteer for the 'Belfast Is for Lovers' tourist campaign, which seeks to establish a reputation for Belfast as a romantic destination: 'The tourists, seeing lovers everywhere they turned, would soon believe Belfast to be a truly European city.'[139] The proximity to a woman in this moment of feigned intimacy arouses him: 'Then I was there, with her lips on my lips and her eyes staring into mine.'[140] This attempt to recast Belfast as a romantic destination is met here by the awkward reality that many attempts at intimate connection are fraught.

When he meets his lover and eventual mother of his child, the experience is deeply unsettling: 'But desire falls far short of the undulating contractions currently waging war on my brain.'[141] Compared to his previously faked emotions, this situation creates a real, destabilizing passion. Jonathan seeks to make sense of her through established mythic parallels. He uses the term 'Siren', replete with all its connotations: 'The Siren's voice has always been pitched towards destruction: shipwrecks, madness and vicious death.'[142] He imagines her deadly qualities: 'Wicked, matchless Siren, and I'll be lucky to survive her or the thing she's making in my bathtub.'[143] And, indeed, in a dream she takes responsibility for the outbreak of violence in the 'Summer of the Tall Fires': 'Bold Siren of a woman, with her hair come loose, snaking down her back. "I did all this … I raised my voice and ruined everything."'[144] Goddesses of war exist across systems of myth, from the Norse Valkyries to Athena in Greek mythology. In Irish mythology, for instance, the Morrigan/Morrigu is a birdlike goddess of war also associated with the figure of the Banshee/bean sí.

In addition to his relationship, the greatest disruption to Jonathan's life is not the fires raging outside but his efforts to care for his baby daughter. Here, Carson represents intimacy as something exceptionally vulnerable and exposing: 'I have made a list of fears that did not exist before you: the fear of people and the fear of lacking people, the fear of money, telephones and time.'[145] In addition to the intimacy of the home depicted in both narrative strands, the novel also represents the intimacy of the general practitioner and the sanctity of the doctor's office. Jonathan casually details the ailments of the people who visit him, and for much of the story, his dispassionate character is useful in keeping his distance. However, this all changes with the visits of Sammy and also Ella, a young girl unwilling or unable to use the wings she has developed. Immediately, his mood changes: 'The presence of this child has changed the atmosphere of my surgery.'[146] His surgery goes from an arena where he can view the bodies of others with a sense of detachment to where he painfully identifies with the bodies of others: 'I touch this place with the tip of my gloved finger and she trembles.'[147] Jonathan is a man, then, who feels comfortable with certain kinds of intimacy and desirous of other forms but who is fearful of the consequences of this closeness.

The end of the novel focuses on Jonathan's intimacy with his daughter. While Jonathan frames his plan to mutilate her as righteous, Carson represents the vulnerability of children in the home from the violence of their parents. The final chapters build up a sense of anxiety and foreboding. He understands his actions through the framework of religious belief: 'I touch her lips with the tip of my smallest finger and think about the man in the Bible – Old Testament most likely – whose lips were burnt by an angel with hot coal.'[148] This moment, in Isaiah, represents purification and renewal through fire, where sin and guilt is taken away. However, while the mouth can be operated transgressively, it is through speech (or, at least, pre-speech babbling) that Jonathan is redeemed:

> One syllable. 'Da'. The possibility of infinite syllables to come. ... I should have covered my ears but it's too late. I've already heard her and nothing now can ever be simple again. Everything will be on Sophie's terms. There isn't anything I won't do for her. ... I know she will destroy me. I wouldn't have it any other way.[149]

It would not be accurate to describe this final scene as a 'love conquers all' ending. Intimacy is represented as something hard won that is not without its complicated, painful drawbacks. This commitment to life makes a point as dramatic as the raging fires that Jonathan can see from his window as he holds his baby daughter. To enter into a relationship with another, whether a lover or family members, requires a vulnerability and openness to potential harms. It demands true courage. This courage is what Carson represents here: both the stark reality that what we love could destroy us and also the enriching powers of intimate life. Carson states her intentions: 'Public and private experience, the external world and my internalised interpretation of it are inseparably merged. Perhaps, this was always inevitable. There seems no other way to write a place with so many lives pressed tightly together, like library books on a too full shelf.'[150] By design, the novel presents a 'too full shelf' with overlapping mythologies and inventive new magical figures. In melding this unique narrative style with a

Belfast setting and the age-old story of intimacy between father and child, she has created a powerful account of the possibilities and difficulties of reimagining our intimate lives.

A 'new form of intimacy': Desire, faith and textuality in Phil Harrison's *The First Day*

Phil Harrison illuminates a different kind of intimacy in his first novel, *The First Day*. The novel focuses on the consequence of an extramarital affair between a preacher, Samuel Orr ('Orr was the pastor of a small mission hall in east Belfast'[151]), and Anna, a 'Beckett Scholar'.[152] The first part of the story details their meeting, sexual relationship, conception of a child and the death of his wife, Sarah. Orr's wife dies in ambiguous circumstances: neither he nor the reader can be sure if she slipped on the train platform or died by suicide. Orr's eldest son Philip expresses his rage and grief by horrifically maiming Orr's illegitimate son in a careful, chilling knife attack. The second part of the story describes this son, also called Samuel, in New York with his ageing, visually impaired father, tries to make sense of the violent act that marked his childhood. For ease, I will refer to the father as Orr and the son as Samuel as Harrison does in the novel. As we reach the end of the first part, the apparently omniscient narrative voice is revealed to be Samuel's: 'I raise my hand to my cheek and take it away. There is blood all over it. This is my first memory.'[153] By turns it is an erotic novel and one that deals with the consequences of violence. Harrison's novel delineates the fixity and impossibility of borders and boundaries in relationships: of the push and pull between intimacy, trauma and the past.

Compared to other fictions of 'post'-conflict Belfast, Harrison wears the direct political context of these representations lightly: 'It was 2012, and a tentative peace was slowly beginning to transform the city.'[154] Anna 'was born in 1986, long after the most horrific days: the no-warning bombs, the Shankill butchers, the bar massacres. 1986 was the year of the last mass demonstration in Belfast'.[155] Indeed, she would have been 12 at the time of the signing of the Good Friday Agreement and had her teenage years marked by hope and the promise of peace. The violence of the Troubles does not drive the narrative, as might be expected, rather it is driven by family violence. In an interview, Harrison noted that 'Belfast right now inhabits an in between space – the Troubles of the recent past abandoned but the future as yet very much open'.[156] The novel thus represents the negotiation of this 'open' future and the forces seeking to close it down. The usual taboo frisson in Northern Irish texts is between protagonists from either side of the religious divide, but here we encounter a different kind of clash of sensibility between two forms of Protestant thinking: the evangelical emphasis on the word of God and the secular writing of Samuel Beckett. Both preacher and academic adhere to similar kinds of work practices: an emphasis not only on solitude and painstaking textual work but also on a potent element of charismatic performance. The relationship to the text is different, compared to the sceptical way that literary texts are often interrogated, the Bible is taken as an instructional document of faith by the faithful.

The novel compares and contrasts these two systems of knowing – both textual and both reliant on the sacredness of men's words. One of the epigraphs to the novel is 'Ne pas céder sur son désir – Jacques Lacan,'[157] which is usually translated as 'Do not give up on your desire.'[158] Indeed, desire and want burn throughout the whole text, and are often shown at odds with intimacy. The novel demands that the reader appreciates women's sexual agency and features an intelligent, creative female protagonist, but Harrison involves an almost exclusively male textual frame, quoting from the Bible and Beckett through to Bataille and Lacan. The text bristles with intellectual and scriptural ways to understand emotional life. In interviews to promote the novel, Harrison cites intellectual influences including Freud, Kierkegaard and Sartre. Male artistic figures also regularly feature, including Cezanne, Rubens and Conrad. Important to note is that Anna eventually moves into a successful creative career of her own and is the only character in the text who begins to transcend the potent pull of other people's words in her mouth. She develops her own critical voice through a reconsideration of the affective and sensual: 'And yet the insights lingered, and formed a vocabulary of their own, and she began to embrace them as truths and build her new work around them.'[159] In a novel replete with the voices of others to understand intimacy, this new vocabulary signals a new option for achieving intimacy.

Language is presented in the novel as a rhythmic, compulsive and intensely physical force. The sensuality of experience is examined through the depiction of the mouth and tongue: 'The touch. And she realised that he had already thought of her naked, imagined the taste of her skin under his tongue. Jesus.'[160] These two tropes, the sacred word and the lascivious mouth, are merged in one of the novel's most transgressive passages: 'What would Jesus do? she asked him. Orr was halfway putting his clothes back on. He stopped, looked at her, and said: He would do this. And he removed his clothes again and moved his mouth between her legs and began to kiss her.'[161] Their initial flirtation is conducted through carefully wrought conversation, right from the moment where Anna meets Orr as he is preaching outside his church. We catch glimpses of both of them in a particular kind of performance as he preaches and she lectures: text-based but inherently performative. Throughout the novel, Anna returns to the words of Beckett to make sense of both her relationship and her subsequent estrangement from Orr. Space does not permit any rehearsal of these tropes within Beckett's fiction, drama and poetry. It is worth noting that his writing is rich with the consideration of the pleasures and pitfalls of intimacy. Beckett writes about a variety of different intimate configurations in his work: sexual entanglements, loneliness, co-dependency. This variety offers Anna ways to think about the varying nature of her relationship with Orr. In many ways, she is exclusively faithful to Beckett throughout the novel, even as she begins to develop her own critical voice in her lauded poetry. For example, a recurring phrase throughout the novel is 'If I do not love you I shall not love'.[162] This is taken from an early Beckett poem, 'Cascando', which is engaged with unrequited love. Moreover, the connection between the visual and the word is highlighted by Anna's thesis topic, which is published as 'an examination of the influence of German romantic painters on Beckett's later plays'.[163] This will be examined later in this chapter as Anna is energized by her connection to a painter, and her son takes a role at the Metropolitan Museum of Art. Samuel, as narrator, repeatedly emphasizes not only Anna's connection to the written word but also how she looks at Orr. Structurally, then, the textual heavily influences the representation of intimacy in the first section of the novel, and the visual comes to the fore in the second.

The writing of Beckett and critical theory function as forms of secular scripture in the text. Such that Anna's adherence to Beckett's words offers her and Orr an early way to connect: 'They talked of Christ and Beckett and anything else into which they could channel their desire indirectly, any container to hold the immediacy of their longing without it spilling into view'.[164] Here Beckett's writing offers an intimate language that simultaneously shows and obscures. His writing even offers Anna a way to make sense of her love for her unborn child: 'She returned repeatedly in her head to Beckett's description of love in *Malone Dies* as "a kind of lethal glue", and lay awake at night – on her back, a new, forced position – trying to imagine what it would be like, holding her own child in her arms'.[165] Hence, the choice of Beckett is not only relevant to broad questions of being in relationship but it also underlies the sexual frankness that the novel portrays. Anna returns to this work in the first year of her son's birth, having dealt with the bodily reality of child-rearing: 'And yet she found herself returning to Beckett, when she could, with a renewed wonder, a feeling for the beauty in his blunt physical descriptiveness and obsession with the body, farting and fucking and so on.'[166]

Orr jokingly refers to Beckett as 'a good Protestant', and his early flirtation with Anna demonstrates their ways of understanding the world and the word. Harrison, like Carson, has discussed the legacy of his Northern Protestant upbringing: 'I grew up in a small religious community not unlike Orr's – and the various complications and frustrations and kindnesses of that have stayed with me long after I abandoned my faith.'[167] This statement makes a much more definite rupture than Carson identified in her writing, and Harrison's depiction of this faith community becomes more ambivalent as the novel meditates on the question of what is sacred. Various objects are subject to reverence in the text, whether sex, the word of God or the writing of Samuel Beckett. The taboo nature of consensual sexual affairs with men of God has been regularly examined in literature and popular culture, from Heloise and Abelard to *The Thorn Birds* and the 'Hot Priest' of the television show *Fleabag*. The figure of the sexually transgressive pastor, while slightly less prominent in Northern Irish culture does find expression in Stuart Neville's novel *Say So the Fallen* (2016). While this figure is free to marry, other sexual transgressions are also highly prohibited for men in the Protestant community in Northern Ireland. Lysaught and Kitchin note that 'the Free Presbyterian Church is highly active in campaigns against the incursion of liberal influences into Northern Ireland',[168] including family planning clinics, sex shops and resources for LGBTQ+ people. Harrison represents Orr, the adulterous man of God, as handsome and charismatic, a man 'around whom stories accumulated, stories rarely troubled by facts'.[169] This physicality has a complex effect on his audience: 'If any man serve me, let him follow me, Orr continued, Christ's words complicated by his own charm.'[170] In particular, he knows how to combine the words that he is preaching with his own physicality and is often depicted using striking hand gestures to convey his meaning: 'She watched his hands move as though levering the words, pumping them up from a well. She watched the hint of a smile form on his mouth from time to time.'[171] The Gospel in Protestant faith traditions is emphasized and Orr performs these words with a sensual zest: 'Some of them sucked on God's words like they were cough drops, but for Orr they were wine and honey.'[172] Harrison even describes the oratory of Ian Paisley in these terms: 'Paisley rallied the crowd, words like butter.'[173] This is an examination of the ways in which intimacy is created between a preacher and their congregants through oratory. Preaching relies on this intimacy, and it is designed to resonate, through the word, to generate affects and set out clear rules for the conduct of intimate life.

The novel follows the conventional narrative trajectory of short-term, passionate love affairs: the initial burst of sexual activity that will prove incompatible with domesticity. At the same time, this trajectory is complicated by the representation of guilt, fear and shame. Their initial sexual attraction is marked by a clear representation of the space between them. The gap between the secular and the spiritual ways of understanding the world stands in for the lack/gap that exists between all lovers. As Berlant argues, 'desire describes a state of attachment to something or someone, and the cloud of possibility that is generated by the gap between an object's specificity and the needs and promises projected onto it'.[174] This 'cloud of possibility' is the undefined future orientation of the love affair which, in this novel, is dashed by the relative certainty of the child and Orr's return to his religion. Faith requires the establishment of certainties in the face of the unknowable. Anna offers Orr a glimpse into uncertainty. He offers her access into a different kind of sensual world, which is similarly textual but not as grounded in interpretation: 'Being courted with scripture. A flirtation of the gospel. Anna had never experienced anything like it; the rhythms and patterns of the poetry pounded inside her.'[175] In addition to this, the narrative voice suggests that she is also attracted by the taboo of infidelity. Anna's parents are rarely mentioned in the novel, but we receive the intimation that her father left the family following an affair: 'She was a virgin at the time, and whilst she was hardly naïve, the destructive joy of sex remained an abstraction.[176] In addition to her affair with Orr, there is also a suggestion that her close friendship with the painter Curran became intimate while his wife was still alive. Later, Samuel notes, 'another married man, Dr Freud?', about this relationship. In a novel that suggests that parental foibles have clear consequences, the narrative voice reveals that her intimate scripts have been forged by infidelity. Using as the focus of the story the extramarital affair between the scholar and the man of God, Harrison is able to meditate on closeness, separation and the nature of subjectivity. While their tryst has an unusual context, Harrison maps some age-old contours within their interactions. While we have not all been 'courted with scripture', most of us have had decisive encounters and felt the waxing and waning of romantic love. The novel focuses on the smaller occasions that map intimate life: 'It was such a tiny moment, insignificant really. And yet, and yet. Kingdoms are won and lost in moments. It was the way he looked around, so imperceptible and so blunt.'[177] This novel offers ways of making sense of intimacy, but all of these feel provisional. It reads as if Samuel, and Harrison, is trying on different kinds of understanding: religious, literary, theoretical and artistic.

Where sexuality is represented as a force to be controlled in the maintenance of the self in faith traditions, here it is a kinetic agent. But, in Harrison's narrative, sex and violence come to be intimately linked. Orr's understanding of the role of faith and family is evidently heavily influenced by the language of scripture: 'It was not lost on Orr: The Lord is longsuffering, and of great mercy, forgiving iniquity and transgression, but by no means clearing the guilty, visiting the iniquity of the fathers upon the children unto the third and fourth generation.'[178] For Orr, the horrific consequences of his infidelity feel natural alongside the prohibitive moral traditions of his evangelical faith: 'She asked him if he thought God would punish him. For what? For this, she said. You and me. Of course He will, he said.'[179] Against the emerging guilt and retribution which inevitably emerge, this scene provides a sense of calm in the relationship. It is the eye of the storm: 'This nakedness a gift, something he gave her which everything that followed could never erase: the feeling of being at home in one's body.'[180] That feeling, also identified in Jenkinson's 'Marie + Finbar', grounds an intimacy with oneself. In the sex itself, significantly, there is no guilt or awkwardness, everything is depicted as easy and natural. It is the moral world outside of the sex that creates the issue.

Accordingly, Harrison takes time to explore the moments between moments of intimacy – how the frisson of the intimate lingers and how the body hungers for it in the interregnum: 'She had both too little of him and too much; even in his absence her body felt more alive, her awareness heightened.'[181] Here, intimacy is represented as not following strict temporal demarcations: here, the after-effects linger. It is not a feeling that can be bounded by literal presence. Their lovemaking is detailed in frank terms, as are the moments of intimacy around them: 'They almost always made love first, no small-talk or awkward uncertainty. After the first month, as their intimacy increasingly matched their desire, Anna would often answer the door naked.'[182]

The novel portrays not only overtly sexual intimacy but also moments of quotidian non-sexual intimacy. Crucially, this kind of intimacy is possible before Anna's pregnancy and the death of Orr's wife. While much of the early passages of the novel focuses on the intensity of their sexual connection, a trip to Scotland allows them moments of intimacy: 'For four days and four nights they drank tea, talked, sat in the shape of each other's bodies on a bench in front of the cottage watching the dusk descend and the mountains fold in on themselves, the colour fading slowly until all was darkness.'[183] As Harrison shows, intimacy is not a fixed, static entity but rather something subject to forces of movement and change throughout a life or within the course of a relationship. To be intimate with someone, whether sexually or otherwise, does not end the story. By beginning with the transgression and then unravelling its consequences, Harrison offers us messiness and complexity: 'They still had sex, but more gently, and less often … Orr still looked at her with longing, with desire, and his hands still moved over her.'[184] Harrison opens out the possibilities of different kinds of love, outside of the narrow possibilities of monogamy: 'Orr spoke so rarely of Sarah to me; but Orr said he did not stop loving Sarah, but rather – now I speculate – he felt his desire widen, expand.'[185] As well as the beginning of a relationship, this novel also examines its ending: 'Their intimacy grew more physical; she knew that the new pressure of his hands on her body, his rough tongue on her skin, held some unsaid, inarticulable truth.'[186] This description tells how we 'read' intimate moments and develop an interpretation of the subtle cues that a relationship is ending. Harrison represents the subtleties of the end of intimacy as Anna feels Orr begin to withdraw: 'But as Anna moved in his caresses, under his hands, he began to sense there an absence, a removal, and the deeper he went into it the further it receded.'[187] Many of the stories in this study consider the moment of intimacy – and the lack of it and desire for it – but this novel examines the slow process of intimacy fading. Here, it is presented as a gradual process of estrangement, as opposed to the 'coming home' of intimate contact.

If Harrison regularly portrays Anna's lust for Orr and her sexual desire, it deserves noting that her son is reconstructing his parents' relationship and his own father's physical desirability and charisma. He also represents the taboo eroticism of mothering:

> For Anna, the sheer physicality of her son was a startling location of pleasure, an eroticism she had not expected but found herself longing for daily, the strange combination of pain and focused, visceral pleasure as his mouth fastened on her, his rough gums on her nipples, first one then the other. On occasion, lying in bed, the sensation rose, spreading like melted butter, and she would orgasm, coming with a shudder, the child, oblivious, on her breast, still feeding.[188]

Clearly, this is a son representing his own mother orgasming while breastfeeding him, another example of the novel breaking the taboos around intimate life. Anna is also represented as having a flicker of inappropriate lust for Orr's son, who maims her own child, and, as we eventually discover, these are told through the narrative voice of that child. There are two ways to read this. The first is as a depiction of a sexual identity that women are not traditionally afforded in fiction, especially writing from Northern Ireland, as not only active desiring subjects but also the possessors of secret, taboo desires. The second interpretation would be that Anna is an almost monstrously sexual mother whose desires wreak havoc throughout the text. She is associated with the death of Orr's wife and her complicated relationship with Philip which allows him access to her home, where he eventually maims her son. It is significant that Philip remains estranged from her at the end of the text.

Alongside this fading of passionate intimacy, the resentments grow in Philip, Orr's oldest child. As in *The Firestarters*, the figure of the malevolent child threatens the family unit. In domestic fictions, the threat often stems from an abusive patriarch, but in these texts the fears of the consequences of violence for the next generation are manifested through an uncontrollable violent child. The narrator describes him as 'a craftsman of hatred'.[189] This figure proves particularly disturbing because they are 'home grown', a very intimate kind of terror. Philip is represented as someone who uses intimacy against people:

> Philip had an extraordinary skill of carefully unpicking a person's weakness, of paying attention as much to what they didn't say as to what they did. He had an ear for the repressed, the skilfully avoided. And he had that rare absence of compassion, a preparedness to use whatever he could get his hands on for his own ends.[190]

In the novel's intimate meditation on the limits of the body, Harrison returns repeatedly to the language of boundary and division, endlessly recreating and collapsing: 'Boundaries dissolved, no reflection, no mediation.'[191] In addition to this dissection of permeable borders, there is the question of the cut: the painting, Samuel's face, decisive breaks in relationships. This is made explicit by the depiction of sex: 'And the lover, bound together to the beloved, penetration eroding for the briefest of moments the lines between, the discontinuity.'[192] The novel, then, engages the reader to imagine what is transgressed, and how this is linked to the violence of the 'cut'. This section ends, significantly, with Philip slashing his young half-brother across the face. After the pivotal moment where Samuel is brutally scarred by Philip, we pivot to the second part of the novel, set years later. The act slices the novel in two: the reader is now fully aware who is narrating the story, and we move to New York to trace Samuel's life since the incident. The second part of the novel draws on thriller conventions, as the threat of Philip's violent return unleashes painful memories of the past. The tone is markedly different in the second part of the novel, as alongside this air of menace we trace Samuel's attempts not only to find sexual intimacy in America but also to renegotiate his relationship with his father. While the first part of the novel involved a son attempting to reimagine his parents' erotic life, this second part offers more uncomfortable revelations and recollections as Samuel seeks to come to terms with his scarring and role within the family. His role at the Metropolitan Museum of Art allows for insights into the kind of artistic practice he favours, the representation of the body, including Caravaggio, Cezanne and Rubens ('I discovered Rubens, the sensualist, his plump people full of life and sex and fat, so much more fleshy than his cautious contemporaries'[193]). This sensuality is heightened for Samuel by the anxiety provoked by his brother: 'The Rubenses bloomed. The flesh practically fell off them. I had been right: threat, danger enlivened the experience of the paintings, made them visceral in a way the austere silence disguised.'[194] Harrison emphasizes the sensuality of Courbet's 'Women with a Parrot' against the violence that has been done to it: 'Her curves are beautiful too. Her breasts are there, obviously, but you actually notice her belly more, a sort of tiny mound, a roundness.'[195] This delicate sensuality contrasted with Philip's actions: 'Courbet's painting is sliced neatly down the middle, a clean, brutal cut.'[196]

Where the mouth was the most significant receiver and transmitter of intimate information in the first part, a consideration of the eye takes place in the second part. In addition to the references to art detailed above, the novel also returns to the eye as a site of knowledge. For a text that directly quotes Bataille several times, it is significant that the father loses his sight following his sexual transgressions. In his reading of *The Story of the Eye*, Roland Barthes traces the metaphorical relationship between ideas of castration and blindness,[197] and the trope has a long history in psychoanalytic criticism.[198] Orr notes that, since his visual degeneration, 'words are my eyes now'.[199] His intimacy with his son is developed through reading aloud and he settles into the New York community through a re-engagement with scripture. In the same way as the first part of the novel illuminates Anna's attempts to make sense of her love affair through the frameworks of literature and critical theory, the second demonstrates the inadequacy of words for Samuel: 'I was so young that it didn't happen only once but rather kept happening, each moment of recollection, as my vocabulary grew, not simply a retelling but a re-enactment, the words themselves palpable, structural.'[200] Here, the body stands in for what cannot be vocalized in the text. Phillip is unwilling or unable to communicate his grief and pain.

While the eye achieves a new prominence in this story of art, blindness and erotic glances, it also foregrounds the role of skin and touch, which will be further explored in Chapter 3. Other than the mouth as a conduit for sensuality and textuality, the novel also represents the power of touch through hands as sensual objects. The hands that Anna was so captivated by as Orr preached were also used to caress her, with no less intensity. Samuel is always aware of his experience of being prominently facially scarred and the way this affects his intimate relationships. As Philip has intended, the scar acts as a constant reminder of the affair. A scar is often imagined as something fixed, but Samuel imagines his as having a kind of agency: 'I stare in the mirror and start to feel that my scar is moving, growing rather, expanding. I literally lift my hand to my face to stop it, and then stop myself.'[201] Samuel returns to think about Philip's motivation: 'But the scar was only the method. Philip's deliberation, his preparedness, settled in me as my own, personal gospel. … A precision that could barely be contemplated, and yet would never leave. And all for me. A gift. Reparation.'[202]

Harrison represents Samuel's search for intimacy in America. His first queer encounters are marked by shame, taboo and internalized homophobia. His desire for intimate contact reminds the reader how he imagined his mother's desires in the first part of the novel: 'But it crept back, the palpable, physical sensation of desire; increasingly at night I would awaken.'[203] Harrison carefully represents the sensuality of his casual encounters: 'But those few visits reminded me (like I had really forgotten) of breath on my neck, skin on my skin.'[204] This is a novel that seriously considers the power of the erotic in the lives of the protagonists: Samuel imagines his relationship with Oki in the same terms as he imagined his parents love affair, that eroticism is a kinetic force which internally destabilizes: 'It was a more visceral, tentative sensation, a spreading; Oki would move along my nerves, push to the edge of my body, as though, as I experienced in one nightmare, I was a host being eaten at from within.'[205] All sexual encounters in this novel have the power to radically destabilize and reshape the lives of the protagonists, and in this representation of a 'visceral' sensation, Harrison examines the power of intimacy to consume the self.

The novel deals with complex processes of intimacy, and the end is no exception. There is a move towards redemption, but the way is not straightforward. Samuel kisses his brother two times. The first time, when he is unconscious ('I lean my face to his, my lips to his lips, and I kiss him'[206]) and the second when he is in recovery ('I put my lips on his cheek – that cheek, yes – and kiss him'[207]). These acts of tenderness against an aggressor may seem like moments of forgiveness, but Philip is bedridden and helpless after Samuel has arranged to have him assaulted. Throughout the course of the narrative, Samuel has tried to make sense of his history through retelling the story of his family and their pivotal encounter, and not until the final pages of the novel does he reach something close to redemption: 'The past, where I had lived for ever, opened up into the present.'[208] Samuel's last comments offer a radical rejection of the past that projects him into the future: 'Fuck lines, fuck borders. Fuck family, fuck the law. Fuck one thing following another. Fuck the past, fuck the future. Fuck apology and disappointment. Fuck fear and shame.'[209] His life has been marked by failed attempts to make sense of a moment of intimate violence: through therapy, education and art. His scar made his history as a victim of violence immediately legible. With these words, he refuses the intimate and affective scripts that have been laid out for him. The lines and boundaries of the novel, so frequently tested to the point of collapse, now dramatically expose the solution to intimacy: 'fuck borders'.

From the beginning of the second part of the novel, Harrison makes the reader aware that its central concern will be the renegotiation of intimate relationships. At the end, Samuel has gained insight on his relationship with his father and 'whatever quantity of intimacy we both required, neither too much nor too little, we stumbled into easily'.[210] However, the casual intimacy with which the novels ends with is uneasy: Orr will continue to lose his sight and become more frail, and Philip is still a potential threat. But against this, a kind of hope endures, that family, whether of origin or by choice: 'The absurdity of it all: we became a family.'[211] In a novel that engages with the failure of heterosexual, monogamous family units to hold together, this is striking. Ostensibly, it covers three generations of a family: grandfather/father, son/uncle and niece/granddaughter. The novel ends with a visit from Sarah and these words from Bataille: 'Between one being and another, there is a gulf, a discontinuity … But I cannot refer to this gulf which separates us without feeling that this is not the whole truth of the matter.'[212] The erotic relationship of the first half of the novel, then, opens up ways of thinking about the complexities of intimate life. In the end, however, all of these attempts to make sense of intimacy, to quantify it theoretically or to use established scripts must be appreciated as limited and limiting. The intimacy at the end of the novel is surprising to all: the queer son, the dying father and the daughter of a violent man form a kind of family. But, intimacy is surprising: as each moment unfurls into the next we are endlessly brought together and separated. We cannot predict the ways in which our intimate relationships will unfurl, or the ways in which the narrative of personal and political history will influence their experience or representation.

'Love being a holding-close and simultaneously a letting-go': Proximity and distance in Lucy Caldwell's *Intimacies* (2021)

Of the texts considered in this study, Lucy Caldwell's *Intimacies* (2021), from the title onwards, telegraphs intimacy as its central concern. Caldwell even traces the history of the term: '*Intimacies*, first used in printed English in 1641'.[213] Rarely in the collection do we learn the first names of our protagonists, but the narrative is from a first-person perspective – offering us an intimacy with their difficult decisions. The stories deal with the choices made about intimate lives and the question of what it means to be proximate to others. They mostly engage with women in their thirties – that key time of choices about relationships, reproduction and the nature of working life. While her earlier collection *Multitudes* (2016) focused on with adolescence, *Intimacies* explores in detail the hard choices of women in their thirties and the ways in which they figure their lives and regrets. Young children and motherhood feature often, as does illness, sexuality and failed attempts to communicate. But key to all of these themes is the intimate life not lived and the loss contained in the choices not made. Taken together, the stories give weight to women's decisions about their own bodies and intimacies and the porous boundaries of these decisions. Caldwell notes that

> *intimate* in its noun-form comes from the Latin *intimus* meaning innermost, from *intus* meaning within. I wanted to write about the greatest intimacies I've known: what it means to conceive and to carry a child inside of you, and then realise that the real work is in learning to let them go. And from the inside-out to the outside-in: I wanted to write, too, about desire, about desiring someone so much you want to be not just inside their clothes, but inside *them*, beyond the boundary of skin.[214]

Caldwell here shows an acute awareness of the variety of forms of intimacy and its radical power to unsettle the self and other. Throughout her work she re-examines this conundrum of the proximity and distance that we need to live within and without each other.

'People will tell you everything' explores a variety of opportunities for intimacy that are not fulfilled. Two female colleagues go out for drinks after work, and both are harbouring intimate secrets: the junior colleague keeps quiet about leaving her last job because of a relationship with her married boss, and the more senior colleague, Rachel, has romantic feelings towards the unnamed narrator. Rachel seems to be constantly discussing her intimate life compared to our more stoic narrator, but we have glimpses into the latter's rich internal monologue as she struggles with navigating her intimate life, including friendships at work, her family, friends and romantic life. There is a clear sense of loneliness and dislocation throughout the text which manifest in attachments to particular times and places. She describes the Christmas season as an evocative time for regret and nostalgia. Like her married lover, she values Christmas Eve: 'It had always been about Christmas Eve for me too – about the build-up, the anticipation, the house full of secrets, the drawing-in – and I was sure that he'd find a moment to write to me'.[215] Christmas Eve can be read as a particularly intimate time, often reserved for close family or long-time friends and steeped in nostalgia. In particular, Caldwell writes about Irish women who have relocated but nonetheless have an uneasy relationship with the city they have left and know intimately:

> Belfast didn't feel like mine exactly, any more, now I'd been gone so many years – I couldn't have told you where the best bars were, and the bus routes had all changed – but it still felt like a part of me: and how badly I wanted him, then, not in an abstract sense, or in some nebulous future, but right there beside me, Corn Market, Christmas Eve. I wanted him to see the city, to walk its streets with me, and I thought: I have to tell you this.[216]

Here, Belfast stands in for a part of her own identity. She is deeply, profoundly sorrowful in parts of the text, as in her question: 'Can I call you up by sheer force of longing?'[217] and this overwhelming feeling manifests itself in churning, anxious sensations because she cannot square herself with the intimacy she has lost.

Several of the stories discuss how the intimate is mediated through the digital and expose that which cannot be fully communicated through virtual means. This first story deals with miscommunication, absence, desire and loss experienced through the digital. Caldwell's protagonists, as women in their thirties, did not grow up with technology mediating every aspect of their intimate lives, but they are still eager adopters of messaging applications, such as iMessage and WhatsApp. Importantly, Caldwell's characters can appreciate what messaging apps lack: nuance, context and the cues of body language. They promise instant intimacy, but this is always at a remove. In particular (as we will also see in the next story), messaging on these apps are haunted by the traces of what is unsaid, particularly in the form of ellipses, which indicate that a communicant is writing but which do not necessarily lead to a message. Our narrator's former lover begins to engage in one of these fault lines of intimacy: 'Twice, after I'd ended things and quit the archive, I'd seen him, *typing … typing …*, and my whole body had been instantly liquid with relief and desire. But the messages never came.'[218] Here, the digital and the physical are intimately brought together: three undulating dots can make her 'whole body' become 'liquid'. Therefore, Caldwell pushes beyond the oft-repeated trope that the digital is simply bad for intimacy to show that technology is changing intimacy rapidly, in ways we do not yet understand and the effect is powerful on both our sense of self and its physiology.

In addition to the reminiscences of loves past, Caldwell also presents a complex negotiation of a different kind of intimate: the office flirtation. Office policy demands that staff give only their first name and to produce photographs for a website that are often idealized and bear little relationship to lived reality. Caldwell brings our awareness back to the ways in which intimacy can be misconstrued: our lonely narrator thought she was making a friendship – a different kind of intimate – but Rachel reads their relationship as courtship. What is striking is that they know so little about each other. Our narrator knows little about Rachel's intimate life, whilst Rachel does not know the secret that our narrator holds about her past relationship. Rachel espouses the virtues of a particular kind of distance: '"I'd also say," she said, "don't rush to give away all of yourself, instantly, because someone has happened to express the slightest interest."' In the end, the narrator's two intimate secrets remain hidden: Rachel does not know about her affair and none of her colleagues are aware of her homesickness, loneliness and regret. In this story of shallow, corporate intimacy undercut by moments of heartache, we see the tension – characteristic of Caldwell's collection – between the pain and pleasures of intimate life.

'Words for things' examines the desires and regrets of a young mother through the digital traces of scandalous women, particularly Monica Lewinsky. The coverage of Lewinsky's relationship with Bill Clinton occurred when the protagonist was a teenage girl. Caldwell depicts this scandal as a pivotal moment in forming how the characters in the story talk about sex and relationships, and, vitally, what is not said. The personal narrative is integrated within the discussion of Bill and Monica's relationship and how it functions as a cultural cypher for guilt, shame and sexual desire. Even our narrator's mother has an opinion on the intimate scandal: 'I remember my mum saying how charismatic he was, I said.'[219] This story, then, examines the cultural and familial scripts of intimacy that we receive, and how these are mediated through digital technologies, such as the search engine and the messaging app. The protagonist uses the search engine predominantly as a nostalgia machine for a time before her current responsibilities. It also provides a way to connect with her fellow new mothers as they bond by discussing women who have taken different paths in their intimate lives. The figure of the ruined, scandalous woman acts as a kind of intimate bogeyman.

Intimate pasts are evoked as the story exhibits a palpable mood of nostalgia for their young adulthood: 'As I walked, I thought of our early twenties … big cities with bright lights, flat shares and failed love affairs and flea markets on Sundays. We'd thought we were living the dream, and if we were unhappy, well, it was our fault, our failure to live up to it all.'[220] A similar lifestyle is depicted in *Expectation* (2019) by Anna Hope, where the narrative moves between the lives of three protagonists who flit between these same kinds of encounters in their twenties, and then they face the realities of parenthood, infertility and infidelity in their thirties. In addition to the boredom and regrets of parenting, Caldwell also depicts the most intimate pleasures of closeness and recognition: 'The baby woke beaming, as if seeing my face was the most wondrous thing ever, and I ached with love for him. We spent the afternoon in bed, feeding, cuddling, practising tummy-time.'[221] These intimate moments can now be easily recorded and shared as small clips: 'The baby was in a playful mood, gurgling and babbling, so I took a video of him squealing with pleasure as I kissed his toes and sent it to my family group.'[222] The digital allows us small, mediated glimpses into intimate life that were once more difficult to capture and transmit. Here, the WhatsApp group transcends the boundaries of geography, device type and operator: anyone with a smartphone can participate in the curated videos and images from family across the world.

However, the promise of intimacy through the digital can be punctuated by small miscommunication. For example, the protagonist's mother seeks to use the new features integrated within the app: 'She had recently discovered gifs and communicated almost exclusively, if often erroneously, through them.'[223] Her mother expresses her happiness at the smiling baby through a gif of *Flashdance*, which she has not seen. At the same time, against this shallow, digital performance of intimacy, comes a profound statement from her mother: '*You'll never be loved so much again.* It was no more than I'd been thinking myself, since my son had woken. But I felt the ache all over again, the inevitable and necessary complication of that love.'[224] This reflects the problems of intimacy – while connection is vital for life, it also brings with it the inevitability of loss.

In a later story, 'Lady Moon', intimacy is mediated through internet fertility chat forums where people share the most private details of their bodies with strangers. Here, the anonymity of these forums allows of the sharing of 'intimate detail'. In 'Words for Things', however, internet search engines easily provide biographical information to slake the protagonist's every curiosity about public figures' intimate lives, from her former teacher to Jade Goody to Nell McCafferty. Potted life stories and biographies are available with a few clicks. In these searches, the narrator focuses on women who have been somehow transgressive, alongside her interest in Lewinsky:

> While my husband was gone, I texted a new name to my friend: Anna Nicole Smith. We'd spent the afternoon sending names back and forth. Tonya Harding, Amy Winehouse, Shannen Doherty, Britney Spears. Because the thing was, it wasn't just Monica Lewinsky. It was all the other women too, who used to be sort-of laughing stocks, and who – you suddenly realised – turned out to be something else entirely.[225]

These celebrity women navigate intimacy in the public eye and their 'value' is directly linked to their perceived 'shameful' lives. Caldwell focuses here on the way these women's intimate experiences are rendered digitally and become part of the popular consciousness. She also recalls a swaggering university lecturer who used the *Starr Report* as a text in their class, and this audacious act shocks her: 'It had been inconceivable to me that you could put a verbatim account of giving a blow job alongside the poems of Wordsworth, and read them with equal attention and care.'[226] But what I think is more interesting than the mere shock factor of studying explicit material in the classroom is how Caldwell again draws out the significance of what is left out – and that redacted material exists beyond the digital sphere: 'I still remembered it, after all these years. Dot, dot, dot. Dot, dot, dot, *dot*. What was said, and wasn't, and why.'[227] Those dots mirror the messaging dots in the previous story: they are an expression of something that has been formed but cannot be read. As the story closes, the protagonist composes a message to her friend and then stops herself: another idea formed and discarded in the search for connection.

'The Children' concerns with futurity as well as being rooted in the past: both the protagonist's own past and the story that she is 'writing … about Caroline Norton, who *changed the lot of mothers forever* with her battle to reform child custody law, or so the blurb on her biography says'.[228] The protagonist, a mother of infants and writer, finds a mass in her breast at the same time as she is writing Norton's story. The story is saturated with references to the intimate: breastfeeding, googling health issues, doctor visits and contemplating the consequences of one's own mortality for children. In contrast, Norton's story indicates a life of intimate misery: domestic violence and being separated from her own children. Our protagonist suffers anxiety about the fear of being separated from her young family: 'Since they were born, I've dreamed of losing my babies too. I dream that I've left my daughter in a Left Luggage unit and there are hundreds of dully gleaming lockers and I don't have a key.'[229] Not only does Caldwell parallel her protagonist's and Norton's lives to articulate universal anxieties, she clearly situates this within the contemporary climate of fear around the Trump administration's 'family separation' policy on its border with Mexico in mid-2018: 'I read Twitter instead, swiping, tapping, swiping. In the US, the children of asylum seekers are being taken from their parents at the border.'[230] This story illuminates the status of refugees, asylum seekers and other migrants, and particularly how these harsh policies affect their intimate bonds, experienced primarily through online sources and social media: the swiping and tapping mentioned above. The media images disturb the central character: social media allows for the worst images of cruelty to be shared across the world. The images of mistreated children cause widespread revulsion in the months that follow, to the extent that even a small child recognizes the horror: 'My son is relieved: worried that the man who steals children will try to take him.'[231] The story demonstrates ways of trying to resist this: protests, signs, sharing on social media. But it also examines the legacy of different kinds of traumatic events and the ways in which viewing these events can be deleterious to physical and mental health. In this story, she offers an analysis of generational trauma:

> But the psychoanalyst uses the image to explain how suffering is passed down the generations; how we become trapped in the behaviours of our parents and theirs, doomed to repeat destructive patterns, unless we find ways of breaking free … We go on. We endure, and go on. The old battles, the same battles, once again and in endlessly new configurations.[232]

This analysis is not a simplistic imperative to 'break free' from the past, but a recognition of the fundamental difficulty of doing so. Caldwell's writing not only acknowledges the learned scripts of intimacy that are passed down in families but also demonstrates awareness of the ways in which the times in which we live can fundamentally change the way we relate to each other. In this story, the personal and the political merge, as do the global and the local, the public and the private. Caldwell shows here the power of a reconsideration of the intimate to span centuries and the globe.

'All the People Were Mean and Bad' deals with a young mother who has been raised as a devout Christian and faces a test of her faith and relationship during a long-haul flight. Caldwell regularly focuses on conversations that happen in the interstitial spaces of travel: car journeys, bus trips and on flights. This story also offers a marked difference from the other collections as it eschews the 'I' voice for a 'you address'. Our protagonist is having a difficult time with her daughter on the flight and a man's kindness and tolerance leads her to relax and open up about her faith and relationship, and even cut up her food ('the bizarre intimacy of a stranger feeding you'[233]). She describes her traditionally religious upbringing to this man: 'I was brought up believing it all, you say. God and Noah, the Flood, the Ark – I was brought up believing it was literal truth. That the world was six thousand years old and the Devil had planted fossils to try to trick us.'[234] At the same time as this verbal intimacy with a stranger, Caldwell allows her protagonist to reminisce internally about her courtship with her husband and their attempts to keep intimacy alive through phone calls while he is travelling for work. The representation of this rich parallel interior draws out both how intimacy changes over time, and after children, and – illustrating one of Caldwell's key themes in this volume – the difficulty of maintaining intimacy over distance and the problems and possibilities of using digital tools to bridge distance. With this stranger she recalls flesh and blood intimacy as they discuss the deaths of close family members. She also describes her relationship with her cousin, who seems to be more spontaneous than our protagonist:

> You think of the books that you and your cousin loved, the ones with multiple pathways through, and dozens of endings. You'd read them lying on your stomachs, heads pressed together, holding various pages, options, open. You'd always be careful, trying to make it through, and she'd choose the most reckless routes possible, just to see what might happen. She would have gone with him. You think: If she was still here, at the other end of a WhatsApp stream or the tap of a FaceTime away, she'd say to you, Do it.[235]

This scene provides a way of understanding Caldwell's project in several of the stories in this volume: the *Choose Your Own Adventure* series, which, like this story, are written in the second person. These books were hugely popular in the 1980s and 1990s, and here Caldwell uses them to explore women's ambivalence about their life choices. Fantasy now replaces the safe exploration of the books. In particular, the story draws out the presence of adulterous fantasies in the imagination of mothers of young children:

> You wonder, can't help yourself wondering, what it would have been like had you gone with him: in his executive car, even back to his hotel, maybe, where he holds you in his arms; kneels before you and presses his face to you; eases your jeans from your hips and unbuttons your shirt and lays you carefully on his

bed; and maybe that's what you want, for someone to undress you and lay you down, to make the decisions for you; but however you try to stage the sequence in your head, you can't get past the fact of your daughter there, and the whole thing dissipates.[236]

These desires, then, are taboo because they bring with them the fear of destabilizing the family unit. In describing this woman's erotic desire and the ambiguities of agency, Caldwell offers an important corrective to the cultural depiction of the sexless mother. What her protagonist wants in her intimate life is to be sexually desirable and, if not quite dominated, then to have the responsibility of parenting lifted from her for a moment. To prioritize the erotic while being a parent is particularly culturally sensitive for women, but in representing a mother as a desiring subject shows Caldwell further complicating the ways in which the desire for different modes of intimacy can be clashing and contradictory.

'Intimacies' deepens Caldwell's presentation of the ambiguities of intimate life through a series of seven short statements about love, grief and intimacy. The imagined audience is a recently born child, the narrator's second, and these statements cover is advice, reminiscence and the difficulty of pregnancy and child-rearing. In this piece, Caldwell contends with loss and grief: 'I should say, at this point, that this was two days after we'd lost you, or lost the baby we thought would be you ... no heartbeat.'[237] But she also offers the affective richness of hope, joy and intimacy. It begins with an encounter between the protagonist and a businessman in an airport – another one of the transitional spaces that the collection deals in. She is short-tempered and self-righteous in her indignation, but this immediately gives her pause about opportunities for compassion. This begins a meditation on the past, present and future of intimacy and the nature of love and mothering. The past becomes something dynamic that has the power to interact in radical ways with the present:

> I read too that time doesn't heal wounds – or that it does, but it can also unheal them. A lack of vitamin C means the body's collagen stores deplete, and old scars resurface and reopen. At sea, sailors in the grip of scurvy would find themselves dying of old, surmounted wounds and childhood injuries considered overcome.[238]

Caldwell exposes here that this is not a linear process – and this concepting of unhealing is a powerful one. Neglect gives rise to the wounds of the past reappearing in the present. This is mediated through a consideration of the vulnerability and fallibility of parents and children, and now his story, as well as several others in the collection, deals with how mothers keep a sense of their own past and present against the demands placed on them by their children and society's expectations. This is expressed by Caldwell's narrator:

> I am terrified of making the wrong choices. Of doing the wrong thing. I am terrified of getting in the way of your life. I mark the margin of Kate Chopin's *The Awakening* where Edna Pontellier says: I would give my money, I would give my life for my children; but I wouldn't give myself.[239]

This is the central intimate issue in the novel – how to parent while still maintaining a sense of oneself and how to be proximate without disappearing. The narrator tries on possibilities for how to be a woman and a mother, reaching for Winnicott's '*good-enough* mother'[240] or through the depiction of her own sensuality – dressing a male partner in her silk dress ('I understood something I hadn't before about desire'[241]) and reflecting on her own eroticism. This figure, the mother who is independent, sexual and regretful, is agentic and potentially troubling. Such 'troubling' must occur if the moral and ethical quandaries of intimacy are to be fully explored. Caldwell discusses the role of the writer in casting new kinds of intimate relations:

> Find someone, I would tell you, to whom you can say all the things you can never say. Look: I can make two people walk into a room, and have them do things to each another of which they may or may not have dreamed. I can make time run backwards, or take a different course entirely. … Art as merely a surfeit of desire, these words the currency of unspent love.[242]

In other words, Caldwell consciously explores here what she weaves into each story – how the choices of a writer mirror the ways in which we continually recast our own lives. She ends the collection with thoughts on the nature of intimacy: 'Love being a holding-close and simultaneously a letting-go / All things, everything, at once.'[243] This twofold movement has been at the crux of Caldwell's project with these stories: how we navigate the tensions of intimacy between this holding-close and letting-go, and across the breadth of our intimate lives. In each encounter, in each moment, we have the chance to remake our relationships with our selves and others – to renegotiate new intimate encounters.

Each of the texts in this chapter, then, engaged with established scripts of intimacy and sought to remake the way relationships have been depicted. In the subsequent chapters, we will focus on narrowing down this concern with intimacy towards pleasure, the haptic and the vital intervention of *Milkman*.

The writing which we have considered thus far has seen a variety of intimate configurations but also had potent figures in the Irish cultural imaginary destabilized, especially the mother and child. There is a sense of openness and expansiveness in the definition of intimacy in these texts. As Berlant reminds us,

> rethinking intimacy calls out not only for redescription but for transformative analyses of the rhetorical and material conditions that enable hegemonic fantasies to thrive in the minds and on the bodies of subjects while, at the same time, attachments are developing that might redirect the different routes taken by history and biography. To rethink intimacy is to appraise how we have been and how we live and how we might imagine lives that make more sense than the ones so many are living.[244]

Following Berlant, it is no coincidence that this new sense can be felt at the end of a decades-long conflict, as we begin a process of reconsidering what our lives might look like. Taken together, this fiction rethinks Northern Irish intimacy and imagines different kinds of lives and configurations. They illuminate how established social and cultural forces are brought to bear on our most private moments and offer imaginative alternatives. To read them opens up space to think through our pivotal attachments. Although that process will be intensified in the coming years as domestic life is scrutinized like never before, this fiction reminds us of the other worlds that are possible even in the smallest of moments. While there have been pleasurable moments in them, and moments of touch, this chapter focused on broad categories of intimacy as a way of making sense of the relationships in this fiction. In the next two chapters, we will focus our glance on intimacy to these two interconnected modalities to unpick how this orientation towards the intimate manifests itself in the barest exchanges.

2

Pleasure

'Pleasure can get out of hand.'[1]

Not all intimacy is pleasurable and not all pleasure is intimate. The previous chapter argued that a reconsideration of intimacy in Northern Ireland would allow for a fuller understanding of the complexities of social life in a 'post'-conflict culture. Developing that, this chapter advocates for something of a critical turn – a movement towards the representation of pleasure in Northern Irish texts. Moments of pleasure within literature and culture will be examined as a space for exploration and contestation of hegemonic ideas of home, sexuality and political life. However, while undertaking this reassessment we must be careful not to set up a false dichotomy between a 'pleasure text' and a 'trauma text': Northern Irish literature and culture has moments of both. The issue here, then, is not with texts but with *readings*, and the aim is not to replicate one overdeterministic critical practice with another. Instead, I propose we seek out moments of pleasure and let them stand beside both moments of pain and neutral everyday events, to do justice to the myriad affective states expressed by Northern Irish writers. This chapter will consider depictions of pleasure in a selection of recent texts which are written by authors from Northern Ireland and which engage directly with both this geographical context and also with pleasure in the 'post'-conflict era: Glenn Patterson's novel *The Rest Just Follows*, Billy Cowan's play *Still Ill*, Lucy Caldwell's short story collection *Multitudes* and two collections by Rosemary Jenkinson – *Catholic Boy* and *Lifestyle Choice 10mg*. The focus will be on the depiction of pleasure, particularly sexual, to see whether these texts offer new ways of being an erotic subject in the changed political climate, or whether the sexual charge still lies in the fissures of unresolved conflict.

There are intellectual and institutional imperatives for a focus on 'trauma texts'. Comparative perspectives with other cultures that are grappling with the legacy of a long violent conflict are often thought to yield a way out of Irish exceptionalism, but an overdeterministic focus on a painful past has come to dominate criticism on Northern literature. In this age of the academic funding imperative, particularly in the British climate with the impact agenda, many projects have sprung up to discuss 'dealing with the past' and the commemoration of violent events.[2] There is a danger that literature and culture have become used in instrumental ways, to discuss what they can tell us about the politics of the author or a particular historical moment and they are often read as palliatives for perceived ethical gaps in a flawed process. The frustration is palpable and understandable; critics want literature to do things that politicians in Northern Ireland seem unable or unwilling to do. But, quite often in these analyses, literature is not set within its cultural contexts, and creative writing is expected to do transformative ethical and political work. This impulse has also led to those texts which are seen to engage most directly with political violence receiving not only disproportionate critical attention but also being widely taught to 'sex up' courses on Northern Irish culture. Through this process, trauma texts come to dominate the focus of Northern Irish literary scholarship, while texts which speak to broader political questions are elided from the cultural landscape. While a focus on trauma is perhaps natural in this political and social context, it is not sufficient to explain contemporary Northern Irish culture's engagement with history, politics and sexuality.

Alexander Beaumont discusses how a representational burden was felt on British fiction during the decline of leftist politics in the 1980s as 'the expectation placed on expressive culture to do the work of political action'. However, he notes that 'today, the British novel is frequently marked by structures of failed utopianism, frustrated or incomplete experiments and even withdrawal and quietism'.[3] Beaumont's identification of the consequences of the critical expectations placed on British fiction can be compared to the current situation in Northern Ireland, and we must guard against the ossifying effects of wanting literature to fit into our critical and political paradigms. The distinction can be made between this sort of broad political desire and the generative possibilities espoused by Eve Sedgwick in her essay, 'Paranoid Reading and Reparative Reading' (2003).[4] As Robyn Wiegman summarizes, Sedgwick's approach to reading and recovering as 'about learning how to build small worlds of sustenance that cultivate a different present and future for the losses one has suffered. You could say that it's about loving what hurts but instead of using that knowledge to prepare for a vigilant stand against repetition, it responds to the future with an affirmative richness.'[5]

In what follows, I will consider how contemporary Northern Irish culture can create these 'small worlds of sustenance' and how writing about the past with pleasure also has the potential to foreground intimacy in a body of work more normally associated with trauma and violence. In this context the writing of mutually enjoyable intimate encounters, which will be broadly conceived of as 'pleasures', has the power to realign traditional cultural narratives of sexuality, family and the domestic. These representations stand against what we might call the 'melancholic erotic' in Northern Irish writing: where intimacy is asked to repeatedly stand in for the politics of the Troubles. Examples of this include Joan Lingard's *Across the Barricades* (1972) series, where Kevin and Sadie's cross-community relationship is set up as a paradigm of political co-operation, or Robert McLiam Wilson's *Eureka Street* (1996), where the ceasefires are met with a surge of sexual activity among Jake Jackson and his friends. However, there could be the suggestion that this is merely replacing one set of ossifying representations for another and expecting the erotic to be a political agent. Instead, we can think of the experiments of pleasure as moments which do not have to stand for anything else but themselves. Pleasure is an easy metonym when it is written in purely orgasmic terms, that is, as an end in itself. As Laura Frost notes, 'in the same way that an orgasm-centred theory of sexuality does not account for vast registers of eroticism, the idea of pleasure as a performance that has ended or a dam that has burst imposes false borders on the experience'.[6] A criticism aware to the powers of pleasure in Northern Ireland will be alert to the imposition of these 'false borders' in more ways than one. This chapter will argue that beginning to account for these 'vast registers of eroticism' is exceptionally powerful in Northern Ireland if we want to loosen the representational stranglehold on sexuality. These moments cannot be forced into dominant reading paradigms but can, instead, be aberrations in texts which have been read as straightforwardly political. I want to follow what, in *Time Binds* (2010), Elizabeth Freeman describes as 'the unintelligible or resistant moment' alongside how Virginia Woolf uses the idea of the 'moment' in *Mrs Dalloway* (1925), to convey a variety of temporally constrained pleasures.[7] While Woolf's repeated use of this term varies contextually in the novel, it is in her iconic encounter with Sally Seton ('Only for a moment; but it was enough') where the moment of pleasure has the sort of power Freeman discusses.[8] For Woolf's characters, these moments are as much about the realization of pleasure than being lost in a moment, the pleasure is one of recognition. The spectre of the First World War recurs throughout Woolf's novel, and this pleasure/trauma representational bind is also prevalent in Northern Irish cultural context.

Pleasures may be politically incorrect, we may find pleasure in trauma or the meaning of an event may shift and change over time. What once gave us pleasure may no longer hold appeal, particularly under scrutiny. Lauren Berlant reminds us that, in criticism, there 'is nothing more alienating than having one's pleasures disputed by someone with a theory'.[9] Literature and culture are sites where we consume for pleasure but also see pleasure represented. That is, to follow Roland Barthes, both the pleasures *in* the text and the pleasure *of* the text. In *The Pleasure of the Text* (1973) he distinguishes between plaisir/pleasure as 'euphoria, fulfilment, comfort' from jouissance/bliss as 'shock, disturbance, even loss'.[10] However, this term is also used by French feminist thinkers to unpack what they see as the radical power of female sexuality, such as in Helene Cixous's essay 'The Laugh of the Medusa' and Julia Kristeva's *Powers of Horror* as 'that sublime affect which shatters or overwhelms the subject's stability in language, identity and therefore also in society. In this conceptualization, women are positioned to generate a radically different kind of language, law and desire'.[11] However, Barthes, Cixous and Kristeva foreground the more extreme sensation rather than explore the symbolic potential of 'euphoria, fulfilment, comfort' to be politically transgressive. To write about bliss can be radical, but to examine everyday intimate life in culture might also reveal a great deal, as the first chapter of this book demonstrated.

Frost notes that pleasure is 'semantically unconstrained and apparently ahistorical, although close attention to the way the word is deployed will reveal that one era's pleasure is not the same as another's'.[12] It is this ambivalent historicity of pleasure that I want to draw out: how it lives in the place between cultural construction and 'pure' feeling. One encounter can waver between these modes and as we slip in out of our minds and bodies. A 'moment' of pleasure, then, can be powerful indeed, particularly in its relationship to ideas around analysis: we have a developed psycho-critical apparatus to discuss desire and a physiological language for orgasm, but less debated is the broader construction of erotic pleasure with and without the assumed end. If pleasure is something which is difficult to critically discuss, or resistant to discussion at all, this process is even more fraught in a society where the dominant critical paradigm is the discussion of trauma. The challenge for this criticism is how to attend to the present moment and also gesture towards futurity. This is well expressed by Heather Love in *Feeling Backwards* (2007) where she argues that a 'central paradox of any transformative criticism is that its dreams for the future are founded on a history of suffering, stigma and violence'.[13] To consider how culture might represent Northern Irish intimate life, we can bear Love's ideas about how queer culture responds to its painful past in mind. Culture can respond to this imperative: it can move beyond this paradigm, be haunted by it or develop new forms of writing about intimate life. It is, of course, complex to foreground pleasure while still acknowledging and respecting the years of suffering in Northern Ireland. Ireland, North and South, has a complex judicial and cultural relationship to pleasure in addition to the mainstream biopolitics by which populations are managed. Fintan Walsh, for example, notes 'the centrality of gender and sexual power dynamics to the maintenance of social and political stability in the North'.[14] Indeed, instances of the perceived danger of sexuality are not hard to find in Northern Irish public life, whether the 'Save Ulster from Sodomy' campaign or the controversy when the pop star Rihanna was chided by a farmer for being scantily clad when filming in Clandeboye.[15] However, this is an over-simplistic view of Northern Ireland as a sexually repressed society which does not necessarily map on to either culture or people's lived experience.

Instead of thinking that all people in Northern Ireland are under the yoke of unassailable prohibition, we can turn to cultural representations where sexuality was so often used metonymically for sectarian politics. Turning towards pleasure as a critical practice should not negate anyone's lived experience of violent conflict and the continuing legacy of the conflict. These two ideas do not have to be competing discussing, as pleasure in culture does not lessen anyone else's experience of victimhood, but it does raise some taboo questions about why, politically, pleasure is a taboo. In Northern Irish political discourse, the language of desire/want/demand occurs quite frequently, but the language of bliss/satiation/fulfilment is less common. The Good Friday Agreement inaugurated a consociationalist political economy that relies on the tacit agreement that neither community has their political wishes fully satisfied. More so than most political settlements, the terms of power sharing in Northern Ireland has relied upon leaders from both communities claiming victory when, in truth, it was impossible to fulfil both national desires concomitantly. The status quo is maintained as long as both parties are satisfied with being dissatisfied. To describe positive, contented feelings can feel inappropriate to the political moment; to claim that you're experiencing pleasure can limit your political bargaining in the discourse of truth and reconciliation.

In addition to this frustrated body politic, the language of desire has a complex relationship with religious and national ideologies. The political power of sexuality in the Northern Irish experience has been detailed by Clair

Wills, in *Improprieties* (1993). Wills notes that 'maternal sexuality, prostitution, homosexuality, or simply explicit sex, sex for pleasure and adolescent sex – become ways of questioning the propriety of political processes, nationalist and unionist concepts of community, and the very basis of the idea of home'.[16] When the denial of sexual autonomy and bodily rights is one of the few things Northern Irish political parties have in common, small worlds of sustenance, small intimacies can be radical. This is not to say that the people of Northern Ireland must 'fuck for peace' but rather turn towards cultural representations of sexuality that resist the overdeterministic focus on one type of experience. As critics, we must embrace these improprieties as moments of pleasure that can refute totalizing narratives of power and rethink the power of cultural depictions of intimate life.

Literature written during the Troubles used the love plot as a political metonym or used the erotic charge of the conflict in a way which often drew its sexual energy solely from asymmetries of power or the charge of the cross-community taboo. Widows were often fetishized, particularly by men, who were implicated in their husband's deaths, such as Marcella in *Cal* (1983), and female combatants on screen were depicted as highly sexualized, such as Jude in *The Crying Game* (1992). In particular, the Troubles novels of Eoin McNamee feature sexual encounters that have a complex relationship with the idea of pleasure, such as the ill-fated brothel in *The Ultras* (2004) or Victor Kelly's relationships in *Resurrection Man* (1994). While that is in keeping with the highly stylized noir aesthetic of his crime fiction, the representational optics are clear: in these fictions, it is often the historical context that is imbued with an erotic charge. When it has occurred, Northern Irish textual pleasure has had a distinct focus on the male orgasm. Women's writing such as Mary Beckett's *Give Them Stones* (1987) and Anna Burns's *No Bones* (2001), often, and for understandable reasons, equate sexuality with forced reproduction, abuse and traumatic pregnancy. This responds to the legacy of moral conservatism and silence around sexual violence in Northern Ireland.[17] But, to draw attention to representation of politically charged sexuality is a certain kind of exceptionalism which ignores kinship with the exploration of this topic by both British and Irish authors. For example, Alan Hollinghurst's novel *The Line of Beauty* (2004) and Colm Tóibín's *The Heather Blazing* (1992) directly contrast homosexuality and the AIDS crisis with their political context, Thatcher and Haughey respectively. Similarly, Jeanette Winterson's depiction of lesbian sexuality is set against the evangelical community in the North of England in *Oranges Are Not the Only Fruit* (1985). Anne Enright's novels often juxtapose sensual and erotic pleasures against the constraints placed upon women in their public and private lives. In these texts authors from Britain and Ireland are equally engaged in placing pleasure alongside political and social concerns. Critics have, thus far, been less interested in seeking out these moments in Northern Irish texts, eliding their richness. This chapter will argue how moving towards a pleasure-seeking impulse when considering contemporary writing from the North of Ireland will allow the fullness of experience and writing to be illuminated.

'To die by yer side …': Queer pleasures in Billy Cowan's *Still Ill*

The interplay of politics and pleasure is explored in the work of Billy Cowan, a playwright from County Down whose plays have been performed in London, Birmingham and in theatres in Greater Manchester, including in the Contact theatre in Manchester and the Lowry in Salford. Cowan details how his own experiences interact with his writing: 'This doesn't mean that everything I write is autobiographical, that my stories are always true, that would be limiting, but the use of autobiographical detail is, for me at any rate, a crucial component in fostering this sense of intimacy.'[18] While this study focuses almost exclusively on fiction, I wanted to include his work here as a really powerful engagement with what we might term the 'Troubles erotic'. Cowan's flash fiction is included in the appendix to this book. His play *Still Ill* follows the return of a gay exile to Strangford to find his brother, Dave, and sister-in-law, Elaine, running a sex shop with proceeds from drug dealing. Elaine claims she bribed the local 'Ulster says No brigade' with pornographic magazines and that 'we're now the sex an' drugs capital of the North. We have swinger nights down at The Oul Cross. And you'll love this … there's even a cruising ground for dirty old queers like yourself.'[19] In this play, Cowan clearly sets out to excavate the secret pleasure seekers from suburban Northern Ireland and to expose the hypocrisy of the way in which the repression of sexuality is used for political gain. Tommy details his happy, bourgeois queer life in Manchester – he even has an allotment – but cannot resist the lure of his former teenage crush, Gary, and this despite the revelation that Gray is involved with the intimidation of Tommy's brother. Here, the traditional Troubles erotic of the 'sexy hardman' is queered to the soundtrack of the Smiths, but as Gary sings 'There is a Light That Never Goes Out', Tommy resits this nostalgic imperative: 'The hunger strikes. The bombings. The Riots.

The unemployment. Great stuff.'[20] The tension in this encounter is between Gary wanting to unravel the minutiae of the past – re-enacting it in their adolescent outdoor adventures – and Tommy wanting to forget the past, a past linked with his mother rejecting him before her death. Finally, the rational, restrained Tommy breaks down his reserve and shares a tactile erotic memory:

> I remember you lifting me up and kissing me on the forehead when I agreed that
> I Know It's Over was a far superior song to There's a Light That Never Goes Out.
> I remember the reflection of the fire in your pupils and thinking how fucking
> beautiful you were.[21]

This emphasizes how pop culture offers a language for how to understand taboo erotic desires. It transpires that during that fateful summer Gary slept with nearly everyone they knew, but it is the legacy of paramilitary gang structures in Northern Ireland, rather than the homosexual love plot, that leads the play to its tragic dénouement.

Cowan's depiction of Northern Irish pleasure is complex, then, and demonstrates the continued hold of the Troubles taboo over the depiction of eroticism in Northern Ireland. Tommy and Gary are each other's fetish: Tommy as the bourgeois queer migrant offers Gary the promise of a different lifestyle while Gary as the queer hardman allows Tommy to reconcile his sexual awakening in Northern Ireland to the present moment. As noted earlier, it was not that politically transgressive erotic encounters, such as Gary and Tommy's, were not happening but that they were not culturally depicted at the time. Not every Loyalist enforcer was rigidly heterosexual: former UDA hitman Sam 'Skelly' McCrory is now a gay rights campaigner and Jim 'Doris Day' Grey was widely regarded to have been bisexual. However, the taboo over homosexual relationships is strong in both communities. Writing about the 'Save Ulster from Sodomy' (1977) campaign, Sean Brady notes that for Ian Paisley,

> Ulster, the hallowed province, had to be made fit for the second coming of
> Christ, and therefore needed 'saving' from sodomy. In a society riven by male-
> dominated violence and religious conflict, LGBT people at the very least would
> be wary about exploring their sexuality, and certainly emotions of guilt shaped
> and directed their lives, freedom of action and sense of agency.[22]

While conflict taboos are still at the root of sexuality in *Still Ill*, the tension between Tommy and Gary can be read as symptomatic of a wider conflict: those who left Ireland during the Troubles and those who stayed. The story of the Irish homecoming is common to the point of cliché, but Cowan allows this story of domestic, intimate life to play as a queer melodrama. In many ways, the structure of the play is fairly conventional: Cowan employs realism in his short scenes over experimental techniques. This serves to contrast the play's queerness against the more straightforwardly 'political' realism of the usual 'Troubles' play. The pleasures in Cowan's text contrast strongly with the rest of the narrative: they are punctures and interruptions in an otherwise standard Troubles drama plot about enforcers and conflicts of family loyalties. The queer sex in the play begins aggressively and fits in with traditional representations of sexuality in Northern Irish writing: 'they start to make passionate, almost violent love'.[23] However, this initial violence is transformed into something approaching real intimacy or, at least, as much as the stage allows. The violence of the Troubles keeps intruding after intimate interludes, as public political life steps on private intimacies.

The sexual other that engenders the intimate encounters in the text is the presence of the North of England, through Tommy's homecoming and the continued references to Steven Morrissey, the lead singer and songwriter for the Smiths. Specific moments of pleasure (lyrical and acoustic) from Morrissey's oeuvre are eroticized when Gary uses their adolescent charge in his seduction of Tommy: 'a few crates a beer, my Smiths CDs and a couple a hundred of condoms'.[24] In this sense, Morrissey becomes a way for them to navigate their erotic lives, to make sense of their moments. The play represents a host of small intimacies from play wrestling to playing cards and bawdy jokes ('Nah, my taste is in your arse').[25] However, these moments of pleasure and queer potential with the narrative do not signal queer futurity. In Cowan's drama, queer representational politics and the conventions of the Troubles drama intersect: the fatalistic catalyst is the spectre of the Troubles rather than of the AIDS epidemic. The play's final moments see the lovers torn apart by the threat of political violence and an ambiguous, possibly fatal, conclusion. Gary's final cry is high melodrama filtered through the language of the Smiths: 'My eyes were closed and all I could see was you … It's always been you. … Tommy don't walk away! … Tommy! To die by yer side …'.[26] Before this, Gary had expressed intimacy to Tommy through sexual jokes, but here he expresses a painful vulnerability. This is filtered through that most fatalistic song, 'There is a Light That Never Goes Out', but instead of a double-decker bus, the legacy of the Troubles appears to be the agent that intervenes in intimacy. As we will see in Patterson's work, popular culture can offer a language for intimacy that is otherwise inaccessible in this political context. Cowan's work forms an important bridge between eroticism in previous Troubles texts and newer rewritings of sexuality in Northern Irish texts. The charge of the past is still present as a powerful erotic force and it can be fetished through a queer perspective. The troubles erotic, rather than just a fatalistic spectacle of heterosexual sex and death, can offer a powerful commentary on queerness in the North.

'Shot by both sides': Formative pleasures in Glenn Patterson's *The Rest Just Follows*

Glenn Patterson has represented bodily and emotional intimacy throughout his writing life. His novels are almost exclusively set in Northern Ireland and deal with various periods of history, whether the decades long sweep on *Number 5* (2003), the birth of the Civil Rights Movement in *The International* (1999), nineteenth-century shipbuilding in *The Mill for Grinding Old People Young* (2012) and the DeLorean factory of the 1970s and 1980s in *Gull* (2016). Yet, despite these ambitious engagements with history, all of this fiction are replete with intimate moments. All of this fiction, even when they deal with the violence of the Troubles, feature characters who experience pleasurable moments. Patterson also co-wrote the screenplay for the film *Good Vibrations* (2012), one of the most notable expressions of Northern Irish joy on screen and, like the novel, deals with the punk movement in Belfast. A similar nostalgia for the era is found in recent novels by Geraldine Quigley (*Music Love Drugs War*, set in Derry) and Henry McDonald (*Two Souls*, set in Belfast): both of which feature many references to 1970s alternative music culture against the love plot and the troubles narrative. Music is foregrounded throughout these texts: for Quigley, it is often the music of Ian Curtis and Joy Division, and McDonald uses Bowie's Low as his reference point. As with Patterson's work, moments of utter pleasure mingle with the horrors of the violence of the Troubles and, in the case of McDonald, football hooliganism.

Patterson's body of work allows histories of pleasure and trauma to weave together but his work is often read overdeterministically for what it can tell us about a 'liberal' Protestant tradition of writing.[27] This, however, is to miss the texture and the complexity of his writing, which treats pleasure with the same narrative power as political violence. *The Rest Just Follows* (2014) deals with a broad swathe of history from the 1970s to the present day and offers a variety of pleasurable encounters. The novel spans the adolescence to middle age of Maxine, St John and Craig and is filled with nostalgic detail, from cigarette brands to fashion and film. Rather than a literary quotation, the title and epigraph is from Tracey Thorn's memoir *Bedsit Disco Queen* (2013) about the nature of adolescent friendship. While diverse sexual encounters are woven throughout the narrative, other connections are also foregrounded. This is not the heightened, politically symbolic coupling of earlier fiction but the smaller intimacies of, for example, teeth brushing before sex or tea and biscuits in front of an electric fire. The significant events in the lives of the characters are their relationships, from family illnesses to new parenthood and infidelity.

Patterson's fiction is significant for the representation of the sort of improprieties that Wills saw as being so significant in poetry. But it is not the thrill of transgression but rather the deep ordinariness of sexual life that is remarkable in Patterson's writing. Gay characters in his novels are not a plot device, or symbolic, rather they are just getting on with both their erotic and quotidian lives. However, his novels are unique in male-authored Northern Irish writing for their representation of potent, active female desire. The adolescent sexuality in *The Rest Just Follows* positively crackles, particularly the sensory stimulation of Maxine's first fashionable haircut. The jukebox in the hairdressers 'was playing a song she had never till that moment heard but would ever associate with that day, that whole period of her life'.[28] The song is Magazine's 'Shot by both Sides', which in a more traditional Troubles novel would be a loaded reference but in this case functions as an ironic commentary on the expectations of popular culture references in Northern Irish fiction. Patterson details life in the hairdressers with relish: every song, every outfit and the 'cocktail' made in the hair-washing basin. As the male stylist Max circles Maxine, she takes pleasure in the details of his appearance: 'He wore a T-shirt ripped at the shoulders (his arms looked to have been knotted together from the discarded material) and a pair of red-and-black-striped jeans so tight you could see the shape of him like something on the butchery counter'.[29] This intimate encounter is full of tactile, aural and visual pleasure, and the intimacy of the moment is carefully constructed: Maxine glimpses a nipple or an Adam's apple or catches his scent, she lets him completely reshape her appearance, to her eventual pleasure. It is significant that the last pleasure is Maxine's, as she stands in that iconic hairdressers and relishes her independence. Patterson prioritizes female pleasure in this novel and offers women multiple ways of experiencing it which are tied to their sense of independence and autonomy.

However, as well as these aesthetic pleasures, the novel also features some moments which carry the charge of a more well-worn Northern Irish history. Craig, our revisionist historian turned Unionist politician, rolls a joint on RF Foster's book on Lord Randolph Churchill and also takes on his own dead mentor's work as the starting point for his PhD. He begins an affair with his former teacher's partner and this is part of a long tradition of what one might call the 'sexy widow' in Northern Irish fiction, where a young man is sexually initiated by a woman whose partner has died during the Troubles. Patterson's language to describe their encounter is similar to Cowan's: 'It was frightening the way they went at one another, scratching and biting … and for a long time after they had rolled apart neither of them could bring themselves to speak.'[30] This charge of history is further extended in Craig's encounters throughout the novel, with his infidelity to Maxine arising from his speaking engagements at peace-building conferences. However, this is not to say that representing pleasure linked to the Troubles is wrong, or regressive, or that people who experience such pleasures are inapposite. What is significant is that Patterson gives us a range of pleasures and desirous engagements with history: all of his characters suffer missed connections or loss; they are affected by the political context to a greater or lesser degree, but all of them know intimate connections that cannot be read easily as political metonyms.

'Bubbles of Joy': Moment of pleasure in Lucy Caldwell's 'Here We Are'

As new generations of writers emerge in Northern Ireland, new variants of pleasure have been explored. Lucy Caldwell is the author of three novels, *Where They Were Missed* (2006), *The Meeting Point* (2011) and *All the Beggars Riding* (2013), which was chosen for Belfast's and Derry's 'One City One Book' initiative. Her short story collection, *Intimacies*, was examined in the first chapter of this book. Her novels, like Patterson's, are often dense with sensuality: *Where They Were Missed* has moments of heady teenage obsession which are observed in careful detail. *All the Beggars Riding* presents a daughter imagining her mother's seduction of her absentee father, right down to the negligee. This novel is deeply concerned with the power of connection and disconnection, and Lara's visceral identification with the city of Belfast as a sensual object is a central narrative catalyst. Under consideration here, though, will be a story from her 2016 collection *Multitudes*. The short story, formally, can be better equipped to consider moments of pleasure, since it does not always have the same narrative baggage as the novel where pleasures can often feel like interludes within the prose. The short story can be read as a self-contained unit, an enclosed structure that can carry the intensity of a pleasurable moment in a manner which would be unsustainable if held over three hundred pages.

Lucy Caldwell's short story 'Here We Are' demonstrates both the possibilities of this genre as well as the power of the representation of female desiring subjects. The story centres around two schoolgirls who fall in love after being asked to perform a duet at a school concert. Angie's father is a staunch Unionist counsellor whose opprobrium eventually separates them. However, rather than focus on the ways in which the story carefully traces the structural operations of homophobia, the narrative concentrates on Belfast as a site of pleasure. The title, 'Here We Are' functions as the lovers' refrain, grounding their romance geographically. The city becomes another character in the lovers' tale, providing long walks from Cutters Wharf 'along the Lagan and through the Holylands; Palestine Street, Jerusalem Street, Damascus Street, Cairo Street … The tide is turning and a two-person canoe is skimming downriver, slate grey and quicksilver'.[31] The story, then, is replete with Belfast pleasures. Indeed, the narrative's most significant spectre is not historical or political but rather an afternoon over coffee in the Other Place on Botanic Avenue where 'I felt as if my blood was singing – that sparks were shooting from me'.[32] This encounter is rendered in intimate detail, where the girls imagine an unselfconscious future where they can express their intimate desires.

When our narrator first begins to feel desire for Angie, she is unable to fully express her longing as anything other than a bodily sensation. Alison Garden notes that the depiction of their relationship 'works to privilege not just female sexuality, but to elevate silenced stories from the margins of recent Northern Irish history'.[33] Their exchanges before their sexual intimacy are fraught with sensual power as Caldwell deftly explores the all-consuming nature of adolescent desire and the power of moments of pleasure. Throughout the story, she represents lesbian sexuality as a joyous, unselfconscious pleasure: 'We started giggling again, ridiculous bubbles of joy'.[34] She repeatedly uses words like 'easy' and 'free', which is directly contrasted with their eventual shaming and break-up. Following the Marriage Equality March, she considers looking up the now married Angela but, walking the streets of East Belfast in her dreams, decides that her desirous memories are enough. These moments are reminiscent of Clarissa Dalloway's and Sally Sexton's carefree adolescent flirtation and are written by Caldwell as snapshots of possibility. Their moments of desire are playful and temporarily unconstrained by political forces. As critics, we should avoid rendering the pure, unconstrained joy that leaps off the page tawdry with an overdeterministic political reading of the politics of Unionist lesbianism. For Caldwell, pleasure and desire are utopian spaces where experimentation can flourish.

'I was pretty sure I was born to live, die, eat, sleep and have sex': Rosemary Jenkinson's Wild Women

Throughout this chapter (and indeed, this book), we have seen authors represent moments of pleasure in their fiction. But in no author's work is the pursuit of pleasure more consistently depicted than in the short fiction of Rosemary Jenkinson. In both the collections under consideration here – *Catholic Boy* and *Lifestyle Choice 10mg* – desire is the major narrative catalyst in most of the stories. This is something new to Northern Irish fiction – a sustained, frank discussion of the intricacies of sexual intimacy from a woman's perspective. There is no guilt or shame in most of their encounters, but rather a commitment to pleasing oneself. *Catholic Boy* explores some broadly similar themes to her other writing: sexuality, cross-cultural encounters and feelings of impermanence – these nagging impulses will be given further expression in *Lifestyle Choice 10mg*. Her stories are filled with pleasure seekers in contemporary Belfast who are not always successful in either gaining their objects or, often, being able to articulate precisely what they desire. The people of Belfast are depicted as hedonistic and headstrong but, critically, open and adventurous to a range of pleasures away from the moral conservativism that previous generations lived with. It is also a collection which examines impermanency and how intimacy is managed in house sharing. For example, in 'Paper Piranhas' a woman must persuade the Government that she is not in a sexual relationship with her housemate by eliding all traces of intimacy. 'Odyssey' features a couple in the process of separating who consider the difference between their public and private shows of intimacy: 'He always like to play the great love story in public.'[35] In both of these stories a key value of Jenkinson's characters is emotional honesty and integrity – they seek to be honest and fair in their interactions with their sexual partners and themselves. This dismantles the idea of the pleasure seeker as exclusively selfish, but rather the pleasure here is in both giving and receiving.

The first story in *Catholic Boy*, 'Revival', sets the tone for the rest of the collection. It describes a woman's encounter with Alex 'Hurricane' Higgins, a world champion snooker player. Higgins died in 2010 from multiple causes[36] and, before his death, was a notable figure in the pubs and streets of Belfast.

Jenkinson's narrator depicts a shabby yet kinetic figure and recalls the physicality of his performance, which marked part of his appeal to his audience: 'When we was on top, he'd strut, preeningly sexual, loose-limbed in the pleasure of predation, and clean up the table in seconds.'[37] It is this enduring aura, of the pleasure-seeking competitor, that fascinates Cara to the point where she briefly entertains the prospect of a tabloid scandal involving Higgins: 'Lascivious lines about tipping the velvet and sinking the pink also sprang to mind.'[38] She thinks about the visceral energy of the actor Richard Dormer, who wrote and starred in a lauded play called *Hurricane*, about the life of Higgins. In addition to its run in Belfast, the play was also performed in Edinburgh, New York and London and has become the dominant cultural depiction of the player's life. In this story, Higgins becomes for Jenkinson emblematic of a kind of Belfast nightlife sensibility which courses through the novel; it is a city which is alive to the touch and full of kinetic energy. Cara describes a sensitivity to stimuli with 'nerve endings that buzzed with a kind of internal tinnitus to the touch, an electrical storm within.'[39] It is important that the collection begins with a younger woman identifying with a pleasure-seeking Belfast icon. In this story, the consequences of excess are noted, considered and dismissed. The lure of self-destruction is too great, and a pleasure in itself.

In 'Travels Round a Room', the story takes places within Gregory's bedroom as he is avoiding calls from the temp agency he works for. While women's restlessness in the collection is expressed through seeking sexual activity, Gregory finds himself seeking respite in a variety of different forms, whether drug-taking, religion or political activity. He self-diagnoses with one of the major diagnostic criteria for depression: 'Gregory knew his own condition. It was anhedonia, defined in the dictionary as, "inability to feel pleasure in normally pleasurable activities".'[40] Following this self-diagnosis, he'd 'decided to devote this year to finding the adrenaline points, to finding out what really made him buzz'.[41] This pleasure chasing manifests itself in a number of ways, beginning with a period of drug-taking. The 'beginning of drug-taking that had opened up new vistas, new trajectories of thinking that had fluted his mind into paeans of sheer pleasure'.[42] In several of her stories, Jenkinson engages with drug-taking in Belfast, which is particularly illicit given the historic distribution of narcotics by paramilitaries.[43] She also emphasizes the communal nature of this activity: 'Those pills and powders and herbs had nailed a gallimaufry of boneless puppets to the walls, dancing and feverishly shaking, while their full-blooded counterparts drifted slowly, their bodies swimming through a communal tide as their brains kept crashing on the same shore.'[44] However, these pleasures become more and more unsustainable: as the highs get higher, the lows get lower. In this story, the peaks of pleasure are, by nature, unsustainable. Gregory eventually turns to a church group to try and orientate himself away from anhedonia: 'Going home his heart was bursting like a pod with seeds of goodness and along the streets cherry blossom bubbled and frost on the branches as if filled with the same impulse.'[45] Again, a large part of his pleasure is in the communal aspect but this eventually fades, leaving him to turn towards another collective – political resistance: 'He craved further fixes so he took his annual leave in the great battleground of international summit where he locked arms with thousands.'[46] After his foray into anarchism, he seeks pleasure in hypochondria, eventually leading to a home visit from management. This leads to the story's ambiguous ending, as Gregory considers whether he might be able to find the pleasures he seeks in the experience of work in late capitalism. As he imagines the rows of workers at their screens, he considers this as a form of rapturous 'messianic radiance'.[47] However, we suspect this will be another failed pleasure for Gregory – he does not consider mutual enjoyment, just his own gratification. In Jenkinson's world, the most powerful pleasures are those which are shared – if only for a moment.

Now to turn to those stories which deal explicitly with women's sexual pleasure. In Caldwell's stories we saw pleasure confined by homophobia and social repression, but Jenkinson's stories have a different focus: they examine women who sleep with men and who are depicted as actively desirous. Vance reminds us that 'the tension between sexual danger and sexual pleasure is a powerful one in women's lives. Sexuality is simultaneously a domain of restriction, repression, and danger as well as a domain of exploration, pleasure, and agency.'[48] This danger, which so often colours the depiction of women's sexuality, is not felt in these stories. What is striking about Jenkinson's stories is that women express their desires with relatively few impediments and the few moments of repression are met with disobedience and ridicule. These are unruly women who, despite the dangers that Vance notes, prioritize their own sexual pleasure. Jenkinson writes about multiple sex acts and positions in a way that is particularly rare in Northern Irish writing, where the expression of sexual freedom often comes at a cost. The worst thing that happens to any of the women in *Catholic Boy* is being evicted from a rented room due to a large volume of gentlemen callers. This does not elide the history of repression and restriction that was the hallmarks of Northern Irish women's lives but rather open up space for a multiplicity of representations. 'Catholic Boy' is one of several stories that explores the dynamics of older women who have sex with younger men. The relationship is consensual and without coercion or power differentials. Ruth meets Jarlath in a bar and their brief relationship still involves ample time for her to consider his body in careful detail: 'That disparity between white unblemished skin and masculine muscle.'[49] In Jenkinson's writing, we are often given a wealth of detail about the male body but rarely about the female body, unless it directly pertains to the pleasure these women are receiving. Women are depicted as actively desirous, and Ruth becomes entranced by the smallest details of her lover's appearance: 'Desire was triggered off in the subtlest of ways.'[50] As she meets his attractive sister, it refers to a kind of 'double desire.'[51] The sectarian erotic taboo is worn lightly in the text: despite the title, physical chemistry trumps political history. It is not a grand symbolic cross community relationship. Jenkinson also examines how the pleasures of sex extend not just to the act itself but also to the after-effects: 'The ache in her legs and womb as she sat down reminded her of the sex and made her happy.'[52] We also see Ruth's vulnerability as she attempts to see Jarlath again by returning his scarf. She muses on the closeness afforded by these sorts of encounters: 'To have sex with someone was akin to knowing their genetic blueprint. There was no greater intimacy – and paradoxically no greater distance.'[53] Pleasure becomes a kind of knowledge, and intimate knowledge of someone's pleasures becomes a pleasure in itself. Some of Jenkinson's women long for more from their lovers, some move on quickly. In showing women who have different relationships to intimacy, she avoids the trap of stereotyping her characters as cold yet insatiable nymphomaniacs. They all seek pleasure, they desire their male partners, but she deftly examines the different ways in which they respond to the encounter and the afterlife of pleasure.

The narrator in 'The Art of Mendacity' is a sexual adventurer who finds herself hiding her many lovers from her house-proud landlady. She tries to be respectful but 'in the end lust got the better of me'.[54] The narrative details her many lovers, their bodies, their peccadillos. In Jenkinson's women, we often get an appreciation of the detail of men's bodies and sexual peccadillos. In particular, this narrator is unashamed about her appetite for sexual pleasure: 'I have a sexual career that keeps me very busy … a serial sleeper.'[55] Jenkinson explores a similar desiring figure with Jess, in 'The Ideal Man' who begins the story by stating that she wants to get married and finds a man who conforms to her idea of 'marriage material'. She is then distracted by a 'perfect ass' in a suit that 'shuddered and shook with shimmering liquidity up and down his whole body'.[56] She is unable to stop thinking of men she has desired and slept with, until she gives into temptation: 'And for the next months she went slumming it, largeing it up joyously on brambling, rootless nights, giving herself up to men with bodies like driftwood.'[57] Here, sexual expression runs the gamut from being a welcome distraction from the pressures of work to being a defining facet of these characters' identities. In 'Valeri', a woman has a brief encounter with her artist flatmate who asks her if she has ever 'made love with a tree', to which she replies, 'Well, there was a rhododendron bush.'[58] She recalls kissing their phallic shaped heads and, when she is disappointed by the distracted Valeri, goes back to her fantasies: 'Then I slowly lay back on top of the bed covers, the painting in my mind letting the boughs of flickering shadows blow over my body.'[59] Where the flower is often used as a symbol for female sexuality, here the budding rhododendrons stand in for the phallic object which here is something natural and beautiful. The tenderness is her kiss is mirrored in the gentleness of her fantasy. Within these stories there is aggressively passionate sex but there are also softer, dreamier moments which allow for the expression of a range of eroticism.

In 'Song for a Polish stranger', Clare is dissatisfied with the casual sex that she finds unfulfilling: 'Microwave sex she turned it: sex that was hot, quick and filling at the time it was ultimately full of salt tears, empty and bad for your health.'[60] She meets Tomasz, a Polish man, who has been subject to racism in Belfast and who lost his arm in a car crash. In Northern Irish writing, often these 'post'-conflict encounters are laden with questions of national politics but in this story the focus is on two bodies connecting through pleasure. On meeting, they immediately click and have sex: 'She was barely in when his mouth swooped to hers, the sheer speed of his move rocking her back against the wall.'[61] She admires his physique ('His whole body felt planed to perfection, grained with light blond'[62]) and only briefly pauses at his severed arm. In one of the most sexually generous comments in the narrative, Tomasz tells Clare before they have sex to 'take whatever you need.'[63] She asks for exactly what will satisfy her, and gives pleasure in return. Like Ruth in 'Catholic Boy', she feels vulnerability afterwards as she hopes for a subsequent encounter. Jenkinson represents many different kinds of casual affair as some have afterlives some do not, some feature tenderness and others do not. Her women range from the voracious to the vulnerable, sometimes both and everything in between. This is not the 'zipless fuck' but rather a varied representation of women's emotional responses to sex.

This variation is most keenly described in 'Love History'. In this story, two former lovers reconnect and our perception of their relationship and libidos change over the course of the narrative. Emma and James begin the story flirting in a bar, with James regaling her with the stories of his adulterous affairs: 'Then one night she came into my room, and after that there was no peace for me. She was hotter than hell.'[64] Emma thinks that 'he had a romantic soul coupled with the love of sluttish women'.[65] It is quickly made clear, however, that despite James's masculine posturing ('He never wore underwear, considering it too feminine'[66]), Emma is the more free-spirited of the pair and unapologetic about her physical appetites: 'I was pretty sure I was born to live, die, eat, sleep and have sex … I never wanted to be pinned down by anyone – except in bed of course.'[67] While out with James, she picks up another man, Liam, for sex. Jenkinson is frank in her depiction of Emma's sexual pleasure and describes her encounters with both men in quite explicit detail. Jenkinson's women are perhaps the most sexually voracious in Northern Irish literature. Emma is disappointed to see James bear the hallmarks of his appetites and notes the ways in which hard living has left him tired and red-eyed. She opines that 'the truth is women have the strength to rage against it all for longer than men'.[68] Jenkinson positions female forbearance in a different way here: as something that can withstand more pleasure in the form of multiple orgasms. Here, the figure of the rootless woman is reclaimed from being a dangerous outlaw to someone resilient through a reconsideration of her relationship to pleasure.

Jenkinson's most recent collection, *Lifestyle Choice 10mg* (2020) not only explores territory familiar in her work but also pushes boundaries of what is expected from fiction set in Northern Ireland and fiction written by women. In an interview she noted that 'I'm a natural short story writer, not a novelist. I think the difference lies in personality: short stories are for promiscuous commitment-phobes; novels are for monogamists. I'm a thrill-seeker and I always want to move on to the next literary buzz.'[69] This sense of thrill-seeking is most acutely palpable in this collection. It is particularly frank in its depiction of sexual pleasure and drug-taking. That is not to suggest that this collection is a constant orgiastic thrill-ride: Jenkinson regularly punctuates her more hedonistic tales with poignant stories of love and loss ('Butterfly Canon in D') and, indeed, sometimes blends the two modes ('What She Does in the Dark'). There is more work to be done on how this collection deals with the representation of the past and memory in Northern Ireland – it is rich in its engagement with the legacy of conflict, the continued presence of the past and social, legal and academic engagement with violence. A story like 'Man of the North', for example, examines a former combatant who is now doing the rounds of academic events:

> Wasn't he off to a peace conference near Auschwitz in the new year and invited to speak at Cambridge at the end of the month? It was his reward for actively trying to heal the pain of the past … The talk was for PhD students in Irish Studies, so he'd have to put on a good show, throw in a few multisyllabic words.[70]

'The Lost Generation' deals with people who moved away for employment and educational opportunities during the Troubles. However, I want the focus in the chapter not to be on this rich vein within the collection but instead to be on those stories that engage most directly with the theme of pleasure, and in this collection, this can be further broken down to stories which deal with sex or drugs. The epigraph sets the tone 'Woe betide the woman who could sleep with a man and who did not do so!' – *Zorba the Greek*, Nikos Kazantzakis.[71] It is this aspect of the collection that I am interested in, which pushes this idea further than *Catholic Boy* as she examines the figure of the 'unruly' (or unruled) woman.[72] *Lifestyle Choice 10mg* goes even further in presenting women's appetites for all kinds of stimulation, be it chemical or clitoral. The tension at the core of the collection is the disjuncture between seeking pleasure, whether erotic or narcotic, and the world of paid work. This is not fully resolved in the stories – we have characters who give up jobs, miss interviews and move regularly in search of new pleasures, but we do not often hear about the consequences of their flitting. But, as restless as they are, you are left with a sense that perpetual movement is the only option available. I want to refer to these women as 'wild', a term Jenkinson uses thirteen times in the collection. The collection ends with a bittersweet high school reunion and the comment, 'Wild, isn't it?' she said, looking out.[73] Wild is used to describe lovers, landscapes and girls expelled from school. Wild is a useful idea not just in this sense, but the word is also used expressively in Northern Ireland, to add emphasis to an adverb or adjective. Her stories are about women who live in that wild space, simultaneously natural and coded as too much by Northern Irish society.

The collection begins as Jenkinson means to go on ('The one thing not to do while the head of a handsome Greek rests between my legs is to remember that work even exists').[74] Regularly there is a tension in the book between the demands of paid work and the desire of her protagonists to be fully rootless. Often, these characters (usually female) haven't achieved the same status markers as their peers. Indeed, the protagonist of 'Millennial Woman' acknowledges both the societal explanations placed on her and her inability to meet them: 'I really have to start upping my game. That way, even if I still fail in life, at least failure will be something I've achieved rather than something I've just let happen to me.'[75] She meets a young man on a night out and takes him home for sex. These are women who are confident in their own bodies and who often lightly, humorously acknowledge a flaw and then immediately forget about it in favour of a remarkable sexual self-confidence: 'I'm in this clinch on the bed and I have these wild, ludicrous visions of taking a selfie right now and putting it on Instagram.'[76] Throughout the stories, Jenkinson represents women who are appreciative of male beauty: 'The head of his penis is as round as a pink rosebud, touched by the dew.'[77] The women in the stories sleep with a variety of men with a variety of bodies. The consequences of this lust are briefly mentioned at the end of the story as she doses herself with contraceptive pills to prevent a pregnancy and then leaves, condoms in bag, for Greece.

'Men' is about a would-be writer, Tara, who finds herself not only dissatisfied in her relationship but also in the concept of monogamy: 'I was twenty-six years old and my family said I hadn't met the right person. I didn't think there was a right or wrong person for me, they were all just different. A person was right one day, and the next he was wrong.'[78] Jenkinson often represents women who acutely feel the weight of social expectation on their intimate lives but instead choose their own, wild path. Jenkinson describes mutual oral sex between Tara and married Max in explicit detail. Indeed, while her stories often feature traditional heterosexual penetrative intercourse, there are also a variety of other sexual acts depicted in her stories. She also examines the hypocrisy in her lover's equivocations: 'The irony was that if he thought he was giving a uniquely special place to his wife by fucking only her, she mightn't make the same distinction … There were no half freedoms in this world.'[79] Jenkinson's women are confronted by men who are often jealous and possessive, such as Tara's boyfriend Joe who is intimidated by the sex scenes she has written and does not think her capable of the creativity ('"Imagination," he scoffed'[80]). However, reading these stories sparks a consideration of his own desires and fetishes – 'They made him dig deep into his subconscious, perhaps even inspired him. The next night he told me his deepest sexual fantasy.'[81] Eventually, Joe articulates his desire to be penetrated by Tara ('And I didn't think it was odd to want your girlfriend to fuck you'[82]), and she approaches this request with cheerfulness and curiosity: 'I couldn't wait – I was about to get his cherry. I wanted to see his face when I was really giving it to him, the lines in his forehead, his perfect teeth bared.'[83] The encounter itself is rendered in some detail and for comic effect as they are interrupted at a vital moment and his fantasy collapses. One might be tempted to theorize the penetrated male and woman wielding a strap on as some sort of symbol of radical feminist reclaiming of the phallus. However, Jenkinson depicts this particular sex act as one among a multitude of ways of fucking in a story which examines an endless variety of body parts, acts and relationships. This begins to move the language of Northern Irish intimacy away from the language of the representational lacunae of the past towards something that might be more generative.

Tara's attempts at publishing her writing are not successful as she does not produce the monogamous heteronormative fantasy that her publishers want: 'I wondered if really I was qualified enough to write a love story. Someone who used the word *clinging* probably wasn't on a wavelength with monogamous love.'[84] The relationship to intimacy and distance that the whole collection engages with can be summarized by the end of this story:

> Though he didn't say it, he knew deep-down that I didn't care for family, that I couldn't stop looking at men and I got bored in one environment. Like a flower, I required constant replanting and different bees to take away the pollen. … And I also knew that I'd find another man to replace him, whether better or worse. I liked being alone, feeling free for a time but not indefinitely.[85]

This desire to be both separate and together is not a paradox, rather it begins to explore the ways in which we find ourselves desirous of both states at different times.

'Night Haze' examines the decisions of a young woman, Mia, who engages in sex work. This is not presented in judgemental terms – she is shown to have some very minor debt issues but otherwise having a family to fall back on financially. She is also presented as desirous – sometimes for her clients but often for men on the street: 'A boy of eighteen or nineteen grinned at her. He was gleamingly clad in white skinny jeans and a white shirt in spite of the grime of the city. Like an urban angel, she thought. A gold chain fell around his neck like a slipped halo and she longed for him.'[86] She is also attracted to Sean, her initial contact with the escort agency, who she begins a sexual relationship with based on mutual lust: 'Within time, their clothes seemed to melt from them. Their bodies were almost impalpable.'[87] Belfast is presented as a city alive to sensual pleasures: 'On the streets, bright-eyed people were merging on the city, infused by party fever.'[88] The theme of displeasure with work is raised again as she muses, 'You could always tell yourself that you were taking control of your body and selling it as a commodity, in exactly the same way you'd sell out your brain to a paltry, mind-numbing admin job.'[89] Her work is presented as no more exploitative than the other women in the collection who work unsatisfying jobs: 'It felt clinical, not lustful. It was exactly what it was, a transaction. She had once read about Van Gogh and what he called his "hygienic excursions" to the brothel.'[90] What seems particularly useful to Mia is the trait that many of Jenkinson's women share the ability to appreciate a variety of male body types. Any sense of danger comes from clients who display overt and covert misogyny. This is displayed most openly in a client from the Orange Order who is obsessed with sexually transmitted diseases: ' "If you give me a disease, I'll track you down and kill you," he warned, his breath still rasping. "Don't think that I won't." '[91] Of course, disease and sexual repression have a long social and literary history, and here this is tied to the Unionist establishment. The criticism of sex work in the story is not of the practice itself, but of the economic control of women by men. The real danger in the story comes not from her clients but from the procurer. At the end of the story, she is in a violent embrace with him: 'He pulled her tight against him. She could feel his hand moving up to the back of her head, as her body locked into his grip.'[92] Mia, in the end, does not have the freedoms of the other women in the collection because of the financial structures around her sex work.

Two stories detail the efforts of anti-drug activists in loyalist communities: 'Bomb Dust' and 'What She Does in the Dark'. In both cases, their efforts are met with resistance ('The reason he'd had to leave the Shankill was because he'd been talking at meetings on the other side of the peace wall, telling them he wanted to live in a drug-free, fearless community'[93]) and detail the complex interplay between ghosts of the past and sins of the present. However, in 'What She Does in the Dark', Fiona copes with her son's death in two ways – campaigning against drug-dealing in the Fountain in Derry and sex with a younger man. In the story, Jenkinson details the variety of colloquial language available to talk about drug-taking: 'Have a brain-bleach, he's off his bollix, steamboats, off on the whirlybirlies, lit to the tits, there's no brakes on a rocket, she's licking the windies, you daze-ball, skull it, lash it into you.'[94] She represents a woman struggling to deal with her grief amidst a community fuelled by drugs. Throughout the story, the language of narcotics is used: 'The moon beat down on the riot, a lurid ecstasy pill, the white powder of sprinkled stars circling the sky.'[95] Again, Jenkinson presents a woman attracted to wildness in another: 'That wildness in Warren was what kept drawing her to him.'[96] So, there are two modes of 'losing yourself' in the story – sex and drugs. Both are presented as potentially fatal, as her partner has major clout in the area. In particular, sex and death and presented as intimately linked. Fiona is depicted as a vampiric succubus 'feasting on his young, hard body, still not able to feel it, like it was buried deep in some country coffin'.[97] For Jenkinson, sex has an unsettling, kinetic power that animates her female characters:

> And she saw herself touching Warren, not with the light touch of a resurrectionist, but with frenzy for life, not with the light breaths of an invocation, but with the rasps of an earthly desire that would keep on waking her, shaking her till the day she died.[98]

In addition to these stories which present anti-drug activism, Jenkinson also presents several stories which examine drug-taking. In 'Ketamine Nights', a would-be teacher is taken to a wild, drug-fuelled party in Dundrum that begins with the offer 'Fancy a wee kidnap?' Well, who wouldn't want to be smuggled away by a legendary party animal?[99] The quaint seaside cottage is full of 'mega hell-rakers and psychedelic psychos holed up in Garrett and Emmy's cottage'[100] and inspired by the host's 'fears of the British Army, we are the start of his own private army, us band of red-eyed, deadbeat, high-as-a-kite tatterdemalion wastrels'.[101] The wild County Down landscape merges with her refreshed sense of herself: 'And all around me the countryside is pulsating with blossom and there's nothing like a bout of self-destructiveness to make you feel truly alive, and, if there's one thing I know, I don't want to be sitting in a classroom on a Friday afternoon ever again.'[102] *Lifestyle Choice 10mg* exposes a different kind of drug use to that featured in her other stories – the abuse of prescription medication, particularly opioids. Between 2017 and 2019, the use of the drug Naxolone to reverse opioid overdoses in Northern Ireland 'sharply rose' by 40 per cent.[103] While the crisis of the abuse of pain medication is well-document in the United States, research on this topic is only beginning to emerge. Annie's housemate Paddy is a small-time drug dealer but he offers her OxyNorm with the description, 'It's little brother to OxyContin – hillbilly heroin they call it in the States.'[104] Jenkinson details the side effects of opioids, including constipation: 'I was horribly bunged up on the meds. I lived on a diet of prune juice and syrup of figs.'[105] She reflects on her addiction: 'I'd ingested more in the past weeks than Prince, or even Elvis. I would be seriously damaging myself at this rate, and all just to survive a meaningless job of never-ending data.'[106] Here, the job rather than the drugs is seen as the central issue as many of the women in the story feel deeply unsatisfied with their employment. In Jenkinson's fiction, then, pleasure is the antidote to the boredom of paid work but it can take many forms. These stories examine the lure, the moment and the aftermath of these pleasures. Different characters have different responses to different pleasures. While not all of these attempts will provide long-term contentment, each of these restless pleasure seekers expose something vitally important in Northern Irish society – that the will to hedonism endures and that women's desires are a powerful force.

It is clear that, in these recent fictions, certain key themes predominate. Adolescent sexual awakenings are set against the morally repressive political regime in Northern Ireland. Queer and non-reproductive sex occurs frequently, and it is difficult to read any one act among many as a grand symbol of political allegiance. Representations of sensuality, whether interpreted as improprieties or resistant moments, are being showcased in recent Northern Irish writing but critical work has yet to catch up with this impulse or to reclaim the texts from the past's limiting paradigms. These texts represent the evolution of 'pleasure writing' in Northern Ireland. Cowan presents a queer erotic that is tied to the past. Patterson demonstrates female pleasure in alternative subcultures alongside the vast sweep of the Troubles history. Caldwell gives women's pleasure time to flourish against the backdrop of repressive homophobia. While Jenkinson's stories are clearly set in contemporary Northern Ireland and are inflected by this setting, her bodies yearn for exactly the right kind of stimulation. The currents of energy they present are markedly different from previous troubles writing – these are wild women, aware of the past but never constrained for it, eternally seeking, never satisfied. Taken together and, indeed, alongside the other texts in the study, they reflect a more sustained focus on pleasure than I have seen in over twenty years of reading fiction from the North of Ireland. When set against a cultural and critical climate where sexuality is used in overdeterministic, instrumental ways these representations can challenge representational and interpretive norms. Berlant notes that 'even if desire fails to find objects adequate to its aim, its errors can still produce pleasure: desire's fundamental ruthlessness is a source of creativity that produces new optimism, new narratives of possibility, even erotic experimentality'.[107] With these directives in mind, we must not treat Northern Irish culture as an instrumental tool to do the ethical work of politicians. Instead, we must listen out for small worlds of sustenance these texts contain, be it in new forms, new desires or new pleasures. There have always been moments of pleasure in the culture produced during the troubles, even in the darkest days. As we can clearly see from the texts in these chapters, these erotic experiments are flourishing in contemporary writing. It is my hope that 'new narratives of possibility' continue to be found in Northern Irish writing, and that the erotic can be a space to open up new ways of being with and for each other.

3

Skin

In Robert McLiam Wilson's novel, *Eureka Street* (1996), the lovelorn protagonist Jake Jackson takes home a barmaid from his local pub in Belfast:

> And I knew when my skin touched her skin that I probably wasn't going to kill myself for a while, that life was fundamentally a pretty sound commodity when it could include a girl like Mary. And when she touched me she touched the matter in me. She touched me through.[1]

In this novel, Jake craves intimacy and often delights in the small moments of his experiences with women. He has the capacity to romanticize the smallest details of their appearances and has regular trysts throughout the novel. But it is in this first encounter of the novel in which the core of his longing is expressed and experienced through the skin. This is an important moment in a novel that considers how male characters negotiate intimacy. While Jake is undoubtedly being melodramatic in this passage, skin contact offers both recovery and a changed outlook on relationships with others and the self. Touch is a narrative catalyst throughout the novel. The second part, the 'touching through', also raises a question of how, culturally, men have understood and expressed the experience of touch in literature and philosophical writing, of which more later. Skin contact is a marker that a barrier has been transgressed. But this novel focuses squarely on the experience of Jake's embodied self, not Mary's skin, which hopefully is also alive to his touch. With these concerns in mind, this chapter will engage with how touch, skin and haptic experience in contemporary writing might 'flesh out' the experience Wilson examines here, of culturally coded masculine vulnerability and feminine silence, and offer something even more complex and transgressive in each moment where skin meets skin. The focus in this chapter will be on short stories and the ways in which they can examine moments of skin contact and how the experience of being an embodied self is related to gendered norms around giving and receiving touch. Under consideration will be selected stories from *Gods and Angels* by David Park, *Aphrodite's Kiss* by Rosemary Jenkinson, *Sleepwalkers* by Bernie McGill and *Wild Quiet* by Roisin O'Donnell. Through Jenkinson, McGill and O'Donell we will examine what it means to touch and be touched for female writers and in the work of Park we will consider his sustained focus on narratives of masculine vulnerability. Some of these stories offer short, poignant haptic encounters but some of them (such as Park's 'The Kiss' and Jenkinson's 'Marie + Finbar') have a sustained engagement with the skin. In these stories, the skin becomes the portal for moments of revelation and gestures towards both old wounds and new possibilities.

Building on from the previous chapters on intimacy and pleasure and sharing obvious thematic correspondences, this chapter will draw out a lot of these 'haptic moments', whether they engage with touch, the desire for touch or the sense of being in your own body. Rereading these texts in 2020 during the coronavirus pandemic brought the bodily politics of these texts into sharp focus. I approached them as representations of how we related to our bodies before the language of contagion through skin contact was uppermost in public discourse. Hands in this fiction are, for the most part, not gloved or seen as entry points for disease. Hopefully when this book is published, we will be able to have all the consensual touch that we desire again. The moment of touch will be examined in these pre-2020 writings in a variety of contexts, from the gentle caress of lovemaking through to the Judas Kiss. Critically, though, it seeks not to recuperate touch away from the violence of the Troubles but to showcase and interpret a variety of touches and skins in 'post'-conflict writing. Many of these stories carefully examine the experience of being a person with skin: themes of whiteness, fragility and sensuality are common, as is a more complex engagement with Northern Irish skin that reorientates the frame of reference away from traditional metaphors of scarring and examines the experience of not only being comfortable in one's own skin but also being in 'skin relation' with others. I do not mean to set up Northern Irish skin as some exceptional entity but rather to chart the ways in which several writers have turned to the surface of the body to explore and expose the contradictions and commonalities in how we relate to each other. This chapter will begin by surveying the recent turn towards the 'haptic' and 'skin studies' within literary and cultural criticism, then consider how far this emerging body of knowledge might interact with our twenty-first century Northern Irish context. To examine this turn I want to engage with *Haptic Modernism*, where Garrington asserts that the word 'haptic' be understood as an umbrella term denoting one or more of the following experiences: touch (the active or passive experience of the human skin, subcutaneous flesh, viscera and related nerve-endings); kinaesthesis (the body's sense of its own movement); proprioception (the body's sense of its orientation in space); and the vestibular sense (that of balance, reliant upon the inner ear).[2]

Of the experiences that Garrington identifies, this chapter will focus mostly on touch, although she usefully draws our attention to how difficult it is to isolate one haptic experience from another. Touch can be a force for connection, it can soothe and heal, but violence and unwanted physical attention also falls under this spectrum. Touch involves a negotiation of a matrix of consent and to touch can be vulnerable or aggressive for both the instigator and the touched.

It is similarly complex to identify where skin ends, as the connective features link the epidermis to the dermis to the hypodermis to subcutaneous fat, via nerve endings, sweat and sebaceous glands and hair follicles. Skin can be broken, scarred or aged. It can be held together by stitches, covered with make-up or hidden from view for cultural or religious reasons. Skin is of different thickness, sensitivity, sweatiness and hairiness on different parts of the body and so responds to touch in a variety of ways. Not only is the meaning of skin culturally variable, it is endlessly physically variable from cell to cell. In this way, it innately refuses order and can give way to a more nuanced view of the embodied self. Recent critical work on the sensuous has made 'a shift from the distance to the proximal sense, that is, from sight and hearing to taste, touch and smell'.[3] Writers have been concerned with skin and touch for centuries (this intellectual history is charted by Steven Connor in *The Book of Skin*, a key touchstone for this chapter), but it is not a stretch to say that recently there has been a revived interest in what is written on the body. For example, Constance Classen argues that touch should be urgently historicized, to 'understand the sensory life of a society'[4] and the history of 'skin studies' is charted by Marc Lafrance[5] in a special issue of *Body and Society*. In their introduction to their 2003 edited collection, *Thinking through the Skin*, Sara Ahmed and Jackie Stacey suggest a reorientation away from traditional ways of conceptualizing the relationship between the skin, body and self. They seek to avoid 'taking "the body" as its privileged figure'[6] and instead position the skin as 'the fleshy interface between bodies and worlds'.[7] Following this, this chapter seeks to move towards the skin as a generative subject for analysis. Skin contact is a specific concern, particularly what Ahmed and Stacey term 'inter-embodiment … the mode of being-with and being-for, where one touches and is touched by others'.[8] It is this ethical imperative that this chapter is particularly animated by: the examination of moments of consensual touch as a kind of exchange of knowledge. In particular, Connor uses the work of Michel Serres to characterize skin as 'a milieu: the skin becomes a place of minglings, a mingling of places ... If all the senses are milieu, or midplaces where inside and outside meet and meld, then the skin is the global integral of these local area networks, the milieu of the milieu.'[9] One of the aims of this chapter, and indeed this book, is to look out for such moments and meeting places in Northern Irish writing. For example, the power of touch can also be seen in the last episode of the first series of *Derry Girls*, as one of the final moments of the series had an overwhelming response from the audience on social media. One user stated she was 'keeping it together until Joe put his hand on Gerry's shoulder'.[10] These two characters had a gently adversarial relationship throughout the series, but in this one moment, touch spoke where words could not. To attend to these moments of skin contact, these meeting places, develops a network of touch that complicates the body politics of Northern Irish culture.

Three concepts emerge that bear relevance to a discussion of the relationship between skin and writing in our Northern Irish context. In *The Body Keeps the Score*, Bessel Van Der Kolk re-examines Peter Sifneos's term 'Alexithymia',[11] or inability to express emotions. Because of the inability to commute extreme emotional states through language, he instead suggests that we turn towards the body to communicate. In his work on the role the body can play in healing from trauma, he advocates a holistic approach: 'It is critical for trauma treatment to engage the entire organism, body, mind and brain.'[12] Often, he discusses how trauma can lead to visceral and immune symptoms that can be treated through physical activity, including yoga, meditation and performance: 'For our physiology to calm down, heal and grow we need a visceral feeling of safety.'[13] What I want to explore in the analysis of these texts from Northern Ireland is how the body can play a role not just in the healing from traumatic events but can also offer a means of communication when words fail us. In the skin encounters to follow, touch often stands in for different kinds of knowledge transmission. Secondly, to draw on this idea of the body being a portal to recovery, I want to use Jackie Stacey's term 'dermographia', which she defines as 'a form of skin writing'.[14] While this is a medical term that means 'writing on the skin', Stacey uses it to foreground the dynamic engage between skin and mind in the way that writing is produced, a writing of and on the skin. The third key concept I want to introduce derives from Jay Prosser's statement that 'skin autobiographies are as layered as the skin itself'.[15] Northern Irish short fiction, then, can be read as a kind of skin autobiography that interweaves the wider political narrative with smaller personal moments to expose the multilayered nature of identity and biography. Prosser reminds us that 'skin is the body's memory of our lives'.[16] So, then, in the moment of touch we bring with us two things – the attention to the past and an engagement with our sensual present. These imperatives will be vital in reconsidering Northern Irish skin.

Following on from these ideas of skin as simultaneously a record of our lives and something that is alive to the present, a more complex relationship between skin and the past exists in a country with a legacy of recent conflict, indeed, some people still 'bear' the literal physical scars of the conflict. Earlier, we noted how 'skin studies' marked a break from other ways of understanding the sensual world, and this is especially true in Northern Irish cultural criticism, where the optical was taken as the primary sensual aestheticizing mode. This is a consequence of two factors: the first is the fact that the beginning of the Northern Irish conflict coincided with the 'satellite revolution' in television news reaching the BBC and also in colour reporting. Northern Ireland became one of the first political conflicts to be beamed, in colour, across the world. The second is the rise in critical discourses theories of the visual, spearheaded by Laura Mulvey's influential essay 'Visual Pleasure and Narrative Cinema', which deals with the gendered nature of the filmic gaze, which chimed with the often-pornographic gaze of Northern Irish culture.[17] What does it mean, against this critical tendency, to turn towards the haptic from the optical? Northern Irish skin is of most theoretical interest when it is pierced or cut, which ignores the idea that skin is constantly engaged in exchange with the outside world through its semipermeable membrane. Several texts explore the ways in which the conflict engages with the language of skin. For example, Christian masochism and mortification expressed through the skin is most graphically realized in Bernard McLaverty's *Cal*. Eoin McNamee's *Resurrection Man* focuses on the skin split open during torture. In David Park's short story, 'Learning to Swim', the 'hard men' are marked by the signs of ageing but also their tattoos: 'the old men's faded blue tattoos decorating their forearms – bluebirds, Indian chiefs in feathered headdresses, serpents coiled round daggers'.[18] Allan Feldman's work stands as a rare interrogation of the hermeneutics of the tortured body, and he identifies how skin was used during incarceration as 'your scars and other identifying marks'[19] were recorded. Previous works, my own included, read Northern Irish literature and culture as a site around which formations of the Kristevan abject could be played out, including in Scott Brewster's analysis of poetry, where he notes, 'It might be argued that Northern Ireland – a territorial and signifying space whose meanings and boundaries have been so violently contested, a body politic sustained and racked by anomalous and permeable partition – has been in the condition of abjection since its foundation.'[20] Northern Irish fiction written since the end of the Troubles, this chapter will argue, offers a way out of this abject body politic towards something more recuperative. I do not seek to claim that there is a 'new haptic' in Northern Irish short fiction where touch is used in a universally positive, restorative way, that it is universally transformative and will heal us all. Instead, I want to argue for the variety and sustained focus on the modalities of touch and the way in which they dynamically interact with the past, present and future.

As I have noted, critical work in Northern Ireland and beyond[21] has focused on the skin as a site of, often political, wounding.[22] A lot of previous writing on skin has to do with cutting, self-harming and tattooing: 'how "the skin" acquires the status of a "fetish"'.[23] Wounding is a key feature of the Northern Irish cultural landscape. The language of scarring is regularly used in Northern Irish social, cultural and political discourse. For example, *Lost Lives* asserts that 'the scars inflicted may never heal'.[24] While not wishing to be glib about such a vitally important book, scars, by their nature, do not heal. This tissue replaces normal skin and stands in for the wound that was caused. Scars bear witness. Scarring is being used here to metaphorically refer to emotional or psychological scarring that followed from troubles trauma and, in particular, the death of a loved one. Scars refers to the wound which has not, and may never, fully heal. This idea of skin that has been irrevocably broken is also used in Michael Longley's poem 'Wounds', or Seamus Heaney's bog gashed open in 'Act of Union'. Scars are often taken as an overdeterministic metaphor for the after-effects of the Troubles, but, as we shall see in Rosemary Jenkinson's short stories, scars can be a narrative focal point for meditation and reflection. For her protagonist, Marie, the changing relationship with scar tissue enacts her move towards rediscovering her sexual independence. Many of these texts propose a different relationship with scars and scarring than the representational trope mentioned above. To be scarred is to be alive, to have survived. But, critically, the survivors, who bear the scars, do not always behave like the malleable, politicizable dead. Scars look different from vantage points: whether up close or barely perceptive from distance. These texts begin to ask who is looking upon the scars, who is regarding them, who is obsessed with them and who turns away.

Alongside the metaphorical language of scars is the more infrequently used but possibly more apposite idea of the 'scab'. It is possible to aestheticize the scar: from the purplish redness of hypertrophic scarring through to silvery criss-crosses of stretch marks. We associate the scab with in-betweenness. A scab has uneven edges and is most often associated with restless picking and the space between healing and self-inflicted prolongment of suffering. As Connor notes, 'a scab is a visual compromise between lesion and healing; it preserves the blemish or disfigurement to the smooth integrity of the skin's surface even as it affirms the skin's successful defence against puncturing or laceration.'[25] Scabbing, however, is a critical and unavoidable phase in the wound healing process. Connor reminds us that the 'scab thus offers the pleasure of an averted threat; by reopening the wound, the child may play with and master the trivial but symbolic risk to its psychic wholeness.'[26] Indeed, this dermal language was used by Bill Clinton to refer to the peace process in Northern Ireland:

> Peacemaking quests came in two kinds: scabs and abscesses. A scab is a sore with a protective crust, which may heal with time and simple care. In fact, if you bother it too much, you can reopen the wound and cause infection. An abscess, on the other hand, inevitably gets worse without painful but cleansing intervention. 'The Middle East is an abscess', he concluded. 'Northern Ireland is a scab.'[27]

The fact that Northern Irish politics have so frequently been described using the language of the skin is important to note, however, there is something specific in the terms that Clinton uses here. He describes a surface level wound in the process of healing, rather eliding the complex, deep economic and social roots of the conflict. But, he does foreground the relationship of broken skin to the touch of the other and suggests the fragility and volatility of skin to outside intervention. Broken skin and its attendant troubles feature throughout the texts under consideration but perhaps in a more ambiguous way than Clinton's scab suggests.

It is worth noting that, for all the focus on different kinds of skin encounters, the skin considered here is almost universally white, or skin written by white writers. In addition to the theme of scars, scarring and scabbing, these texts also begin to address questions of race. Academic criticism has focused, in particular, on the ways in which the Irish were compared to other colonial racial others during the nineteenth century in British popular culture.[28] Irishness and whiteness have been contrasting and comparable discourses, particularly in British and American history. Dyer notes that Irish have been considered white 'under particular historical circumstances'.[29] However, despite the prevalence of sectarian identity markers (school uniforms, paramilitary tattoos), 'passing' in Northern Ireland is a luxury most people in other sites of civil conflict do not have access to. Critically, however, ideas of the cultural construction of whiteness are interrogated through the texts, particularly in the work of Rosemary Jenkinson and David Park. Whiteness is not exalted or privileged in most cases, but rather examined and deconstructed. Despite some of the attitudes considered in these stories, it is clear that the continued rise in racism in Northern Ireland[30] is an unwelcome development in the 'post'-conflict landscape. This is particularly well examined in Chris Gilligan's *Northern Ireland and the Crisis of Anti-racism*[31] and Shannon Yee's important short story 'The Brightening Up Side'. This short story, part of the North Belfast section of *Belfast Stories*, traces a short walk taken by a mother with her child through part of the city. Firstly, the story presents a woman who is frustrated by her sleepless child and the pressures of new parenting. She keeps repeating 'Keep it together' as her 'mantra'[32] as she is overwhelmed by the task of taking her baby outside to a potentially hostile world. Perhaps, in a longer story, we might have discovered that she was suffering from post-natal depression but here we are only given a glimpse of her mental state, which is mirrored by the greying skies and dark architecture. Eventually, however, Yee also infers that there could be more to this character's unsettled state than her maternal responsibilities when she is confronted by racist graffiti. She details the horrible moment where the protagonist is confronted by the words painted on Cliftonville Football Club's stadium, and she tries to deflect from the visceral, stomach churning feeling by imagining the materials used to produce the graffiti. She tried to imagine possible redress and whether the city council would take action. She imagines young offenders tasked with the job: 'Street cleansing. Atonement via bleach. That's one approach to truth and justice.'[33] In the chapter on *Milkman*, I examine how access to the city is curtailed by class, misogyny and sectarianism, but here Yee layers on something else vital: how racism affects the experience of 'post'-conflict Belfast and the ability to move freely without discrimination made visible. Yee contrasts this with the signs of 'progress' visible in the more affluent areas of the city: 'Progress is evidenced by the artisan coffee served tepid and trendy on pressed ply in concrete-floored Cathedral Quartered coffee shops run by nouveau-Christians who tolerate the gays.'[34] As the protagonist received harassment from an 8-year-old child, she weighs up her options in retaliating: 'Because in the bigger picture you don't know who lives in that boy's house and tribal tendencies run deep, get historic; who would take her word against his?'[35] She imagines the wider consequences for the young boy's hatred: a difficult home life punctuated by harsh words. This evidences her capacity for empathy despite unbearable circumstances but still begs the question of how to react to the scourge of racism in Northern

Ireland. While racism continues to be a scourge on contemporary British and Irish society, it takes on a particular dimension in a society with a very recent history of group violence and the desire to protect one's own community. In particular, she focuses on the issue of explaining racism to the child in her pram: 'How does she explain to her baby why the photo of the only Chinese politician was on the top of a July bonfire?'[36] At the end of the story, we get glimpses of hope: the sky brightens a little and a man covers over the racist story with an invitation to 'think'. Yee here acknowledges the long, painful history of racism in Northern Ireland and how it affects people in the present and also gestures towards possibility with her 'something new, something transformed'.[37] In the years to come, I expect the landscape of literature from the North of Ireland to be transformed and enriched by voices writing against racism and also celebrating cultures outside of the dominant traditions. In addition to my suggestion that we listen out for pleasure in the previous chapter, it is our duty as critics to attend to this new writing and celebrate diverse voices.

A 'moment of illumination': Dermographic exchange in David Park's *Gods and Angels*

David Park is the author of ten novels, one novella and one short story collection. This collection, *Gods and Angels*, shares thematic preoccupations with his novels as his prose writing, both deal with men who do not live up to hegemonic, masculine ideals and focus on small, intimate encounters. In interview, he noted,

> Well, all the stories are about men and exploring men's lives – different ages and geographical locations – some here, some beyond ... It's not a sociological or psychological statement, but it does explore and illuminate aspects of masculinity ... I think men find it more difficult to share what's inside and they feel the need to conform to stereotype and many don't have a network of support. It's a generalisation, but it can be a problem. They don't have enough trust to open up about themselves.[38]

This collection is deeply concerned with the male body as a potential site of redemption and knowledge, and the skin is overwhelmingly displayed as the conduit. The stories portray a clear aching for physical connection and examine the social and technological constraints that restrict men from intimacy. Park notes, 'Human intimacy might take a sexual form but equally it can be found in a momentary glance, the slightest of touches, the briefest exchange of words. I think I am always searching for such intimate moments in my writing.'[39] The body is represented as a betrayer and a calmative and the skin is the evidence of this inner turmoil. Park's characters often find a pleasure in the skin as a meeting point which is at odds with the language of religious texts. This is most clearly realized in Caravaggio's sneering at religious hypocrisy in 'The Kiss'. Skin becomes a vital signifier of interiority for Park, and haptic encounters feature in stories where it is not the main theme. In 'Crossing the River' the subsuming of identity is revealed through handprints ('My palms are long sanded smooth by the oars and fingers white-whorled with calluses –no one could take my fingerprints any more').[40] In 'The Painted Cave', tenacity is contrasted with skin texture as our protagonist 'is always surprised at how soft and smooth her skin feels – he expects it should have some of the toughness of her spirit.'[41] In 'Skype', Park is concerned with the physical encounter mediated through technology and making a distinction between digital content and the 'real' moment. A chance encounter is given particular credence here as Gabriel lingers on his most significant human interaction, with Anna who runs the coffee shop: 'Her sleeves are rolled to the elbow and for a second the light catches the fine lattice of blonde hairs on her forearms.'[42] This is contrasted with his attempts to engage with his family as 'on the screen her face is shadowed.'[43] Park's characters show a discomfort with the virtual way skin can be experienced in the twenty-first century.

In the first story in the collection, 'Learning to Swim', a young English academic named Henry gets his first teaching position in Belfast. His area of interest is the poetry of John Donne, and the poet's lifelong preoccupation with the sacred and profane echoes throughout the story. Henry is obsessed with the disjuncture between academic study of the literature of the body and what Donne called 'The Ecstasy of the Spirit and the Flesh'.[44] John Donne might well be regarded as a poet who is invested in the symbolic and sensual power of the skin. Poems such as 'The Flea', 'Elegy V: His Picture' and 'Elegy VIII: The Comparison' showcase the different ways that Donne uses the skin. It may be something of a cliché to assert that Donne's work exists between the word and the flesh, but the use of his work within Park's writing is significant. While Park was raised into the Baptist faith in East Belfast, his current engagement with the divine is more complex, as he asserts in interview:

> My aim as a writer – and it's a religious thing, although I'm not conventionally
> religious – is I want to take human experience and somehow find a moment

of transfiguration; a moment of illumination that just illuminates the beauty of something even though its mundane, even though it seems ordinary. It's to find those little moments of human experience that are symbolic of something beyond us.[45]

While this impulse will be considered throughout all of Park's work, his interest in this relationship is mostly clearly visible in 'Learning to Swim'. In interview, Park said of the story, 'I just wanted to bring two very different worlds together – the cerebral and the physical.'[46] By these different worlds, Park is referring to two different discourses of masculinity and, by extension, two different conceptions of the body and skin. Park's work has largely been invested in a self-critical exploration of masculinity, frailty and vulnerability which manifests itself through the body. This is pivotal for the way that Park approaches the relationship between body and mind throughout his work: he often begins with a Cartesian dualism and, as the stories progress, exposes the fragility of these binaries. At the beginning, Henry and Eddie are set up as complete opposites. We meet Henry as he is failing to learn how to swim, and we are repeatedly reminded that his realm is the scholarly and intellectual. He is nervous with women and views them from a remove as he idolizes Eddie's younger girlfriend and is bashful when she is in a cocktail dress. He is represented as someone lacking in action but with barely sublimated appetites. Henry rarely touches or is touched during the story, except when he dances with Eddie's new wife Alana at their wedding. Eddie, by contrast, is flash, fleshy and carnal, a man who visibly celebrates his appetites.

Learning to swim in a Belfast pool, he is befriended by a group of older Belfast men. Henry, being an outsider to the subtleties of Northern Irish politics, cannot 'read' them so he is not aware of their past history of violence. Park offers the reader glimpses into their 'skin autobiography' via their physical appearance with 'their bodies over-ripened and fleshy'[47] and their leader, Eddie, showing the effects of his lifestyle as 'his face bore the hints of a heavy drinker'.[48] The weathered, lined face of the drunkard will be a recurring trope in several of our Belfast stories. By contrast, the narrator has focused on the life of the mind and in his crush, the words of Donne come alive: 'I realised that all those thousands of theoretical words I had written didn't mean anything compared to this, when the pure physical reality of a woman brought Donne's lines spinning off the page in a way I had never experienced.'[49] Park's stories, as we shall see, often feature tender love scenes but the overall sense here is palpable frustration and longing. The erotic, for Henry, could be a site of transformation as it is for

Donne, Guibbory notes that the poet's 'boldest intervention was representing erotic love as a spiritual experience that provides fulfilment that the public world, and even its religious institutions, cannot'.[50] Henry's longing for human physical connection manifests itself through his own skin's response to Alana's skin: 'I felt myself blush like a teenager but even when I glanced away my senses were still steeped in her brown eyes, the layered fall of her black hair and her skin's patina, all pulsing to the involuntary rush of words shaken free from the dusty page.'[51] The skin, here, speaks when the protagonist cannot. This chimes with Connor's comment: 'There is a strongly held prejudice in favour of seeing the skin as the part of the body most likely to register emotions and states, such as shock, trauma, grief, fear, anxiety and shame, in which the reasoning subject appears to be, if only momentarily, taken over or set aside.'[52] The skin buzzes, strains to be touched, but in nearly all cases, the moment is elusive.

It is clear with Eddie and his friends, however, that hand shaking and back slapping are part of their masculine camaraderie. Hands become a symbol of their masculine identity as Henry attends a boxing match and is invigorated by the masculine displays of bodily prowess. This is contrasted with his own bookish, bloodless, body: 'I looked at my soft hands, splayed the fingers before clenching them into tight fists.'[53] Boxing has legacy in Northern Ireland, particularly the bare knuckle street fighting of Buck Alec and other pre-Troubles 'hardmen'.[54] The hand is what Abbie Garrington calls the 'poster boy of the haptic'. Hands are a potent metaphor in Northern Ireland: the red hand of Ulster is a rare cross community symbol, with such diverse usages as Great War UVF emblems and on the flags of both the Province of Ulster and the Northern Irish Parliament (1953–72). It is, however, not a touching, sensuous hand but a resolute, blood-red emblem. It is also worth noting that in both Loyalist and Republican iconography, the gloved hand is prominent. While paramilitaries wear gloves for obvious practical reasons, the leather covered hand became an iconic visual representation of the Troubles. This is not the recipient or the giver of the gentle touch, but rather a symbol of anonymous masculine force. Similarly, Henry is fascinated by the fighters 'whose gloved hands looked like the heads of sledgehammers'.[55] Just as the violence of the street fighter was displaced by the Troubles, the peace process has led to sanctioned public displays of masculine violence being mostly confined to the sporting arena. After the fight, there is a physical confrontation at the boxing match by a man whose father has been presumably murdered by Henry's new friends. This altercation is presented as quick and physical, an alternative to the moments of transcendence characterized by Park above. As Sam physically restrains the man, Henry considers the significance of it as 'probably one of those events whose physical reality presses itself indelibly into the memory and which is liable to reassert itself at any given time'.[56]

Whereas Donne's work neatly melds the physical and the cerebral, Park's characters are less successful. Henry concocts an elaborate fantasy of masculine derring-do but is quickly brought down to earth: 'I felt foolish and the euphoric sense of living in the body, instead of the head, seemed nothing more than an embarrassing drink-fueled fantasy'.[57] However, the proposed opposite, of the fleshly appetites of his new acquaintances, is not valorized or celebrated. Indeed, the two need each other by the end of the story as Henry helps Eddie by finding him a suitable love poem for his deathbed wedding. Throughout this story, touch has been a near miss, always at a remove. The narrator is regularly preoccupied with the intimacy he thinks he is missing as he imagines the casual touches between the dying ex-paramilitary and his younger wife. On leaving Belfast, and the situation, he again turns to hands as the key metaphor for proximity and intimacy: 'All of us equally uncertain about when fortune's favours might fade and whether our outstretched hands were ever going to reach'.[58] This recalls Michelangelo's Creation of Adam on ceiling of Sistine Chapel and also gestures to two important things: the act of stretching out your hand and the difficulty of physical and emotional connection for Park's characters. Park's representative of male desire here is significant: it is not a purely sexual impulse but also a profound hunger for intimacy that is registered through the skin.

This duality is also present in the third story in the collection, 'The Kiss', which intertwines the story of Caravaggio painting 'The Taking of Christ' with a brief interlude with a woman guiltily contemplating her extramarital affair in front of the artwork in Dublin's National Gallery. The title refers to the Judas Kiss of the scene in the Garden of Gethsemane and also our modern-day protagonist's dual life. It is significant, then, that Park's reimagining of Caravaggio is much more sensual than his representation of the flesh-and-blood affair. The story centres on Caravaggio's insistent attempts to capture the skin tones for this painting. Park's earlier novel *The Light of Amsterdam* (2012) was similarly concerned with the use of light and dark but this time in Dutch art, such as the paintings of Vermeer. In this novel, it was used as a metaphor for hidden secrets coming to light, or moments of self-revelation. However, while this story is similarly full of revelations, the frames of reference is nestled in the Catholic language of the relationship between the spirit and the flesh. Park regularly uses the term 'flesh' throughout: his work is heavy on biblical symbolism, and 'flesh' is used throughout the New Testament to refer to carnality and supposed weakness.

Indeed, the Book of Common Prayer includes the entreaty to be spared 'from all the deceits of the world, the flesh, and the devil'.[59] 'Flesh' usually refers to the soft matter between the bones and the skin, it is the skin that acts as a site of possibility, transference and transformation in this story. The skin is the portal to the deeper layers of embodiment.

Caravaggio is well known for his use of chiaroscuro and, in particular, the interplay of the shadows on the skin. This is often referred to as tenebrism, a 'type of painting in which significant details such as faces and hands are illuminated by highlights which are contrasted with a predominantly dark setting'.[60] While Connor asserts that 'religious thought and representation has been much taken up with phantasms of the radiant skin',[61] Dyer makes us aware that within 'Western art the dead white body has often been a sight of veneration, an object of beauty … Chiaroscuro becomes a key feature of the representation of whiteness'.[62] Park refers to this religious whiteness as 'the spit-thin, perfect alabaster skin'.[63] As noted, ideal white skin is culturally imagined to be both vulnerably thin and also flawless. The first part of the story is a meditation on the supreme difficulty of replicating this imperative. These painterly difficulties are highlighted by Connor: 'The painter of flesh must strike, through all the delicacy of his means and technique, to give the impression of a flesh which is in fact immaculate, untouched by human hand, and therefore illuminated by its own light and by radiant, rather than pigmented, colour.'[64] Park's Caravaggio is all too aware that his representation of fleshly corporeality offers a portal to the divine: 'What is it gives them their annunciations and beatifications, the gilded transfigurations and their holy miracles, but his flesh?'[65] With the exception of portrayals of Christ on the cross and the stigmata, religious art must rely on the skin as the portal through which this sense of other-worldly flesh is rendered. This representation of the pure, spotless divine body is directly contrasted with the sheer physical effort of painting: 'They're incarnated only through the tightening rack of pain in his shoulders, the throat's dry river-bed, his tired eyes that feel as if he's swimming through gravel.'[66] Park contrasts the representation of the flesh versus an ascetic life throughout the story. He examines how these two modes intermingle in the audience for his paintings:

> Strange how it's always different with his women and while the robed cardinals and their lackeys stand at the unveiling with sagging mouths – he's even seen one lick his lips – there isn't one of them who doesn't shuffle a little closer to touch with hungry eyes and store something for the lonely comfort of the night.[67]

Against this backdrop of Caravaggio's antipathy towards religious hypocrisy, Park emphasizes the sheer graft of the artist's work. Throughout the story, the paint speckles Caravaggio's skin, blurring the lines between the skin of the subject and his own: 'He needs to paint Christ's face and as if to see it afresh changes the angle of his vision, then walks closer before pulling back again, pushing a lock of hair from his brow and tinting it white.'[68]

Park shows the vulnerability and frailty of 'the flesh' as Caravaggio was 'always shocked by the flesh's willingness to shamelessly expose its vulnerability, its willingness to bleed and bruise, its bones to snap and splinter as though everything on the seemingly invincible surface was nothing but a vain boast'.[69] Hands can be the portal to divine creation but they can also be soiled, with the dirt becoming deep in the skin: 'He looks at the outstretched hand with its ingrained grime, the thick rim of dirt under the nails, and presses the few coins into Judas's palm, for a second feels their skin touch.'[70] Again, here we have the hand outstretched, as we did in the previous story. Caravaggio expends a great deal of energy on getting every sinew and dimension of the skin right and is particularly concerned over the effect these labours will have on his hands, which he observes carefully: 'Then he splashes his face, still smelling the paint on his hands that makes him think it has wormed under his skin … raising his palms together again to smell them and holding them there for a second as if he is praying.'[71] This effect is mirrored by Park's careful, painstaking description of skin, hands and the body throughout this story. Park also allows us glimpses into the sexual qualities of exposed skin: 'Caravaggio's face is fully hidden from him, seemingly inspecting the throat of the serving girl who slops across his lap, her laughter tinkling out as now he examines the skin tones of her breasts.'[72] He is obsessed with perfecting the skin tones necessary for divine art. When his friend is stabbed, it not only recalls the permeability of the skin ('Pietro's is a flesh wound'[73]) but also, in his friends exsanguinated complexion, finds the inspiration he needs to finish his painting.

As Caravaggio disappears into the night, we are brought back into the present, as an unnamed woman sits in the National Gallery waiting to travel to a Temple Bar hotel to meet her lover, 'a man she has failed to persuade herself that she is in love with. She wants to be in love because she tells herself that love exonerates, gives its license, and without the belief in love there are only uglier words that clamour on the consciousness.'[74] Her cover story is an art class, and while Park fills this section of the story with painterly detail, it is not as vividly drawn as the scenes with Caravaggio, to match her ambivalence. She finds temporary beauty in the marks on his skin: 'She watches the smooth stretch of his back, the thin swathe of freckles that stipple his shoulders, and feels the urge to touch them, to get back in the bed and snuggling behind him try to blow them gently away like dandelion seeds.'[75] There is a tenderness in this, despite her claim that she does not love him. Instead, in the skin there is a moment of recognition of shared humanity and vulnerability that offers something else. Both Caravaggio and the unfaithful wife seek to find in encounters with the body a portal to something beyond, but it is in inscribing the surface with meaning where they both find a sense of themselves.

In 'Keeping Watch', a police detective who is stalking his estranged wife experiences both painful memories and his current degradation through the skin. He emphasizes the permeable membrane that acts, in Prosser's terms, as his 'skin autobiography':

> It's not just the body's natural reaction to being locked up in a small space while being fed cheap coffee, junk food and lurid-coloured energy drinks, it's as if other toxins seep silently out through the skin – all the years of encounters with piss and blood and puke, all the hours rubbing up against the scum of the world have to find their own release. It's inevitable, I suppose.[76]

The skin here is an entrance point for the traumatic encounters that Van Der Kolk examines: although the body keeps the score, it is the treacherous skin that allows the cumulative effect of persistent negative affect to seep through. The skin is an autobiography, not just of the cumulative past but also of the current environmental conditions. For Park, the functions of the body are inseparable: the visual, the haptic and the somatic are all orientated towards unsuccessfully dealing with the trauma of police work:

> And the spores that lodge in the brain, those dark spots like malignant growths, sired out of what you've seen, what your hand had to touch – these things don't wash away with the shower you always try to take after work. So there's no soap or gel, however expensive, and I've a work locker full of them, ever cleans that stuff off.[77]

In Renaissance writing, there is an 'obsession with the skin's function as a vehicle for carrying away malignancy, waste and toxins.'[78] This is evident in Park's writing, which shows a fascination with Renaissance artistic and cultural depictions of the body. As with Caravaggio's handwashing, the skin is shown as something which can never be fully cleaned and continually interpellates and excretes matter, much to the troubling of its inhabitants. The journey from the car offers, for him, a kind of baptismal cleansing away from the filthy stultified air of the car: 'The mist-raddled morning air clings to my face and crimps the skin so it feels as if I'm wearing a mask'.[79] His skin moves from being the portal to transmit the degradation of the world to his viscera, but instead he holds his ex-wife's 'slip and savour[s] the scent that she's been wearing longer than I can remember'.[80] His every move has gone from rigidity and torque to a softer mode of yield, he is even portrayed 'gently caressing each of the steps into silence'.[81] He cannot see the difference between the violence he engages with on a daily basis and how he violates this domestic space. This is a subtle commentary by Park on the ways in which abusers compartmentalize aspects of their life, but here the body betrays these distinctions.

In 'Boxing Day', the body becomes the conduit through which a teenager, Robbie, comes to have empathy for his mentally-ill mother, Jane. As a young teenager, Robbie has little empathy for his mother as she grapples with her illness. He prefers his father's new partner and her daughter, and their easy physical affection. In this story, touch and skin act as languages for what cannot be said between father and son, and mother and son. This is akin to the Van Der Kolk's concept of alexithymia. Robbie recalls his mother's habit of lightly patting his head and 'began to think of it as the closest she could come to giving me her blessing'.[82] This act has two functions. In Christianity, the laying on of hands during a sacrament invokes the Holy Spirit but is used during practices of faith healing, which are often practised outside of mainstream religion. It also raises a point about the memory of touches past and how our history can be read as a network of touches. In addition to touch, this short story engages with the trope of scarring, another way of confronting and reconsidering past hurts. As in the work of Rosemary Jenkinson, scars have complex meanings and we interact with them on multiple levels, whether as bearer, inflictor or witness. She gives Robbie the tool to see her more closely and make her pain legible: a magnifying glass, that she thinks will help him play detective. Instead of becoming Sherlock Holmes, he turns it first on her while she falls asleep. Park conveys the experience of Robbie never really having properly looked at his mother before, seeing her not just as an extension of himself but rather something shameful that he wishes to forget:

But it was after I had moved the glass to her hands and looked at the white-flecked nails that I saw the cross-hatching on her right wrist and stopped looking through the glass. The marks were no longer red as they must once have been and were now scabbed over and dulled but they were there all the same. I went and sat down again. I wanted my father to come, wanted him to take me where

the reality of such things didn't exist, and as the shadows in the room thickened
I didn't want us to be the people who were to blame.[83]

The mother's scars bear witness to the unspoken undercurrent in Robbie's
interactions with his father. Her body tells the story he cannot. Earlier in this
chapter, we considered the use of scars in Northern Irish culture, but this story
broadens the dermal terrain. The troubles are not the only cause of scarring, and
this story raises the spectre of the post-conflict mental health crisis in Northern
Ireland and the silencing of inconvenient others. In the first half of 'Boxing Day',
the drive to the house by the sea is undercut by painful, half spoken memories
of the past but, as a teenager, Robbie simply sees his happy new life and wants
to bury the memory of his mentally ill mother. In shards, the memory comes
back to him of his father kissing his mother on the cheek in the hospital as she
grasps him to stay. These moments of painful, unwanted touch haunt father and
son throughout the story. Where initially Jane seemed to be an archetypal wild
woman by the sea of Irish literature, so prevalent in the works of Synge and
McDonagh, it becomes clear that her son feels deeply complicit in her current
status. The story ends with a scene that recalls two of Park's other novels: the
falling flakes of *The Big Snow* and the frosty car journey of *Travelling in a Strange
Land*. As Robbie's father awkwardly sings along to the fatalistic Smiths song
'There is a Light that Never Goes Out', so much remains unspoken between
them, revealed only in glances, light touches and the memory of connection.

In 'The Strong Silent Type', a young woman called Abi takes a shop dummy to
her school dance as a prank. In a rare moment of whimsy for Park, whose work
is usually solidly realist, the story is told from the perspective of the dummy,
who Abi dubs Simon. Throughout, the story examines beauty standards as
the dummy, with his pristine manufactured skin, not only observes the flaws
of humans ('I see the imperfections of skin'[84]) but also acutely desires contact
with them. This yearning begins in the silent tableaux of family life that he is
positioned into in shop window displays: 'I've stared into their eyes all day and
all night but their bald orbs of heads gave nothing back despite my outstretched
hand that reached out invitingly to them.'[85] The outstretched hand recalls the
ending of 'Learning to Swim', and again gestures towards an unspoken need. The
title of the story uses a cultural trope of masculinity – the 'strong silent type' as
the stoic epitome of on-screen manhood. This lack of verbal communication
is a recurrent theme for Park's men, but this is the most literal embodiment of
this theme. His is a visual not a haptic world, as he feels the pressure of eyes
bearing down on him from the glass. He has internalized the visual culture in

which women are usually expected to perform as objects of the gaze. Many of Park's stories attempt to draw lines between authentic, imperfect intimacy and synthetic encounters. Smell is an important sense here, as he returns to the language of 'flesh' used in 'The Kiss': She doesn't smell of the perfume counter but something for which I have no name and what must be the scent of flesh as she presses me tightly to her.'[86] Smell also recurs in the later story, 'Old Fool', where the narrator recalls erotic events past through sensual memory: 'their touch, their smell, the memories that each might have evoked'.[87]

In particular, the various shades of white skin strike him. Unlike his own, uniform colouring, Abi's skin tone is less than perfect ('And her skin is white, not white like snow but like the pages of a second-hand book'[88]) which she tries to cover as 'she does her make-up and paints and shades her face so it hides the limpid paleness of her skin and makes it closer to the colour of mine'.[89] The dummy begins to be intrigued by her body, especially those things he codes as 'flaws', such as uneven breasts and her disintegrating hairdo. This recognition of beauty in imperfection and difference is centred on the skin: 'Each one of them is a different size and shape, each one has a different scent, and up this close all of their skins are different.'[90] As we have seen with most of Park's other stories, this one ends on a forlorn note of missed connections and outstretched hands that never meet:

> But my hand is stretched out vainly forever in a window. I want to apply words to her hurt like a salve as all the things I need to say course uncontrollably through my being, rising and falling on a whelming tide of love, but no matter how hard I try, none can breach the sewn seam of my mouth.[91]

In his eventual realization that Abi will require a flesh-and-blood man who can have skin contact with her, Simon is an exaggerated version of Park's stoic men seeking connection, kept in place by rigid ideas of behaviour.

'Heatwave' and 'Gecko' offer two ways of relating to the skin of a long-term partner: the former showcases disgust and infidelity and the latter demonstrates how a new eroticism can be discovered in familiar flesh. In Heatwave, bodily disgust seeps through the narrative from the beginning: 'The city wore half-moon damp patches under its arms and on the buses and tube trains commuters fanned their faces with the free newspapers and avoided pressing against each other in the fear that they would stick, flesh to flesh, an instant Siamese twin with a stranger.'[92] Throughout the story, skin is unattractively moist, as Daisy is even a little disgusted by the sweatiness of her own son as she is 'repulsed a little by the clammy pulse of his body'.[93] Against this backdrop of sweaty, messy bodies falling foul of humidity, Daisy's husband Marcus is obsessed with clean lines and minimal design in his home. This extends to the bodies and skin that populate it: he expects them to be tanned and gym honed, like their nanny, Angelica. Daisy, by contrast, sporadically attends a yoga class for the company and seeks warmth and companionship over hours spent mortifying the flesh. Skin recurs throughout the story as both a marker of intimacy and as a sign of the disintegrating marriage at the core of the narrative. As Angelica rubs sun cream on the couple's son Theo, Marcus watches the scene greedily, observing every detail of the tenderness between them as Theo wriggles and giggles as she makes it into a game. Throughout, Angelica's tanned skin, free of imperfections, is contrasted with Daisy's paler skin. In particular, Marcus disdains Daisy's use of make-up against Angelica's bare faced skin: 'He thought of how right she looked in the morning without make-up and devoid of artifice.'[94] Women are all too aware quite how many products can go into developing the perfect natural look, making a skin that appears flawless can often be the result of painstaking work, much as Caravaggio painstakingly produced luminosity on the canvas. In contrast, he observes his wife's tide lines of foundation with horror and lingers on her make-up 'mistakes'. He also looks at her skin as a bad augury for their future life together:

> He looked again at the bright red of her toenails and how the colour only served to accentuate the whiteness of her legs. He saw too how there were thin threadlines of veins on her thigh as if she had been scratched by a cat and it struck him that she wasn't going to age well.[95]

His sureness over his masculinity (hard, toned, discrete) is challenged when he gets the family car stuck on a beach and needs to be rescued by some bare-chested men who flirt with his wife. A deep, simmering resentment boils up against their bodies, which are not just exercised in an airless gym, but are practical and hard-working. He tries to conjure up Angelica's smooth, tanned skin but keeps circling round the idea of meat carcasses hanging in a fridge, no matter how hard he tries to banish it 'there was only a frozen unyielding solidity and not a single trace of the softness of flesh.'[96] Here Park draws our attention to the socially constructed ideals of both male and female skin. In eschewing the mess and disintegration that are part of being in skin relation with other, imperfect humans, he has rendered these encounters sterile. Angelica exists as a perfect object for him because her body has not yet let him down, her skin has not yet yielded to time. Jackie Stacey reminds us of the inevitability of this process: 'Skin is temporal in the sense that it is affected by the passing of time, or, to put it differently, it materialises that passing in the accumulation of marks, of wrinkles, line and creases, as well as in the literal disintegration of skin.'[97] Marcus's life is depicted by Park as a kind of death, of the impossible quest for a body that is not betrayed by sweaty, ageing skin. In his callous reception to the bodies of others, we see the perils of a lack of empathy towards the body of the other that can only reap an inevitable return for his own, imperfect body.

'Gecko' features a couple who, for their twenty-five-year marriage anniversary, decide to go to see the Northern Lights. They are never named, which adds to a sense of familiarity. The title refers to a school pet, dubbed Gordon by the students (who are unlikely to be familiar with Wall Street), and also to two key elements within the story. He mentions that geckos do not blink, and central to the relationship is the idea of constantly regarding someone without looking at them afresh. Also, it is noted that some species can reproduce without having sex with the male, and their marriage is haunted by the secret that their childlessness was due to his undisclosed infertility. Their lives before the trip are depicted as humdrum: he is five years from retiring as a science teacher and she works for the registry of births, marriages and deaths. He is more private and taciturn, she enjoys chatting with colleagues and is emotionally invested in the lives that come through her office. This trip, then, is a pivotal moment for them to take stock of their marriage and direction of their life together. Though, given the collection's interest in masculinity, it is focalized through the husband with only speculation about his wife's mindset. We hear of a brief flirtation at work and the careful negotiation of how stability and the desire for excitement are managed within a marriage. The trip, then, offers a turning point as he 'told himself he felt lighter, cleaner, as if something was being slowly scraped from his skin'.[98] Prior to their trip, their lovemaking is described as perfunctory and a comfortable kindness. On a snowy excursion, Park depicts a couple who have been sensible and safe finally taking a chance and venturing out on a trip along the icy landscape. The husband's fear and his wife's enjoyment spur a realization of the intimacy that they have:

> Then as his desire quickened she was taking off his clothes and slipping out of hers but trying to do it while she still held him close so for a few minutes they were a tangle of skirmishing arms and scrunching legs that momentarily reminded him of the awkwardness of long-gone courtship in cars … And everything seemed to fall away, both uncertainty and all predictability, so that what he felt was an overwhelming sense of the moment's passion and he let himself be carried by it not caring where it was taking him and when it broke in

a sudden rush he heard himself whisper words that he had no control over and he was telling her the stars were in her eyes and in her hair.[99]

Following this, he sees her afresh again and notices every detail, from the way she holds her head while brushing her hair to the glance she gives herself in the mirror. Specifically, he notices the 'final smooth with the palm of her hand' and how she 'held her palms to it as if gesturing her surrender'.[100] A raised palm can be a defensive stop sign, but here it is something more, a radical vulnerability. Again, the metaphor of the outstretched hand recurs, but in this story, we see a greater deal of connection as their hands gently meet, as he 'stretched out his hand and she stretched hers, the distance between allowing them only to touch at the tips of their fingers'.[101]

This encounter, then, demonstrates an important orientation for this whole study – questions of how intimacy is mediated through proximity and distance. In Park's work, then, this is experienced primarily through failures of communication, but the important thing to note is that all his characters actively seek intimacy. Park's profoundly empathetic fictions of the skin embody Stacey and Ahmed's imperative that 'thinking through the skin is a thinking that attends not only to the sensuality of being with others, but also to the ethical implications of the impossibility of inhabiting the other's skin'.[102] To attend to the skin, then, is to attend to moments of pain, touch and tenderness and to think through the relationality of the skin encounter.

She found it beautiful, this small white flaw: Encounters with another skin in Rosemary Jenkinson's *Aphrodite's Kiss*

The rest of this chapter will focus on three short story writers who depict, mostly, women's intimate experiences and the experience of being in one's own skin: Rosemary Jenkinson, Bernie McGill and Roisin O'Donnell. In Rosemary Jenkinson's collection of short stories, *Aphrodite's Kiss*, the body is clearly a repository of images and history that are regularly manifested through the depiction of the skin and touch. As we have seen in the previous chapters, Jenkinson has most readily written about the pleasures and pitfalls of female sexuality and, in this collection, her frank sensibility is explored through the short story form. The stories span Ireland and Europe, and can be read as a coming from a particular post-Good Friday pre-Brexit Northern Ireland, with characters who are depicted as outward looking and welcoming to other cultures.

Or, at least, the attractive members of other cultures. While Park's work focused mostly on moments of masculine vulnerability, Jenkinson's stories deal more consciously with female agency, whether in relation to sexuality or in the politics of access to medical treatment. The three aspects of skin that I want to draw out in her work are vulnerability, communication and sexual intimacy. Jenkinson notes how these forces contrast and complement each other: 'Intimacy is at its most piquant when physical proximity contrasts with an underlying inner loneliness.'[103] Jenkinson is also one of the few authors who examines Northern Irish whiteness as something frail, vulnerable and particularly susceptible to external influences. She noted that 'white Northern Irish skin is as soft as soda bread!'[104] As well as this frailty, the body is emphasized through her work as an expressive medium: language is represented as something almost physical, as she often notes the movement of lips, tongue and teeth. However, as with Park's outstretched hands, there can be a fundamental lack of connection in most of the stories. As she notes in interview, 'most of the stories mean something autobiographically to me and, while you could say the overriding theme is loneliness, it's not a conscious one.'[105] Her stories manifest this loneliness through a yearning for touch, contact and connection through the skin.

Jenkinson's stories examine the skin as recipient and giver of pleasure. In 2020, she noted that 'it strikes me that I didn't realise how tactile I was till social distancing arrived. How I long for those brief halcyon days in March of the elbow rub or the toe tap.'[106] To develop the argument of the previous chapter, touch is often intimately connected with sexual pleasure. Skin is the largest organ of the body and is erogenous, so it is referred to as the body's largest sex organ. Roland Barthes, in *A Lovers' Discourse*, reminds us of the relationship between language and the erotic body: 'Language is a skin: I rub my language against the other. It is as if I had words instead of fingers, or fingers at the tip of my words. My language trembles with desire.'[107] In Jenkinson's work language and skin are intimately connected. Deutscher usefully moves the discussion of the erotic potential of skin away from a purely penetrative discourse using the work of Simone de Beauvoir, suggesting that her concepts deviate from Sartre's reading of eroticism as follows:

> To touch the skin of the other, to experience one's own, and the other's desire, is a complex recognition both of similitude (in so far as I can experience desire at once and at one with my partner) and difference (for I can never assume that the other desires as I do). The touch is at once a moment of greatest proximity and greatest distance.[108]

Throughout the collection, Jenkinson plays with proximity and distance in the lives of almost all her characters and the touch as a method of communication of desire. In these stories, moments of intimacy often puncture a specific kind of loneliness that her characters exhibit and embody what Deutscher describes as when touch 'occurs as part of a being in the world which thrills to disturbance, being unsettled or tantalised by objects and others'.[109] Jenkinson's short stories embody the subject who thrills to disturbance with the other but wants to maintain their distance – they want to be intimate with the skin of others, but in their own time and on their own terms.

In 'Scenes from an Empty Attic', Angelina's skin acts as a barometer for her physical and mental health: 'The late nights were telling on her skin. The scar on her forehead appeared whiter than usual against the shadows under her eyes.'[110] In Jenkinson's fiction, post-troubles Belfast is often a chemically altered, booze-sodden night town. Jenkinson describes how these experiences are semi-autobiographical: 'I couldn't settle anywhere and it was like I was collecting cities – once I'd lived in one, got to know it, made some new friends, I would go off to the next and try to conquer it, in the same kind of addictive way you do with sexual encounters as in "Scenes from an Empty Attic".'[111] Angelina's hedonistic lifestyle is detailed in somatic terms, as she and her friends are 'inflamed and burnt-out, rubbing coke on to their pale gums, showing their teeth in the candlelight like vampires'.[112] In Jenkinson's fiction, whiteness is not valorized or celebrated, but often cast as something fragile and permeable that absorbs the toxic quality of the atmosphere: 'His tanned skin glowed next to the Irish faces that were the shade of pink-grey limestone, scored by years of drink and cigarettes'.[113] By contrast, Cosme, the Spanish student of the aforementioned tanned skin, has a vibrancy and natural curiosity. Angelina notes an 'an old injection mark on his arm, white against the tan of his skin. She found it beautiful, this small white flaw'.[114] White here is the flaw, against the perfect tanned skin. The beauty of scars will recur in 'Marie + Finbar'. Jenkinson's representation of the sexy European other might be exploitative if it were not also so pleading and desperate for connection: the characters of her novels seek to prolong their encounters with any influence outside of Northern Ireland. It is reminiscent of the end of Sinéad Morrissey's poem 'Tourism':

> Diffuse the gene pool, confuse the local kings,
> infect us with your radical ideas; be carried here
> on a sea breeze from the European superstate
> we long to join; bring us new symbols,
> a new national flag, a xylophone. Stay.[115]

Angelica embodies that last, plaintive 'Stay' – she desires the skin of the other as an erotic escapism. She works in a bank with foreign currency and even the encounters with the notes have a sensual frisson for her: her longing for new, foreign experiences is communicated through the skin. Cosme is depicted as 'like an animal rippling under its pelt'[116] with a 'tight-fitting coat'[117] like a second skin. He is an erotic object for Angelica that is experienced primarily through her relationship with his skin. Because Cosme and Angelica struggle to communicate, he uses a lot of body language, specifically his hands. Communication through the haptic is vitally important to sexuality, particularly the expression of enthusiastic consent. He gestures upstairs when he wants to initiate sex and leads her to bed ('Cosme took her hand').[118] In the stories of David Park, hands were so often outstretched and only rarely met, but in Jenkinson's work, hands are grasping, desirous and sensual ('he brushed the side of her cheek gently with his knuckles … his fingers like creepers slowly moving up his face').[119] As Cosme leaves to catch his plane, Angelica has to leave the fantasy she projected onto his tanned skin and instead numbs her desire for escapism through drink and drugs. Sensuality and skin memory, however, comfort her after this encounter. Northern Irish literature is so often concerned with the after-effects of violent physical conflict, but Jenkinson's work is invested with the afterglow of bodies: 'She pulled off her clothes, slowly touching her skin with her fingers, like she could feel the heat, the food, the voice of a sun-filled land, a beautiful language written on her body.'[120] The need for the other that cannot be spoken is communicated in Jenkinson's writing through a network of exchange of touches. 'Aphrodite's Kiss' has a similar preoccupation to 'Scenes from an Empty Attic'. It takes place in Athens, with Sarah, an English language teacher, engaging in sex and hedonism but ultimately keen to come back to Northern Ireland. The story is heavy with sexual experimentation and, again, the aching desire for the other. This is embodied in a chance encounter with a man on leave from military service: 'At that moment, she decided she would give her love to Dimitris. Her skin ached all over. Her muscles felt as if she had been carrying heavy weights around with her. Dimitris would make her light again.'[121] In these texts, we have often seen skin aching to be touched. However, when imagining her return home, the image of skin contact is more comforting: 'In two weeks' time she would be back in Belfast, back to the sweet lick of her own mother tongue.'[122] The stories which are set in Belfast feature a yearning to be elsewhere and the stories set elsewhere ache for the touch of Belfast.

In 'Marie + Finbar', the representation of the body charts both the deterioration of a romantic relationship and the renegotiation of a joyful relationship with the body. The protagonist, Marie, is a French woman who falls in love with an Irish traditional musician in a Belfast bar. Marie is depicted as sexually voracious and confident in her possession of her body and sexuality. Indeed, the short story begins with a bold sentence: 'The important thing, the French say, is to love your own body. It's good to be heureux dans sa peau, happy in your own skin.'[123] The story, then, depicts a journey away from and a homecoming to this sensation, an easy comfort which has eluded so many of our Northern Irish encounters. While the story quickly depicts her physical difficulties such as 'scars on her ankle and a slight twist in her calf'[124] as the result of surgery on her ankle for a club foot, Jenkinson is also quick to depict Marie overcoming them to gain agency over her body. Her youth is described as a communion with nature, she 'would walk naked'[125] as a 'child of the sun'.[126] Jenkinson depicts Marie as comfortable, relaxed and natural within her own body, with a lack of self-consciousness or shame until her father's penis, once an object of curiosity ('something she longed to touch'[127]), is banned from her and she 'lost her pure communion with nature'.[128] She begins to ask questions about nature and the natural world and how they function alongside norms of shame and prohibition. Marie does, however, clearly seek to reclaim her sensuality as she progresses into adolescence and adulthood, and this is expressed through a connection to both foreign languages and erotic literature. For many of Jenkinson's characters, language, the mouth and sexuality are presented as delicately intertwined. Many of them have an appreciation for the erogenous qualities of language, particularly Marie, who 'loved the sound of strange words in her mouth'.[129] Originally having decided she was going to become a writer, she 'read a quote by Hrabal, which said "you should write like you're fucking in a passageway"'.[130] Her appetite, however, is much more for the latter than the former, as she indulges a passion for both sex and erotic literature:

> She loved sex. In the same way that some people go to university and discover a talent for drinking, drug-taking or supporting hopeless political causes, she found her true vocation in sex. She read voraciously all that Colette, Anaïs Nin and Henry Miller had ever written. The more she read of this stuff, the more sex she needed. She could hardly get through a poem of Musset's without plunging a hand into her pants.[131]

Throughout the story, the representation of skin stands in for Marie's sensuality and relationship with her own body. As in Jenkinson's other stories, European skin is fascinating to the Belfast locals: 'The Irish men were captivated by her warm skin'.[132] She arrives in Belfast to find 'the legacy of a sleepless city at war with itself'.[133] She is disappointed, as she had hoped for erotic liberation but found only alcoholic hedonism. She soon adapts to the culture of Belfast and manages to displace her erotic impulses into other sensual pleasures: 'She found it suited her constitution to go "buck-mad".'[134] The story charts Marie's attempts to find a way to be both a writer and an embodied self: 'the desire to become a writer – was getting lost among the bare flesh and hallucinations and soaked hair and emptiness.'[135] In Jenkinson's work the erotic is often redemptive and skin is transformative, as we saw in Chapter 2. Sex and desire can lead to a kind of renewal for her characters.

However, this redemption through the flesh is not evident in the central relationship in the story. When she meets Finbar, an Irish traditional musician, in a pub, their attraction is immediate and expressed through an initial yielding to each other's skin: 'His softness was as welcoming to her as the plumped-up duvet she wanted to sink beneath that night. Her softness to him was like the soothing foreignness of his mother's tongue when he was a baby.'[136] Here, skin becomes a yielding comfort for her, something to lose oneself in, rather than the difference that he experiences. However, it soon becomes clear than he is deeply threatened by her sensuality and seeks to use the flaws of her skin to bind her to him: 'He said he wanted her breasts all to himself … He kissed the scars on her ankle. He loved the scars. He loved them because they were private to him, and he wanted her to know that she was flawed and lucky to have him.'[137] He becomes jealous of all the men she has slept with and imagines her bed 'impressed with a man-shaped indentation smelling of sweat and sex'.[138] As their possessive, unhappy relationship progresses she gets progressively lighter and he gets heavier, and his once comforting skin becomes impossible for her to bear ('the white of his milky skin within white walls'[139]). As she parts from her relationship with the ever more possessive Finbar, the rediscovery of her body and sensuality is immediate:

> She drew her future intentions in bold colours on her lips. She licked them, remembering how, as a child, she had stained them with blackberry juice. She ate the food of her youth – potatoes in goose fat, rich tapenades, saucisson – and her curves increased with every waxing of the moon … And Marie laughed now, with a flash of her eyes at the men, to let them know she was proud of her appetites. Her voice was louder, her manners more vulgar, freed of Finbar's confining prudery.[140]

Marie is one of the most actively desirous and sensual characters in Northern Irish writing, her body one of many expressive tools at her disposal. Her eroticism flourishes without the confining other, and it delights in the pleasures of her flesh. She decides to become a writer who shows skin: 'She made it her mission to upstage every other writer she met, if not through intellect, then through the body. There were no depths now to which her cleavage would not plunge!'[141] This story enacts a homecoming to an authentic self and a rediscovery of a sensuality. But, in many ways, Marie is an exaggeration of a key impulse of Jenkinson's work: the question of how to write joyfully and sensually about being comfortable in your own body in Northern Ireland.

A few of Jenkinson's stories focus on encounters in Poland, one a tender story of eroticism in a cold climate and another on the consequences of reproductive injustice. 'Poronin' details a brief encounter where the body, again, acts as a way of expression that transcends cultural barriers. The narrator, an English teacher, finds comfort in her lonely existence in the arms of a local she meets at the bar and their encounter is rendered in careful sensual terms as 'their eyes flitting across at each other, trying to preserve the memory of their naked forms for ever, before they were buried under successive layers of clothing'.[142] However, while this and the other stories mentioned showcase skin as a sensual portal to another world, 'Silent Giving', another Polish story, offers skin as something which indicates women's suffering. A TV weathergirl, Alicja, enters into an affair with a Scottish teacher of English, only to become pregnant. Alicja can be read as the counterpoint to Marie, as she is similarly keen for outside experiences, as 'her headstrong nature and the desire to experience every pain and pleasure in the world' is noted.[143] The beginning of the story not only foreshadows the colour palette of its tragic end but also emphasizes the social pressure on women to cosmetically alter their skin: 'When she pulled her hands away, her palms were streaked with studio make-up, a seascape of beachy brown and blue.'[144] Of her two suiters, Tomek and Ewan, she finds something attractive in the latter's 'untoned whiteness, which nevertheless was attractive in its fleshy carnality'.[145] In particular, she is attracted to the social cachet of his profession. Unlike the Northern Irish faces Jenkinson depicts in earlier stories, Scottish Ewan is depicted as having surprisingly unlined skin:

> Then she looked deeper and noticed that his pale skin had hardly a wrinkle, his eyes had only a few smile lines. It was the face of someone living on the margins of existence or in some secret world where suffering was unknown. It was incredible – he was thirty-six yet he seemed unmarked and uninformed by life's tribulations.[146]

Ewan is feckless and irresponsible: he has a girlfriend in Scotland and lets Alicja down when she needs him most. Poland's abortion laws are some of the most repressive in Europe. Alicja faces complications due to having an illegal procedure, facing a prison sentence, a hysterectomy or even death. She is abandoned by Ewan and her family doctor and left to get increasingly sicker in the bathroom where her younger brother died. At the end, Alicja's skin bears witness to the repression of these regulations and the unspoken harm done to women: 'The tips of her fingers were purple, almost a bright violet, and she tried to stifle the rising fear. Nothing mattered any more.'[147] The title, 'Silent Witness', we are told, relates to the women who have sex but are considered quiet and not ostentatiously sexual. However, it stands in for a more general concept of female bodily forbearance. The term 'witness' connotes a kind of detached passivity, which contrasts with the fact that these women's bodies are engaged in sexual intercourse. It suggests they are watching something happen to them, and their body becomes the witness, as does Alicja's. As her skin ominously changes colour, possibly to indicate sepsis, Alicja stands in for generations of Polish and Northern Irish women who have kept quiet during the most unbearable moments. The skin bears witness when the repressive regimes of reproductive justice silence women.

A similar fascination is evident in 'The Girl Who Fell from the Sky', where Ruth deals with a grim medical prognosis which makes her recall a pivotal moment from her childhood. While it is a marked change in tone from the first half of the collection, the story is still primarily navigated through touch and, in particular, the laying on of hands. The lusty, hedonistic tone of the first few stories is gone, replaced by someone whose health has led them to give up on sexual intimacy entirely: 'The last time she'd had sex she'd been in the throes of pain, not passion. Her body was more ravaged now than ravished.'[148] The touch that leads to her to the reminiscences of the past comes from her affable Doctor in the Royal Victoria Hospital, who inspects her body with touch: 'His hands gently circled her lower back. She could feel the boiling pain of his fingertip on her scar.'[149] This is a different kind of scar to Marie's – this is a scar that exists as a constant reminder of illness. As we saw in Jan Carson's *The Firestarters*, doctors are privy to some of the most intimate moments of our lives, and Jenkinson frames this clearly as a haptic encounter. In particular, the touch using hands 'suddenly reminded her of a priest she had known over thirty years before.'[150] When Ruth was a young Protestant girl, she was sent to live with her uncle and his Catholic wife, who enthusiastically brought her to Church. Twice she mentions the impact of the alabaster skin of the saints against the flagellated body of the Christ figure in the iconography of the Church, which sets up the two central ways that skin is used in the faith as both marker of purity and sacrifice.

When Ruth sees that a female soldier has fallen from the sky on television, she retells the story as if she witnesses it and this is interpreted as a holy vision. The priest ministers to her in much the same way as her Doctor, holding out his hands and seeking answers through a skin encounter: 'The priest's hands felt tomb-dry around her own, like he was looking to her for some great answer.'[151] When the misunderstanding is discovered, the embarrassment leads to the child thinking about mortification: 'It means you whip yourself with knotted leather. Why would Aunt Maggie feel she had to whip herself?'[152] The skin here acts not as a conduit for giving and receiving pleasure but is the object of violent penance. It is very much a skin autobiography for Ruth – the skin of the present is simultaneously the skin of the past. In Jenkinson's work, then, we have an immense variety of skin encounters – sensual, medical, cross-cultural. The skin functions in her work as communicator, pleasure-giver and a repository of the story of our lives.

'Each of them marked by the place' – skin autobiographies in Bernie McGill's *Sleepwalkers*

Bernie McGill's short story collection *Sleepwalkers*, published in 2013, shares some thematic affinities with Jenkinson's work, particularly in the representation of the sensual body and the skin in relation. McGill is particularly deft at using the body in her stories as a communicative tool. She notes that, in writing, 'it's the intimacy of the encounter that draws me in'.[153] In addition to the stories which deal directly with skin-based experience and haptic sensations, representations of these kinds of experiences saturate the narrative. McGill has an interest in mindfulness and meditative techniques and runs workshops with a hatha yoga teacher on the relationship between the 'calm body and writing focus'.[154] There is a similar kind of interaction in these stories – the body is very much present in each of them and sensations are often experienced through the skin in contact with others. In 'Home', the skin is used as a conduit to both powerful, painful memories and also the rediscovery of sexuality. The unnamed protagonist leaves for the South of France from Ireland after her young son dies in a horrific farming accident and her marriage breaks down. The full story of their break-up is never fully articulated and she often thinks about her husband – how they met, their moments of small intimacies, how he might react to her current situation. The title of the story gestures towards her in-between life:

she is a cleaner and caretaker of people's homes while feeling nowhere at home. She takes time on the small details of her employers' domestic lives, carefully cleaning and caring for their belongings as she tries on their lives. McGill metes out the tale of her life in Ireland carefully, but from the beginning of the story, an acute sense of grief drives the narrative. This story asks how one can be at home after grief: not only in the domestic sense of home but another sort of homecoming – to oneself. This returns to the question of being comfortable in your skin which was raised by Jenkinson in a much different context but is worth bearing in mind here, as the grieving mother tries to negotiate the relationship between touch and intimacy against the thrum of the past. He fantasises about keeping out the icy grip of a painful past from her present as one might exclude a draft. A draft is first felt through the shivers of the skin. The past is imagined in domestic, sensual terms:

> When she reaches for it, and her fingernails sink in, she thinks of the thick white candles on the table at Christmas and how Robbie would pinch the molten wax with his small fingers, make indentations that would harden into castellated towers where knights would sleep, he said, and guard the flame until it could be lit again.[155]

Here, hands are used for childish creativity. Like Park, the metaphor of reaching hands is used to convey difficulties in communication and connection which haunt the protagonist.

As noted, skin is often represented in Northern Irish fiction as something susceptible to the elements. Our protagonist takes special precautions to keep her own skin as unmarked by the Mediterranean climate as she can:

> Each morning she applies sun block to her face, hands and feet, rubs mint-tasting salve into her lips, wraps her head in a blue scarf. She has no desire to be marked. She looks like a person playing at being a nomad, her eyes and skin and hair too pale for someone who has been much exposed to weather.[156]

This mirrors the ways in which she seeks not to be marked by the place, as she takes care to limit her relationships with the locals to the absolute essential interactions. She avoids intimacy, but it is through two figures: the baker and the artist, that she eventually comes back to her own skin. McGill emphasizes the tactile qualities of the baker's profession and the ease with which he performs transformations: 'It's understandable, she thought, that he should come to believe that heat and time and touch can fix anything.'[157] Hands provide a source of comfort, and this extends to her relationship with Harper, who she initially wary of. As in Jenkinson's short story 'Marie + Finbar', scars can be emblematic of a desire for intimacy but here they are linked to a female desire to touch a man's skin and explore the boundaries of his body: 'At his left temple there is a small scar the shape of a hen's foot, livid against his sun-browned face. She would like to put her hand on it, trace the outline with her fingertips, test the depth of it.'[158] This is a desire not just to reach out and touch the other, but for them to let you explore their imperfections right to the edge of the skin. It is a desire for another's vulnerability. Their sexual encounter is described in similar terms with her agency foregrounded in the narrative:

> She sits down on the edge of the bed beside him and he reaches up and puts his hand in her hair. … She can feel the hairs on his legs against the damp skin of her thighs. He reaches up and under her shirt, traces the beads of water along her spine, and she leans down, closes his mouth under hers.[159]

After their encounter, she returns to the home that she has been caretaking in a pensive but hopeful mood, and goes from watching the boats on the sea to focusing on people, in particular noting that 'a grey-haired couple are swimming, their backs to the sun, naked in the sea [and] she thinks that if she could follow them, maybe she would find her way home.'[160] McGill's writing often focuses on the idea that to deny yourself sensuality after a tragic event denies something fundamental to your personhood. In this story, her skin autobiography involves not only the grooves of hurt and pain but is also alive to sensual touch. The resolution is not easy: we do not know if she is referring to a literal homecoming or to a sense of self, but it is clear after the touch of a lover, there is a glimmer of hope and transformation: 'And she thinks that maybe the baker does know something, after all, about heat and touch and time.'[161]

In 'The Importance of Being Rhonda', a woman's recovery from a brain haemorrhage is experienced through the rediscovery of the tactile world. Rhonda has amnesia and cannot remember her life before hospitalization: she speaks of 'Rhonda' as a separate entity to her conception of herself. In the story, McGill represents a woman pushing against her prescribed identity before her condition, which is defined by the influence of her family and experienced through skin and touch relations. In particular, McGill juxtaposes Rhonda's appearance with her sister's: 'She is tinted and blushed and glossed and mascaraed, nothing like the fleshy-faced shorn-headed woman who looks out of the mirror back at me … It's a hard thing to have your meal choices dictated by a woman whose eyebrows are pencilled on.'[162] As in Jenkinson's work, the experience of receiving medical treatment is a fraught, intimate encounter with the skin. Modern medicine allows Rhonda's skin to be recovered through advanced technology but it also necessitates the contact between the skin of the doctor and her own:

> The doctor leans over to examine the scar on the right side of my head and his fingers are cool. I've seen the graft in the mirror. It looks like a disc of pale wax, like the cooled drippings from a candle, like you could slide your thumbnail underneath and prise it off in one piece without breaking it. I can't help but wonder if Rhonda is trapped underneath.[163]

Here we have the language of scarring again – but Rhonda is able to look at her own body with a kind of detachment due to her amnesia. Prosser reminds us that 'skin re-members, both literally in its material surface and metaphorically in resignifying on this surface, not only race, sex and age, but the quite detailed specificities of life histories'.[164] Rhonda's body is now marked by her scar, which divides her life into a before and after. This extract also draws our attention to medical attempts to mimic skin, which are often unsuccessful in capturing its unique qualities, which reminds one of Park detailing artist's struggles to render luminosity. For Rhonda, skin is also a kind of knowledge, not just a way to think about her past. Her 'skin autobiography' gives her glimpses into a past life of hard labour on her feet: 'I know about the hard skin under the balls of my feet when I shuffle across the floor to the toilet on a walking frame, a nurse's hand at my elbow.'[165] The experience of hapticity here is powerful: she is touching on two levels, both the calloused soles of her feet to the floor but she also the gentle touch of the nurse. While the nurse isn't holding her up, McGill emphasizes the feeling of support that comes from a gentle touch. The work of nurses, in addition to their vital medical role, is often to provide these kinds of invaluable small kindnesses. McGill demonstrates here that touch does not have to be rough or intense to make a profound impact. Also, this moment demonstrates that skin can feel multiple things at multiple times that can both bring us into the present and echo through the past.

The story details both her experience of estrangement from the body, where Rhonda is separate, towards a kind of homecoming through sensory experience:

> I can't sleep on my left side: my forearm is tender where they removed the skin for the graft. … My arms are pale and freckled, bruised at the wrist from where the IVs have been. A delta of blue veins rises on the back of my hand. The skin on my stomach is a little loose, like it has been stretched over a larger woman.[166]

The experience of recovery can be profoundly unsettling as it is often an acute reminder of the permeability of the skin and, therefore, of its impermanence and the inevitability of death. Veins are an aspect of the skin that are rarely considered unless they become a problem, such as varicose veins, deep vein thrombosis or abscessed veins. Superficial veins are close to the body and have vital physiological functions: they are one of the few parts of the circulatory system that can be seen. Another aspect McGill draws attention to is the limits of the skin's elasticity as Rhonda has loose skin, presumably caused by weight loss in hospital. This image is contrasted with the photographs of a trip to Venice with her sister and niece, paid for with her cleaning money: 'Rhonda seated in a gondola with round cheeks and plump arms in a vest-top that wrinkles over her belly, white cut-off trousers that show blue-veined legs.'[167] The Rhonda that is reconstructed is of a smiling, hard-working woman who is determined to please everyone but appears to put her own needs last. McGill asks questions here of female compliance and resistance. As her sister sits at the end of her bed and recalls stories of Rhonda's skill with a toothbrush on the grouting of wealthy houses on the Malone Road, one thinks of the pernicious effect of the discourse identified by Sara Ahmed in *The Promise of Happiness* where she notes the particular affective power of the statement 'I just want you to be happy.'[168] Rhonda is an exaggerated version of the 'happy housewife': she is the happy cleaner, who treats her family with her meagre wages and never complains.

At the end of the story, McGill presents a resolutely determined woman, who cannot reconcile her own embodied self-image with the description her sister presents to her: 'I'm not climbing back inside the shell of that woman they want me to be. I turn down the blanket and find the label and stroke the silk with my fingers.'[169] This subtle moment brings her into the present and offers a hope for the future that is not tied to the past. The last lines recall Heaney's poem 'Digging' ('Between my finger and my thumb/The squat pen rests'[170]), which is similarly concerned with writing as an act of self-determination: 'I pick up the pen, squeeze the foam between my thumb and forefinger, angle it at the lines on the pad.'[171] Heaney, however, seeks a kind of continuation between his own writing and his father's manual labour. Rhonda seeks a more definitive break from her compliant past or, as Ahmed has it, 'to share what deviates from happiness is to open up possibility, to be alive to possibility'.[172] McGill offers us this possibility through writing and self-expression but, importantly, the portal to this possibility is through a radical, meditative embodiment, a feeling comfortable in one's own skin that only came from estrangement and coming home.

As with the setting of many of Jenkinson's stories in *Aphrodite's Kiss*, 'The Language Thing' is concerned with the experience of Northern Irish language teachers abroad. The protagonist in this story, set during the Troubles, experiences a sense of foreignness throughout: 'You don't understand how they can tell that you are foreign. Some Italians have skin and hair as pale as yours, but they know just to look at you that you're not from here.'[173] Here, skin colour is one marker among many of belonging and ease in a story where the narrative voice is frequently disjointed and uncertain, to mirror the place of the protagonist. Her experiences of the conflict are through snatched images on covers of newspapers and letters from her friends, who have also chosen to exile themselves rather than live through the bodily danger threatened by the conflict. Given her relatively poor Italian, she experiences the violence from home through the images presented in the newspaper: 'He is naked to the waist, his ribs visible, his legs and feet are bare. The picture is in black and white but there is no mistaking the marks on the body, on the head. Even from this angle you can tell it would not have been an easy face to look on.'[174] This recalls the depiction of the suffering male body in Eoin McNamee's novel *Resurrection Man*, a fictionalized account of the Shankill Butcher murders which makes repeated reference to the ways in which the cadaver is photographed and displayed. In a collection that often deals with healing and recovery, to have this flash of brutality is a powerful reminder of the ongoing vulnerability of bodies in Northern Ireland. McGill emphasizes the frailty of nakedness and skin exposure here, too, remarking upon his naked torso and feet further compound the sense of a victimized male body as spectacle. This experience is brief, however, as the protagonist turns towards it, turns away and then retreats to a world of foreignness, estrangement and popular culture. This encounter with the tortured skin brings her back to a past she has travelled to get away from – again demonstrating how skin can bridge the gap between past and present.

In 'No Angel', a Belfast woman, Annie, is haunted by the spectre of her father, in a story which shares a distinct mood with Jan Carson's 'Settling', which sees a grandmother reappear in a cupboard. Annie uses a close inspection of his skin to identify his authenticity: 'When he turned his face to scrape the razor along his jaw I could see that the scar was healing well where the surgeon had removed the growth from the side of his nose. His skin was still yellow at the nicotine-stained fingertips.'[175] Her father bears not only the large, visible scars of surgery but also the subtler markers of the effects of his lifestyle. When he appears, the imperfections in his appearance such as missing teeth coexist with his warm recollections of the past. Her father insists on having the body of her murdered brother who defied paramilitaries on display with 'Jamesie's eyebrow like a burst plum, his buckled nose, the rainbow of bruises that spanned his battered face'.[176] Skin broken open here is as a witness to acts of violence. This is contrasted with the experience of Annie as a student in Belfast, with violence simultaneously intimate and distant: 'Eight girls on the landing in their pyjamas and then down to the kitchen to stand bare-footed on the cracked, snail-slimed lino, warming our hands around cups of tea, listening for the sirens; second-hand drama'.[177] Bare feet are a marker not only of domestic safety but also of vulnerability. Annie's childhood fears manifest themselves in a fear of the dark, which is then expressed through marking on her skin: 'A small black crescent of soot was ingrained above my knuckles. The sound of his skin-roughened finger and thumb, rubbing together. "Knocking the door against the back of my heels," I said. "You know I don't like the dark." '[178] This past comes particularly vividly to the forefront of Annie's mind as she prepares to marry a man from a more privileged family and feels her own heritage acutely, despite her hard work to get an education and a job. The bodies of the past intrude on her present. The story ends with a kind of recovery: her deceased father, mother and brother appear to her at the opera following her break-up with the unsuitable man who reminded her of the latter. In the clapping hands of the audience, we feel a sense of an ending, of a story she can now confront.

'Sleepwalkers' is a sun-dappled story of childhood innocence and the intensity of early experience. Kate travels to Andalusia with her family following the suicide of her estranged husband. The experience of the holiday is expressed through the skin, whether through 'a constellation of mosquito bites on her left foot'[179] or a stranger's languid stare at 'Kate's white shoulders, at her pink-faced children, at the biro tattoo on her sandaled foot'.[180] The story is told through the experience of the skin: particularly the experiences of alternating hot and cold. The story is full of these tactile moments: hot air when a door opens, or the sensation of cold ice on the skin. This leads to a sensation of a family oscillating between intense emotional experiences felt through the skin, never quite able to regulate their external environment, which clearly maps on to Kate's struggle to deal with the complicated emotions around Owen's death. The relaxing break does not go quite as planned: Kate saves her son Marcus from drowning in the pool, and she is so ravaged by mosquito bites that her daughter joins them up with biro to form a crown. Despite all this, the family holiday is written on each of their bodies: 'On the last morning, they walk out of the house, the four of them – Kate with her legs covered in bites; Marcus with a bellyful of pool water; Florrie with a sunburnt ear; Abigail with her heart a little melted – each of them marked by the place'.[181] As with McGill's other stories, we get the sense that despite these marks, recovery is possible. Indeed, in her work, the marks are something to be cherished and meditated upon.

'Islander' is the story of Sarah, who plans to travel to the Amalfi Coast with her schoolfriends after finishing her exams but instead finds herself falling in love on Rathlin, 6 miles from home: 'I sneaked a look at Charlie, and the torch of light from Rue Point swept across the green island and touched my bare face and then his. When he felt for and found my hand, it was like a choice he'd made.'[182] Following his accidental death, Sarah struggles with her grief, and despite Charlie's mother trying to physically comfort her ('I looked into her lined face and saw the long road ahead of me'),[183] she is consumed by fear. In this story, women stoically bear pain that is marked on their skin. In the ambiguous beginning and ending of the story, Sarah is confronted with a doppelganger vision of herself, perhaps the self that did not keep the baby, perhaps the self that travelled to the Italian islands rather than Rathlin: 'We do what we can,' she is saying, 'they with their stories and their clatter, and us with ours. We carry the living, and we do whatever it takes to wake the dead.'[184] As with Rhonda, McGill presents a woman who gains insight into her own life through distancing techniques. Here, in this story of skin touching for the briefest of moments, we see how the body and the memory of touch can act to anchor us to past, present and future.

In 'Marked', a fourteen-year-old girl with a large birthmark around her mouth navigates the travails of adolescence and family tragedy. Shunned and mocked by her classmates for her skin, one of her few friends attempts to conceal the mark:

> One day Becca brought round her mum's make-up bag and painted concealer all round my mouth. She said I looked great and I should wear it all the time, but when I looked in the mirror I got a real shock, like my whole face had been rubbed out; like those cartoon characters you see on TV when the animator's hand appears with an eraser and wipes them away, limb by limb. I cleaned it off. Becca said I was mad, that nobody would ever go out with me if I didn't make an effort, but I just ignored her. I don't like how the birth mark makes people behave towards me but I don't want to disappear.[185]

Here, she displays a clear comfort in her own skin but a discomfort with social responses to that skin. Despite her skin being perceived as a 'flaw' by her friends, it is a fundamental part of her identity. The narrator's central concern, though, is not the teasing she receives in school or this perceived sense of inferiority but a text from a boy who wants to meet her after school and the anticipation of a kiss. The surface of the skin is not the important thing here, but rather the anticipation of skin contact. This contrasts with the way in which the fairy tales her mother read to her described ideal femininity as something unblemished and passive: 'I used to think that maybe, when I met my prince and he kissed me on the lips, the mark would disappear.'[186] After declaring that she does not believe in these tales, we are in the realm of the present, where her presence in the world is informed by the reactions of those around her. The story is alive with the power and presence of the body, as the teacher points out 'the shape of Cavehill ... how it looked like a man lying on his back, the peak they call Napoleon's nose.'[187] Her grandmother's carer, 'not white at all, she's black',[188] is portrayed as kind and understanding to both our narrator and to her racially insensitive grandmother. As in the painting in 'A Cure for Too Much Feeling', intergenerational hair washing is a powerful, transformative moment of intimacy. As the narrator helps her grandmother she notices 'a mound at the back of her neck, and when I looked, there it was – a port wine stain, the same colour and shape as mine, normally hidden by her hair'.[189] The portrayal here is of a young woman beginning to feel comfortable in her own skin, despite the attempts of others to shame and degrade her for a birthmark. In particular, McGill displays her empathy, whether for her grandmother or Mr Kenny, the old man in the library that she takes an interest in. The power of the appearance of the skin is repeatedly emphasized but so are moments of commonality, where she seeks to inhabit the skin of the other.

In a collection that exposes the variety of intimate encounters, 'First Tooth' ends the collection on a hopeful note of renewal. A mother, herself the youngest of eleven children, misses her child's first tooth coming out, and McGill uses this moment to describe the joys and pains of the intimacy of mother and child. Our narrator describes the moment when her child wouldn't sleep in a travel cot, and the only thing that soothed was skin contact, with 'you on my chest and your left cheek on mine ... heartbeat to heartbeat, cheek to cheek'.[190] Here, skin contact is a calmative. McGill emphasizes the ability of the body to renew itself: 'We make ourselves over and over again. Your teeth are my teeth, and my bones are hers and her skin is her mother's, and her mother's blood is the blood of hers. Who better to have found your tooth?'[191] Skin, then, in McGill's writing, ultimately is a site on which possibility can be written regardless of the content of the past. Of the writers under consideration in this chapter, McGill makes the past of the skin most visible. She features a network of scars, sunburn, birthmarks and other 'aberrations' to the dermis alongside a network of touches, from the medical to the erotic. McGill reminds us of the skin's past, examines the skin's present and gestures towards a rich, embodied future.

'My skin was singing to be touched': The otherworldly haptic in Roisín O'Donnell's *Wild Quiet*

Roisín O'Donnell's collection *Wild Quiet* is playful with the conventions of genre, with some more realist stories of love and loss and others which engage with the fantastic – ghosts, spirts and mythical creatures. But this is filtered through an acute awareness of how intimacy and the body might affect these representations: 'As the saying goes, the body doesn't lie. In writing fiction, I find the most profound intimacy is to step completely into a character's skin and speak through their bodily senses.'[192] In Chapter 1, we considered how Jan Carson's East Belfast magic realism intersected with her representation of intimacy and, in this section, we will examine how O'Donnell's writing examines the representation of skin and touch through her genre-hopping collection. To begin with, we will consider those stories which feature magical realist elements and then move on to those which examine a more everyday intimacy. Dawn Sherratt-Bado frames 'Ebenezer's Memories' around what it might tell us about post-Agreement politics,[193] and this story considers how memory might be experienced through the body, particularly the skin – the 'feeling' of memory. Catherine's grandfather tells her stories about a monster who lives under the stairs and eats bad news and painful memories, and this story situates the past in the present via sense memory. As noted, skin encounters can mediate between the present and the past. Catherine's deep unease is felt primarily through her skin: 'I was jolted out of my daydream by an outburst from Ebenezer's cupboard – a sound so different from his previous noises that it sent goosebumps crawling up my arms, like an army of ice-legged ants creeping over my skin.'[194] Also referred to as skin-crawling or horripilation, this sensation is where the skin becomes rough-textured due to a heightened emotional state. Again, the skin often reveals subtle things that are unspoken and the sympathetic nervous system and the surface of the body work in tandem to indicate the unsaid. Indeed, the whole narrative of traumatic memories in this story is told through skin and touch, as the images Catherine is presented with are often deeply sensual and domestic. The painful memories which are unleashed by Ebenezer's escape are experienced through Catherine touching the cupboard door: 'I pulled back my hand, from which the blood had drained almost entirely … I wanted to pull my hand back, to step out of the memory, but I couldn't.'[195] The touching, exploring hand is the catalyst for the narrative. The story ends with Catherine older, and lines etched into her palms, reflecting the cumulative effect of age and experience.

In 'Infinite Landscapes', the permeability of skin is identified, not just for its porosity: here the dermis acts as a portal between worlds. Abeyomi gives birth to an abiku, or 'spirit child', following several miscarriages. Simedele O'Doherty's birth is represented as portal to the spirit world: 'As Abeyomi had dreaded, through her umbilical cord Simi had absorbed the spirits of all the other lost babies gone before. Simi would never settle in the skin of one personality.'[196] Where the umbilical cord is usually understood as a conduit for nutrition, here it becomes another meeting point that Connor identified, for the living and the dead. As she becomes an artist, her canvases often focus on these meeting points between worlds, as artist and subject matter intertwine: 'Simi resembles one of her own creations, with her wild hair, green eyes and paint-sparked skin.'[197] This dermographia allows the skin to become both tool of the artist and expressive medium – this is different to the controlled paintbrush of Caravaggio. The artist becomes their art through a return to the skin.

In 'Titanium Heart', grief over a miscarriage turns the buildings of the city of Sheffield into liquid metal: 'Eva would touch the steel bars of the empty cradle, only to find a thin film of silver coming away on her fingertips.'[198] As she descends further into grief, the melting city becomes uninhabitable. In this story, touching hands are often met with not the warm skin previously identified, but with Stephen 'surprised to find that her fingers were deep – river cold'.[199] The qualities of metal are quite different to skin: metal is renowned for its strength, unlike soft, pierceable skin. Metal not only has been used to stand in for skin's vulnerabilities, such as in a suit of armour, but also is one of the most dangerous substances against skin, when it is fashioned into a knife blade or a bullet. Against this powerful language of metal and skin, O'Donnell examines a woman's grief. Her writing often focuses on the powerful, elemental nature of women's emotional lives. The force of feeling is disruptive to the bodies in the text and here, Emma, is closer to a pagan deity. Goddesses of fire appear in nearly every system of mythology, from Hestia in Greek myth to Vesta in Roman myth and Agni in Hinduism. Emma's cold affect manifests itself as a raging force which smelts the city so it can be built anew. Eventually, the process ends and the city becomes one of horticultural renewal and rebirth, mirroring the process of grief. This story, which powerfully expresses the visceral operation of women's pain, ends with a reaching out from the world beyond. Emma haunts the city, as a metal monument to her overlooks the new, lush city of Sheffield: 'Rusty leaves dance and shiver around the woman's shoulders, and in her arms she clutches a deathly small bundle, whose tiny fingers reach up towards her face.'[200] O'Donnell's ambiguity deliberately fits in with the narrative: Stephen is unclear whether the woman is smiling or weeping and we are unclear if the statue is Emma ossified in metal or a memorial to her pain. In this final act of touch, of the child reaching for a mother, O'Donnell offers us an interpretation of the physical, visceral operations of mourning and the way grief is textured through the skin.

'Kamikaze Love' is told from the perspective of a dead Japanese student, Anju, who appears to be stuck in a kind of purgatory. She commences a suicide attempt but then regrets a text she sent to an ex-boyfriend and is tragically killed on her way to rectify the situation. Her attempts to delete the text appear to Oisin as a kind of haunting that is expressed primarily through an eerie feeling on the skin. Oisin's fear is also shown through his inability to keep his hands steady: 'With trembling hands, he takes out his lighter and lights up a cigarette.'[201] We are reminded that the figure of the spectre is prominent in Japanese culture and engage with powerful, complex 'emotions of revenge, fury, obligation, and frustration'.[202] Similar figures which exist between worlds are common in folk legends across the world, and particularly in Irish myth. Skin and touch are everywhere in this story and are primarily a way of knowing that is elusive for Oisin: 'If you're here, can you touch my hand? Just touch my hand to show me you're here or SOMETHING.'[203] Their encounters expose the power the mind has over the skin, as Anju's ghostly presence leaves a lasting haptic impression: 'I float close to him and breathe on his skin. Oisín moans, 'Oh God, what is this?' He digs his hands into his hair.'[204] Skin is regularly washed in the narrative, whether she 'scrubbed flaking skin'[205] or 'loud water gurgled and streamed off my shivering skin'.[206] Skin washing becomes a metaphor for trying to slough off the past. O'Donnell conveys that the haptic senses are vital to a sense of personhood: 'Without touch, without smell, without taste I float in a body that no longer exists.'[207] This uncanny betweeness manifests itself in profound sensations on the skin. The ghost's 'presence in magical realist fiction is inherently oppositional, because they represent an assault on the basic scientific and materialist assumptions of western modernity: that reality is knowable, predictable, controllable'.[208] The ghost can produce feeling on the skin but does not have a skin itself. Oisin keeps trying to relocate his sense of himself within his experiences of the body but O'Donnell presents skin here as a treacherous entity that responds to psychic disturbance. This traitor-skin offers no certainties. O'Donnell intertwines Japanese and Irish mythic resonances to offer an eerie in-betweenness, where even the sense of being in your own skin can be disrupted by ghostly memories.

The more realist stories in the collection can be broadly divided into two categories: those which deal with cultural difference and those which examine women's relationship to the skin. In 'How to be a Billionaire', 'Crushed' and 'Wild Quiet', O'Donnell considers the experience of migrant children who are subject to racist abuse in Ireland and how this is felt through the skin. In the first of these stories, a young Nigerian migrant to Galway encounters racism and first love in Galway. Kingsley has a crush on Shanika, whose 'skin smells like chips and strawberry gum'.[209] In a story about a chaste teenage crush, hands are used to express these burgeoning feelings:

> But one time when we were washing our hands after doing Art, Shanika's hand touched mine, and I felt sort of funny, and ever since then I've just known I like her and nothing can stop it … So I climb up the side of the hut and then I grab Shanika's hand to help her up and Oh Lord, I'm holding Shanika's hand![210]

In adolescence, such brief encounters are monumental and, as we progress to adulthood, the experience of brief touch can dull against more intense experiences. In her teenage stories, then, O'Donnell offers us back this network of formative touches. Hands are used in a dual way in the narrative, both as a way of communication between Shanika and Kingsley and also to emphasize his exclusion from the dynamics of the classroom: 'That means Hands Up, but I don't never put my hand up, coz I don't never know none of the answers.'[211] O'Donnell attempts to set these stories of first love and the failures of the education system to deal with the needs of migrants within the context of racism in Irish society. This demonstrates not only the universal experience of being-in-skin but also the vulnerability of non-white skins. Kingsley has a tragic end in the final story of the collection, 'Crushed', which sees him intimidated by men in 'grey tracksuits and shaven heads. Greyish skin, like something dead already'.[212] O'Donnell not only represents skin as something which can offer hope and intimacy but also begins to expose the vulnerabilities to racist abuse that a different skin colour poses in contemporary Ireland.

In 'Wild Quiet', a young Somali refugee does not speak in her new school in Ireland. O'Donnell uses her silence to reflect on the power of childish touch to communicate friendship: 'You're watching the birds when Saoirse comes over and touches the side of your hijab, where no one at school is allowed to see.'[213] Saoirse is friendly but forthright with Khadra, asking her questions about her faith and customs, but also getting her into trouble for laughing in class. Khadra's communication with her new 'best friend' is non-verbal, but her memories of her traumatic upbringing stay with her, as if they are embedded into her body: 'And the silence seeps into your skin, until it becomes bone-deep'.[214] She distances herself from what she has endured as she is worried that 'if you made one sound, you might say everything. From the trapdoor of your lips, machine-gun fire would pour'.[215] O'Donnell uses the second person narrative to make us empathize with not only Khadra's plight but also that of the other refugees who cross the Mediterranean. Her silence means she is unable to integrate into her class, but the story also offers touch and a coming back to the body as glimpses of possibility for the future. She holds her little brother's hand as he feeds the birds: 'You approach the swans holding Hamza's chubby fist in one hand, a bag of week – old Brennan's bread crusts in the other'.[216] This hand-holding communicates familial love, safety and security. As she imagines being able to communicate with her classmates, she takes a private, intimate moment to pray to Allah for the return of her sister. In the last sentence of the story, the skin becomes a touchstone for reflection and a moment of stillness: 'Just before you go to sleep, you'll untie your braid, and your hair will wave against your skin, as wild and as quiet as water'.[217]

'Time Stretches' follows a man, Alex, travelling from Ireland to Indonesia in search of the resolution of issues from his past. As a boy, he lived in Yogyakarta due to his father's academic scholarship of Indonesian music. His mother, while agitated by her unhappy marriage, is said to have 'skin pale as the inside of potato peel'.[218] This story illuminates the distinction between the temporal nature of skin damage ('Your nutmeg skin was doing its best to camouflage a blue-and-yellow bruise'[219]) versus prolonged, ongoing damage caused by environment and social factors ('their skins the colour and texture of chamois leather'[220]). In this story, a young local boy is victimized for bearing witness to the infidelity of Alex's mother and the trauma affects the course of both their lives. O'Donnell describes this pain through the language of the skin: 'Yogyakarta is etched on my mind like the memory of a lover's skin'.[221] This is a sensual description of a memory tinged with grief and regret, emphasizing how heightened emotions register with our memories. At the end of the story, skin offers a kind of consolation and gestures towards forgiveness: 'But your palms remember. Your fingers close around mine with a newborn's instinctive grip'.[222] In this moment, of friendship, care and empathy, we see O'Donnell use the hands to speak across decades.

In 'Under the Jasmine Tree', Alma has a dream where the Virgin Mary tells her that her estranged son will visit. Ciaran was adopted by an Irish Catholic family at birth. His skin, however, marks his parentage out: 'His sallow skin has been deprived of sunlight for so long it has drained to the colour of old books'.[223] The reappearance of Ciaran makes Alma reminisce about her love affair with the parish deacon, Francisco, which begins with him pressing a jasmine bud into her open palm. This act is somewhere between the religious and the sensual. The sensuality of her youthful encounter is told through the skin, as she viscerally remembers the feelings from that night: 'My skin was coated in a film of sweat, strands of hair stuck to my forehead, and I could feel the bulge of my breasts in the girlish dress Mamma had made me wear.'[224] After she faints and is brought to the sacristy, they have sex in this sacred space. Traditionally used for housing vestments and sacred vessels, this area is carefully hidden from view. Mixing the sacred and the profane, Alma is changed not only by the conception of her son but also the lasting impression of this fleeting encounter: 'Francisco's robes smelt of incense, and afterwards my skin smelt of incense too.'[225] Having distanced herself from her community and her lover many years ago, she now prepares to disengage from Ciaran's life. Hands are used to express not only her tenderness towards him but also his confusion and frustration with her disappearance: 'I can see the nebulas of further questions clouding Ciaran's eyes, but I touch his hand ... From Ciaran's helpless hand gestures I can imagine what he's saying.'[226] From the scent on the skin to the attempts at making intimate contact, this story uses the skin as the primary object of identification. In the end, though, the discrete qualities are challenged by the legacy of trauma, and the reopened wound is not merely painful but also suggests complete collapse: 'No matter how hard I try to keep my skin together, my organs are dividing and pieces of me are spilling all over the dark-veined tiles of Casa Siete Revueltas.'[227] O'Donnell, then, reflects here on what we must bear, what the skin can withstand and those moments when the skin cannot hold.

In 'How to Learn Irish in Seventeen Steps', language takes on the same sensual qualities that it has in Jenkinson's cross-cultural encounters. Luana Paula de Silva, from Brazil, needs to pass Irish language exams to gain a teaching position in the country after marrying an Irishman. The story tells the narrative of their marriage in decline while, at the same time, her proficiency in Irish increases. O'Donnell deals with sensual memory in this story, remembering how her mother's needle pricked her 'nutmeg skin'[228] and her first evening with her husband: 'His sandalwood aftershave will take you back to the night you met, when his first touch evoked a type of muscle – memory, as if your body already knew him from a previous life.'[229] Here, the memory of touch, the haptic trace, lingers on as their affection fades. O'Donnell explicitly links the skin to her attempts to learn the language: 'Like salt crystallising on summer-beach skin, or the solidifying whites of poached eggs on a Sunday morning, begin to find patterns emerging from the embryonic mess of the Irish language.'[230] At the moment the patterns of the language come together, contempt begins to grow in her marriage and their culture clash, once exotic for them both, comes to wear and they split up and she returns home to Sao Paolo. Luana is uneasily caught between two languages and two cultures: skin and touch remain the constants of communication and exchange throughout this story.

'On Cosmology' looks at the aftermath of sexual attraction and intercourse on the skin. Sinéad, a lecturer in cosmology, has a fleeting affair with David which results in the possible conception of a child. The story is addressed to her imagined unborn child after the morning after pill fails and shows a woman simultaneously worried and excited by the prospect of raising a family. Sexuality has a complex role within the story. O'Donnell is careful to draw out the other bodily affects of their encounter: 'But I can tell you now, there was nothing "passionate" about the bruise the colour of cheese mould that he left on the inside of my thigh ... I pulled off my purple snood to find an ugly bruise on my neck the colour of summer fruit about to darken into sticky-sweet rot.'[231] Love bites are temporary reminders of intimacy which can cause not only social awkwardness but also fond nostalgia. Here, they expose the inconsistencies of their encounter, between her initial enthusiasm and desire for intimacy ('But my breasts were traitors, shouting to be caressed. My skin was singing to be touched.'[232]) to her resentful gazing upon this purplish skin as witness. Sinead's encounter goes from being just disappointing sex to non-consensual as she sees the 'shrivelled snake-skin of the condom'.[233] Condomless sex is sometimes described by men as 'feeling better', despite the increased risks. This is attributed to skin-on-skin contact, and, in their research, Braun evidenced 'imagery [which] evokes a massively reduced sensory experience for men'.[234] However, in Sinead's case it is clear that the evening was not as pleasurable as she had hoped, and yet her partner put her at risk for his own desire for a full skin contact experience. Full of anxiety about her future, she climbs the hills around Glendalough and strips down to a camisole as she climbs. Among nature, with her skin touching the air, she has a critical moment of realization: 'A Baltic wind whistled over my bare shoulders, and I remembered when my sisters and I used to swim in the Atlantic as kids. When we'd had enough of the icy water, we'd slipslap out of the waves and run up the beach, skins tinged a deathly hue.'[235] This blue-tinged skin, invigorated by the cold, is far away from the purplish bruise of a love bite given during anticlimactic sex. Here, she recovers a joy in her own body that is not needy or grasping but rather free, invigorated and with her blood rushing to her skin.

Skin, as we have seen, is used by Northern Irish writers in rich, complex ways. These texts are concerned largely with the redemptive power of touch but also on the skin as a repository of a complicated history where the politics of the collective and the individual intersect. They ask what it means to reclaim your bodily autonomy after violence. They open up new encounters and, as new networks of touch are formed, change the way we relate to each other. David Park's stories demonstrated the complexity of how men relate to touch and how fiction can be a place to foreground masculine vulnerability in a society which does not praise it. Northern Irish men's skin becomes a tender, fragile thing in his work, instead of the tattooed or fatally wounded flesh more common in earlier texts. For Rosemary Jenkinson, the skin is a portal to the newness her characters desire – it opens up new worlds of pleasure and connects them with the foreign bodies of others. In Bernie McGill's stories, the past hurts and present pleasures of skin coexist alongside the everyday marks and temporary changes to the surface of the body. Skin charts our past and offers us possibility in her writing. O'Donnell takes up this mantle in her fantastical short stories where skin spans the globe and often has a deeply uneasy relationship with the individual's sense of themselves. This reimagining of the Troubles body, troubled and troubling, injects a necessary complication into the representation of Northern Irish corporeality. As Ahmed and Stacey note,

> This relationship to the past, which is neither simply absent not present on the surface of the skin, is hence also an opening up of a different future. It is precisely by paying attention to the already written, to what has already taken shape (for example, the colonial, racialized and sexed histories of touch as ownership and possession) that one can open up that which has yet to be written, and even touch the skin that has yet to be lived.[236]

Skin, in the work of Park, Jenkinson, McGill and O'Donnell has presented a variety of haptic moments that revealed a great deal about self and other. Touch brings with it the past and gestures towards the future. As we enter a period of being hyperconscious of our own skin, hands and the dangers of touch, this representation will doubtless be rewritten anew. This is Ahmed and Stacey's 'skin that has yet to be lived', and it offers a rich possibility for the creative body to be reworked, retheorized and re-experienced.

4

Milkman

Anna Burns's 2018 novel, *Milkman*, is the most critically and commercially successful novel featured in this book. Before this lauding, Burns published *No Bones* (2001)[1] and *Little Constructions* (2007), the latter described in the *Irish Times* as 'bold, terrifying, funny and profound',[2] as well as a novella, *Mostly Hero* (2014). In *Milkman*, Burns presents the central themes that this study has been organized around: intimacy, touch and pleasure. As a result, I have chosen to give this novel its own chapter, not just due to its singular literary achievement but also because of the way in which it weaves together these themes and offers something rooted in the past but attendant to the possibilities of the future. In the discussion of this novel, I want to foreground how these ideas are mediated through Burns's creation of specific 'moods' and sensations throughout the text and the possibilities she offers for a reimagining of the locus of trauma and recovery in Northern Irish writing. Following the novel's win of the Booker Prize in 2018, it quick acquired the reputation of being a difficult read:

> Kwame Anthony Appiah, chair of the judges, had called the novel 'challenging' when announcing its win, 'but in the way a walk up Snowdon is challenging. It is definitely worth it because the view is terrific when you get to the top,' he said. 'Because of the flow of the language and the fact some of the language is unfamiliar, it is not a light read [but] I think it is going to last.'[3]

If it is not light reading, it is *heavy* reading, which suggests a kind of affective power: a thick, soupy density which requires powers of concentration and forbearance. The novels which win the Booker Prize are not traditionally 'light' reading, so what does it mean to be singled out as a 'heavy' read? Recent winners have included texts which deal with difficult, 'heavy' topics, including Anne Enright's *The Gathering* (2007) and Marlon James's *The History of Seven Killings* (2014), so to have Burns's work singled out as a difficult winner of the prize suggests some particular forces at work. The first section of this chapter will examine these forces and how they drive the narrative in order to foreground the way in which Burns manages the emotional currents of the novel.

In addition to the success at the Booker Prize, it was praised by broadsheet critics on both sides of the Atlantic. Claire Kilroy, in *The Guardian*, said that '*Milkman* has its own energy, its own voice. … Despite the surreality, everything about this novel rings true.'[4] Ron Charles, in *The Washington Post*, stated that 'it's as though the intense pressure of this place has compressed the elements of comedy and horror to produce some new alloy'.[5] Responses to the novel often centre around the atmosphere it creates, and I want to foreground the 'intense pressure' that Charles notes. In *The New Yorker*, Laura Miller praises Anna Burns's technique: 'The voice that Burns conjures for middle sister fits a personality still under construction, cobbled together from bits of books, eavesdropped adult conversations, children's lore, and a stubborn fumbling toward her own, hard-won understanding.'[6] A rare dissenting voice came from Dwight Garner in the *New York Times*: 'I found "Milkman" to be interminable, and would not recommend it to anyone I liked.'[7] However, despite some critics and the judges of the prize wanting to pigeonhole this as a difficult, complex book, it has become a bestseller. Faber publisher Alex Bowler said that it had been 'a beautiful, joyous week for all of us at Faber, witnessing first-hand what happens when the full transformative force of the Booker is focused on a work of art somehow perfectly fitted to our times, to this very moment'.[8] The language that Bowler uses here is notable: it is the language of joy, of beauty and of 'the moment'. As the reviews above demonstrate, responses to the novel from critic and publisher alike use the language of feeling: whether elation, empathy or abject dislike. It is not a novel that people are generally ambivalent about. However, many readers reported online that they did not find the voice that challenging once they got into the 'flow' of the narrative. This reminds me of teaching *Ulysses* to a group of undergraduates, and one of them explained that it 'was like drowning, only I liked it'. There is a similarly fluid quality to Burns's prose, the rhythm of her language interacting with the dangerous current underneath.

This chapter will consider how Burns creates this palpable sense of heaviness within her work, using some insights from contemporary affect theory. We might consider whether *Milkman*'s description as a 'difficult' or 'experimental' text might alter our experience of reading it. Many reviewers of *Milkman*, in an attempt to grasp its singular voice, gestured towards modernist writers, particularly James Joyce and Samuel Beckett. Writing about Eimear McBride, Ruth Gilligan alerts us to the dangers of understanding Irish women's experimental writing primarily through the lens of male modernist authors.[9] I want to be careful not to call all writing which is experimental 'modernist' or, indeed, apply the label 'experimental' to a novel which has a complex relationship to questions of form and technique. The language in the novel is not complex: rather, the technique of defamiliarization that Burns uses is one of elision, particularly the lack of names and places, which plunges the reader into unfamiliar territory, despite the textual clues to 1970s Belfast. The sense of time also adds to the sense of disorientation; for example, when Middle Sister[10] describes relating her story to longest friend, the description could hold for her own narrative structure: 'The fact this had come out organically – even plausibly unchronologically.'[11] The significance of the novel is such that critics will attend to its influences and formal features at length in the years to come, but I want instead to focus on something different – how the novel *feels*. Burns succeeds in creating something innovative that reorientates our understanding of emotional life in Northern Ireland, and while the puzzle of its perceived difficulty will preoccupy critics, I instead seek to develop an understanding of a gut feeling about the book – how it establishes a climate of repression that affects the body and the body as a tool to navigate away from bad feeling.

'It's amazing the feelings that are in you': Navigating emotional life in *Milkman*

Northern Irish culture has a distinct relationship to affect, feeling and mood due in part to the legacy of the Troubles. In *The Promise of Happiness*, Sara Ahmed reminds us, 'When feelings become atmospheric, we can catch the feeling simply by walking into a room, from a crowd or the collective body, or from being proximate to another.'[12] In this chapter, we will consider how Northern Irish texts engage in this production of atmosphere, enable the reader to 'catch' these complex feelings and then carefully detail the dynamics of resisting a dominant mood. Broadly, the first half of the chapter will set up the relationship to what we might term 'negative' affect and the second half will examine attempts to transcend this homogenizing climate of feeling. While there is no doubt that emotional life has been a concern of critical and aesthetic theorists for centuries, it is clear there is a renewed interest in what we can loosely term 'affect theory'. Brinkema, in her introduction to *The Forms of the Affects*, asks 'Is there any remaining doubt that we are now fully within the Episteme of the Affect?' (p. xi). While work on emotions has endured through intellectual history, from the Stoics to Raymond Williams, there is certainly a new energy around these debates, galvanized by Eve Kosofsky Sedgwick's readings of Silvan Tomkins.[13] In *Depression: A Public Feeling*, Anne Cvetkovich accepts that the terminology of this kind of enquiry can necessarily bleed into each other and that she prefers the intentionally imprecise use of 'feeling': 'Terms such as affect, emotion, and feeling are more like keywords, points of departure for discussion rather than definition.'[14] While this is often broadly termed 'affect' by critics, this analysis will also stray into using terms like feeling, emotion and mood to map how these concepts are interrelated but also the use of them by authors, protagonists and readers. Cvetkovich describes this developing body of critical enquiry: 'In a narrower sense, the affective turn has been signifying a body of scholarship inspired by Deleuzian theories of affect as force, intensity, or the capacity to move and be moved.'[15] In this chapter I will use the terms 'positive' and 'negative' for affect and emotions, while realizing their inadequacy for the ways in which individual actors relate to prevailing moods. Emotional states are complex and mutable, and Burns's text explores the issues that surround how we code our rich inner lives. Part of the reason that affect is so tantalizing for literary critics is that it manages to capture something intangible that texts regularly produce. In their introduction to *The Affect Theory Reader*, Melissa Gregg and Gregory J. Seigworth chime with Cvetkovich when they assert that

> affect, at its most anthropomorphic, is the name we give to those forces – visceral forces beneath, alongside, or generally *other than* conscious knowing, vital forces insisting beyond emotion – that can serve to drive us toward movement, toward thought and extension, that can likewise suspend us (as if in neutral) across a barely registering accretion of force-relations, or that can even leave us overwhelmed by the world's apparent intractability.[16]

In *Milkman*, physical movement is foregrounded as a bellwether of these 'force-relations' and how they can have often debilitating consequences. Later, this chapter will explore how these forces are enacted and resisted through the body. Indeed, 'those forces' entirely disrupt the life of Middle Sister and cause her physical and mental harm. They exist at two levels: not only the overwhelming negative affect of the Troubles but also the specific vulnerabilities of being a young woman.

Cvetkovich uses the term 'public feelings' to refer to a large academic project at the University of Chicago which focuses on cultural and academic responses to the most significant public events of the early twenty-first century such as the September 11 attacks and the Iraq War, in order to 'generate the affective foundation of hope that is necessary for political action'.[17] She weaves her own personal narrative of depression with an attempt to capture the mood on the political left. This is important work to consider as we move to an analysis of the relationship between the overall mood of Northern Irish society created by the author and the representation of individual emotional states of their characters: how the collective feeling interacts with the individual. *Milkman*, in particular, meditates directly on the idea of 'public feelings', such as shame, fear and disgust. This chapter will not just deal in negative affect but also in how positive feelings are dealt with, responded to and represented. Even in a text like *Milkman*, which deals with a spectrum of violence, there are a variety of emotions represented: we see joy, hope and relief against the rhythmic pressure of negative emotional states. The two main aspects of this that I want to consider are how a dominant culture of feeling is maintained and the penalties for transgressing a homogenous affective climate.

The novel follows Middle Sister as she attempts to navigate life during a conflict. This is never named as the Troubles, and the city is never named as Belfast. Burns has said in an interview, 'Although it is recognisable as this skewed form of Belfast, it's not really Belfast in the 70s. I would like to think it could be seen as any sort of totalitarian, closed society existing in similarly oppressive conditions'.[18] To anyone familiar with the rhythms of Troubles fiction, it becomes clear that this novel shares the same ominous vibe as something like McLaverty's *Cal*, but, unlike these Troubles novels, there is a promise of lightness at the end. The way in which we traditionally discuss the impact of the Troubles is, rightly, in terms of fatalities, casualties and the ongoing crisis in mental health. There is another element that is less tangible, and cannot be quantified in terms of statistics, but that fiction in the twenty-first century is beginning to attend to. One might, for example, think of the pervasive mood of Eoin McNamee's *Resurrection Man*, but rather than consider the shocking depiction of acts of violence, focus on the downbeat mood of fear he creates. I am tempted to use rhythmic language for this emotional landscape, as it feels like something kinetic: a pulse, a hum, a rumble.

In many Troubles texts, the mood is ominous and tense: the violent act is the main narrative catalyst, the reader's expectations are formed and so the story is taut with its promise. The sense of foreboding captured in fiction is also visible in Willie Doherty's video installation 'Non Specific Threat' (2004), where we watch a shaven-headed man who appears tense while Kenneth Branagh's voice-over adds to the portentous feeling. While Doherty has spoken about the context for the piece being Northern Irish paramilitary violence, it is noted that the work 'indicates a general feeling of danger'.[19] It is this palpable yet nebulous feeling that these contemporary authors seek to evoke. There are a mix of responses to the conflict in fiction: some texts hold an omnipresent mood throughout the narrative that offers little chance of a break in the tension for lightness. However, others vary the prevailing mood or even offer some sense of hope or futurity. Against the representation of violence, this can be a kind of catharsis, and is particularly prevalent in 'post'-conflict texts rather than those written at a time when the end of violence was not in sight. In particular, this chapter is invested in how particular affects are managed and broken: not only in the representation of 'mood' in a text but also how characters navigate emotional life in conflicted situations. I use this term as it is also how, in *Milkman*, Middle Sister describes depressive episodes. While the slipperiness of critical terms appeal, I want to use the same language as the working-class characters in the novel to describe their own emotional states and the consequences of a lack of vocabulary for inner life.

Burns has Middle Sister describe the prevailing mood throughout the novel: 'There was now a feeling in the room to which nobody was admitting: unpleasant, ominous, grey.'[20] The novel presents an acute awareness of feelings and a sensitivity towards change in individual and collective moods. Women, in particular, seem acutely aware of the landscape of feeling. The atmosphere that Burns creates in the novel can best be summarized in this passage:

> At the time, age eighteen, having been brought up in a hair-trigger society where the ground rules were – if no physically violent touch was being laid upon you, and no outright verbal insults were being levelled at you, and no taunting looks in the vicinity either, then nothing was happening, so how could you be under attack from something that wasn't there? … I had a feeling for them, an intuition, a sense of repugnance for some situations and some people, but I did not know intuition and repugnance counted, did not know I had a right not to like, not to have to put up with, anybody and everybody coming near.[21]

This is the difficult bind that Middle Sister finds herself in: she can feel that something is wrong but is unable to act on that feeling. Therefore, she feels uneasy and never at home in herself. What she clearly articulates here is that she has a 'feeling' or 'intuition' towards people or situations that she finds disconcerting. Indeed, she has difficulty articulating what she is feeling, even to her maybe-boyfriend: 'I spoke of feelings even less than he spoke of feelings, I mustn't have believed in any of that all along.'[22] While we will examine silence and passivity later, here we must briefly touch on what it means to speak of feelings in Northern Irish Society. In Chapter 2, the representation of touch and skin was used by writers focusing on 'post'-conflict Northern Ireland to tell stories which could not be articulated by their characters due to taboos over vocalizing their emotional life. As we shall see in *Milkman*, the body is often inaccessible to Middle Sister, so she lacks a channel to articulate her feelings.

One of the feelings that is easily articulated, however, is shame:

> Certainly I knew the feeling of shame and I knew everybody around me knew that feeling as well. In no way was it a weak feeling, for it seemed more potent than anger, more potent than hatred, stronger even than that most disguised of emotions, fear ... Another thing was that often it was a public feeling, needing numbers to swell its effectiveness, regardless of whether you were the one doing the shaming, the one witnessing the shaming, or the one having the shame done unto you.[23]

Burns examines the communal experience of shame, a public emotion which is particularly corrosive to self-esteem and which is monitored and policed by the community. Both the individual and the community are involved in the production, maintenance and management of shame. It is the emotion which is most often named in the text, and Middle Sister describes it as the most powerful feeling she encounters. Kaye Mitchell describes the function of shame in contemporary writing: 'Shame ... returns us to our bodies; it is an incontrovertible ground of (physical and affective) experience. Shame is internal, individual, personal to each of us, while also being a feature of the (external) "social relations" that connect us to others and take us outside, beyond our solipsistic worldview toward some encounter with the other.'[24] Mitchell's argument draws us towards two key themes in *Milkman*: the relationship of emotional states to the body and also the relationship of individual feelings to the collective affective mood.

Shame is a technique of control that is often imposed on teenage girls. It is important in this consideration of how the novel 'feels' to note that the central cypher for these emotions is a young woman in her late teens. This, in itself, marks the text out in fictional accounts of Northern Ireland. Novels and films based on the Troubles often foreground teenage male protagonists, due to the potential for the drama of their involvement as paramilitary foot soldiers. This is perhaps most potently realized in Bernard MacLaverty's novel *Cal*, in which the eponymous protagonist grapples with sectarian violence, Catholic guilt and his attraction to a taboo widow. Even accounts of transgression, such as the joyous film *Good Vibrations*, focus on 'teenage kicks' which are, almost exclusively, male. It is clear that young Northern Irish women's stories are often left out of the conversation. The young adult novels of Shirley Anne MacMillan and Sheila Wilkinson also seek to take seriously the concerns of teenage girls. Previous representations of teenage girls in Northern Irish texts include Sadie in Joan Lingard's *Across the Barricades* series, which were set reading in schools during the 1990s and presumably inspired *Derry Girls*' 'friends across the barricades' – a cross community initiative for teenagers. Some films have also dealt with how young women have been erased from the popular canon of Northern Irish culture, such as Margo Harkin's film *Hush-A-Bye Baby* and *The Venus de Milo Instead*, written by Anne Devlin and directed by Danny Boyle. Perhaps the most sustained engagement with the concerns of Northern Irish teenage girls in recent times have been the television show *Derry Girls* and Lucy Caldwell's short story collection *Multitudes*, which was explored in Chapter 2.

It is, of course, not just in Northern Irish literature where the experiences of young women are culturally marginalized. It is perhaps telling that when the novelist Will Self sought to denigrate the literary achievements of Sally Rooney, he suggested that readers would be better served by reading Nabokov's *Lolita*.[25] Self's suggestion that one should turn to a novel about an adolescent's sexual exploitation over Rooney's novel is telling: in *Normal People*, Rooney gives voice to a young woman's complex relationship with her sexuality, violence and power. Just as Rooney examines difficult questions in her novel, Burns gives her readers no easy answers about Middle Sister's desires. Middle Sister does not have a language available to her to describe her emotions or her body. In particular, Burns explores how young women experience their bodies and the forces that try to alienate them from their experiences. A teenage girl's body is something that is acutely subject to control, particularly in a society like Middle Sister's, where Catholic morality and paramilitary control mingles with the dictates of patriarchy. Teenage girls are often not trusted with their own bodily integrity, instead being subject to taboos, from silence around menstruation to their developing sense of sexuality. The teen girl becomes a site for anxiety while she is continually told to control her own body. This process is intensified through not only the strictures of Catholic morality but also the threats of surveillance from within and without. *Milkman* details this process of doubting one's sense of self as Middle Sister gradually gives up herself to the accepted norms of the community. Importantly, Burns does not portray someone who is uncertain about her feelings throughout the novel. Middle Sister is clear about her lack of attraction to Somebody McSomebody: 'Not my fault though. Not my fault either, that I didn't find him attractive.'[26] Burns portrays a young woman who is internally very sure of her desires but has this sureness ground down by social circumstances. She builds up a picture of how clarity turns into doubt and how this erosion of integrity leads to serious physical symptoms. Middle Sister is clear about her experiences: 'Over time, with experience, you sense that something is wrong or you have a feeling of being wronged.'[27] Where she often seeks to present a neutral affect in her interactions, as will be examined in the section on passivity and silence, Burns offers us her rich inner life and attempts to describe her often overwhelming emotions: 'It's amazing the feelings that are in you.'[28] Despite years of being emotionally 'ground down', it is clear that she is still brimming over with complex feelings. Against cultural accounts which elide the complexity of feeling in Northern Ireland, *Milkman* reinserts the messiness of emotional life that rages despite the best efforts of repressive affective regimes.

In addition to the context of the alienation of teenage girls, the setting of the novel is profoundly important. In *Cruel Optimism*, Lauren Berlant discusses how our relationship with the objects that promise happiness can be fraught. Arguably, both fantasies of national ideology can be read as a kind of cruel optimism, which promise much and ask a lot. They can keep adherents tethered to things despite them causing pain: 'Cruel optimism might be one way of explaining how we do not snap the bonds that are, at some level, compromising, maybe of our existence; maybe of our capacity to realize an idea of an existence.'[29] It may not be a commonplace to suggest that the central political narratives in Northern Ireland promise happiness but, for any political ideology to thrive, it must have futurity embedded within it. While political movements in Ireland and elsewhere are often critiqued for being obsessed with the past, they must simultaneously mobilize the offer of a brighter future to motivate involvement of the lead actors and the active support of the community. *Milkman* examines the ways in which some of these attachments serve to cause widespread harm, or Berlant's *Cruel Optimism*. She describes significant moments in cultural texts as doing important work: 'By staging the impasse in which break-down does its work on suspending the rules and norms of the world … Knowing how to assess what's unravelling there is one way to measure the impasse of living in the overwhelmingly present moment.'[30] This chapter will attend to these moments of unravelling in *Milkman* to discover what they can reveal about the representations of objects of attachment in Northern Ireland. Burns consider these 'survival scenarios' and the way in which authors negotiate structural issues and individual harms. In depicting these sites of unravelling, where the centre cannot hold, she offers rich examples of how these moments of breakdown can also be spaces of possibility.

Feeling feminist: The (im)possibility of solidarity in *Milkman*

In Sara Ahmed's *Living a Feminist Life*, which will be used throughout this chapter, feminist solidarity is seen as a balm for years of living against the grain of society, but *Milkman* has a complicated relationship with the notion of the feminist collective. For much of the novel, Middle Sister prefers the solitary pursuits of reading and running, and, often, she does not fit in with the female collectives in her local area. Broadly, these can be demarcated as three groups: the pious women (including her mother and the other women who attend to real milkman), the 'paramilitary groupies' and the 'issue women'. The latter are a feminist collective, referred to as 'these aborting homosexual insurrectionists',[31] who go from being tolerated as eccentrics to being thought of as an active threat to the community. Middle Sister does not share the Catholic-marriage values of her mother's generation and the 'sudden erotic alarm' of the second. While she appears to share some of the broad values of the 'issue women', she does not seem to approve of their tactics and recoils from their willingness to vocalize their discontent. Each of these three groups provides a different happiness script, which Middle Sister in turn refuses: either heteronormativity, selective promiscuity or vocal activism. In both *The Promise of Happiness* and *Living a Feminist Life*, Ahmed uses the figure of the feminist killjoy to examine the difficulty of resistance to dominant affective scripts. The act of speaking up about women's issues during the Troubles is an ultimate killjoy act: in refusing the traditional scripts, one rejects not only one's assigned gender identity but also by extension the will of the community. Middle Sister becomes what Ahmed terms, in *The Promise of Happiness*, an 'affect alien':[32] someone who does not share the same objects of happiness that their community appears to value. Within her community, there are subgroups who are orientated towards fundamentally different objects of happiness. Therefore, being an 'affect alien' occurs at many levels for Middle Sister. She has her own intrinsic values (reading, physical activity) which might be considered worthwhile if she had been raised in a different environment. But she is unable to fit in with the assigned 'happiness scripts' of either the renouncers and their lovers or the traditional Catholic family that her mother seeks for her. She is also unable or unwilling to be a full 'feminist killjoy' due to the omnipresent threat to limb and life this stance would present.

However, throughout the text, Burns reasserts the power of female solidarity. The force of women in a collective can temporarily disrupt the patriarchal order of Northern Irish society as they disrupt the curfew: 'Local women en masse, however, did so command, and on the rare occasions when they rose up against some civic, social or local circumstance, they presented a surprising formidable force of which other forces, usually considered more formidable, had no choice but to take note.'[33] While this does acknowledge the power of solidarity, it also presents it as a temporary aberration from politics as usual. Not only does the text explore questions of women and solidarity, it also examines the limits of this solidarity: who is the proper object for solidarity and how gender-based collectives sit against other loyalties. Here, women's solidarity is a force that can change the atmosphere and counteract the dominant affective state. We considered earlier the power of 'force-relations' in the construction of subjectivity, and here we can see these relations having a powerful effect on the 'mood' of a community. In addition to the question of how we want a Northern Irish text to make the reader feel is a consideration of how we want a feminist text to make us feel: what are the assumptions we bring to bear to a text we code as 'feminist'? Often, texts create a mood of stultifying oppression, which is either presented as day-to-day drudgery or in the ongoing threat of violence, which builds to a critical incident. From the beginning of the novel, we are aware that Milkman will die, so the tension in the novel is whether Middle Sister will kill her harasser. In feminist cinema, such as *9 to 5* and *Thelma and Louise*, cathartic power comes from humiliating or killing the man who represents patriarchal dominance. Indeed Claire Henry argues that the 'rape-revenge thriller' has been an enduring feature of modern cinema.'[34] The affective power of Burns's writing is such that the tension builds up to a moment of critical 'snap' which never fully arrives. She does not kill her harasser but the mood critically shifts after his murder: 'What I did know was that relief was coursing through me with an intensity I had not ever in my life felt before. My body was proclaiming, "Halleluiah! He's dead. Thank fuck halleluiah!" even if those were not the actual words at the forefront of my mind.'[35] Middle Sister clearly articulates how her body and mind are in concert and offers the reader a palpable sense of relief.

In diagnosing the subtle and overt ways in which misogyny weaves itself around Northern Irish society, Burns produces a rich glimpse at not just the workings of oppression but also the possibility of futurity. The issue women seek to reconcile their own experiences with the experiences of women across the world:

> There would be the injustices too, thought the traditional women, those big ones, the famous ones, the international ones – witch – burnings, footbindings,

suttee, honour killings, female circumcision, rape, child marriages, retributions by stoning, female infanticide, gynaecological practices, maternal mortality, domestic servitude, treatment as chattels, as breeding stock, as possessions, girls going missing, girls being sold and all those other worldwide cultural, tribal and religious socialisations and scandalisations, also the warnings given against things throughout patriarchal history that were seen as uncommon for a woman to do or think or say.[36]

What Burns emphasizes here is important: that misogynistic violence occurs in every society and takes a variety of shapes. The novel examines a young woman who, despite remaining quiet, is acutely aware of the history of violence towards women. Important moments of solidarity come as the issue women are defended from the threat of physical harm: 'They're simpletons. Intellectual simpletons. Academe! That's all they're fit for.'[37] While it may seem like the feminists are being belittled in these comments, these works are designed to shield them from aggression. In this small act, we see the possibility of gender-based solidarity. For Ahmed, the figure of the killjoy is 'the wrong sort, or bad sort, the one who speaks her mind',[38] which chimes more with the tactics of the issue women. Middle Sister's forms of resistance, however, are in silence, reading and physical activity as speaking her mind would put her in immediate physical danger. What Burns draws out, though, is the myriad subtle ways in which Middle Sister fails to perform her assigned role of 'Working-Class Catholic Nationalist Woman', which she defines against the figure of the 'female wayward': 'This was certain girls not being tolerated if it was deemed they did not defer to males, did not acknowledge the superiority of males, might even go so far as almost to contradict males, basically, the female wayward, a species insolent and far too sure of herself.'[39]

Throughout the novel, Middle Sister is clear to draw a distinction between herself and this figure, until her behaviour codes her as the 'wrong sort'. Katie Markham, discussing Black Taxi Tours, notes, 'Affective synecdoche, in its broadest form, is the process through which the affects attendant, or "stuck", on certain bodies begin to speak to other bodies and self- reflexively of the sticking process.'[40] This involves a process of mediation between large-scale cultural production of affect and smaller, more intimate encounters. Middle Sister does not realize that she is coded as an 'affect alien' and, therefore, a killjoy who produces bad feeling both for her mother and for her community. In Markham's formulation, bad feeling 'sticks' to her. As Ahmed notes in *The Promise of Happiness*, the 'female troublemaker might be trouble because she gets in the way of the happiness of others'.[41] To think of Middle Sister as troublemaker is complex: she does not actively seek to trouble anyone in the novel, preferring instead her own interior monologue, but in refusing to cleave to the roles expected of her, she is deeply troubling to her own community. However, despite this difficult relationship to ideas of feminist solidarity, there are moments of collective action among women in the novel that are striking in how they disrupt patriarchal order. Ahmed discusses the power of such moments of what she terms as 'snap': 'Snap, snap: the end of the line. In a feminist and queer genealogy, life unfolds from such points. Snap, snap: begin again.'[42] These moments of snap abound in the novel, most powerfully as women break the curfew en masse:

> But when also you had to factor in the other side with their equally ridiculous runners and riders, it was out of the question really, that the traditional woman's forbearance would not, in these circumstances, snap. So it would snap – because life was going on – children to be fed, nappies to be changed, housework to be done, shopping to be got in, political problems, … these women would break the curfew by taking off their aprons, putting on their coats, shawls, scarves.[43]

The snap is not due to solidarity with a sectarian political cause, but rather due to the vital everyday business of keeping home and family together despite overlapping restrictions on women's freedoms. Women reclaim the streets in small, important acts which are personally dangerous to them. We get a sense of an atmosphere of oppression gradually building in multiple scenarios during the text until this critical moment. Burns uses the term 'snap' several times in the novel to demarcate small moments of resistance where women decide that their current situation is intolerable and rebel against it, culminating in Middle Sister wresting a gun from Somebody McSomebody in a nightclub toilet: 'I snapped the gun off him, getting it by the barrel, the muzzle, the end, whatever that bit was called. He wasn't expecting that and before I did it, neither was I.'[44] A powerful moment of snap happens when, in the nightclub, women attack Somebody McSomebody as a proxy for the cumulative effects of misogynistic oppression: 'This called for bare hands, stilettos, booted feet, flesh-on-flesh, bone-on-bone, hearing the cracks, causing the cracks, venting all that pent-up anger.'[45] A history of the Northern Irish feminist movement will reveal lots of small moments of snap and while they are not depicted as historic in the grand Troubles narrative, each of them marks out a small, distinct break from a homogenizing climate of fear.

As mentioned, one of the ways in which Middle Sister navigates the emotional politics of living during the Troubles is through refusing to participate in this discourse by remaining silent.[46] However, as the novel demonstrates, not even this passive refusal is enough to exempt her from continuous scrutiny. Audre Lorde reminds us, 'Your silence will not protect you.'[47] She discusses the reasons why women stay silent – 'fear of contempt, of censure, or some judgement, or recognition, of challenge, of annihilation'[48] and the lasting effects of choking down the emotional reactions to injustice: 'What are the words you do not yet have? What do you need to say? What are the tyrannies you swallow day by day and attempt to make your own, until you will sicken and die of them, still in silence?'[49] It is clear from the way that Middle Sister discusses her own harassment and that of others that she recognizes these 'tyrannies', but her coping strategy is silence. Middle Sister, soon learns that feigned ignorance is better than exposing her feelings to the community: 'I'd launch my "I don't know" as the biggest player in my verbal defence repertoire and I'd be prepared to carry on saying it because another thing I'd learned by the end of primary school was that it was best not to open my mouth in the interests of truth except to a trusted few persons.'[50] Indeed, the tries to present herself as 'inert' and 'vapid' despite the fact that the narrative voice reveals her to be thoughtful and quick-witted:

> I'd hoped the sheer nullity of me would lead them to doubt their inventions and their convictions, even to suspect that a renouncer – especially that Man of Men, Warrior of Warriors, our high – celebrity, local community hero – could ever have developed lust for such an inert, vapid person as myself. … Of course I believed myself sentient. Of course I knew I was angry. Of course I knew I was frightened, that I had no doubt my body, to me, was brimming with a natural reaction.[51]

The clearest representation of asymmetries of power in the novel is who gets to speak freely, and to whom and about what they speak, and how this affects the mood of interactions. Where Middle Sister notes that she is 'brimming' with feeling, she tersely maintains her silence in order not to disturb the prevailing climate of feeling. The novel opens with Middle Sister attempting to exercise by running in her local area, but she is joined by a man who seeks to make her feel uneasy: 'He made lewd remarks about me to me from the first moment he met me – about my quainte, my tail, my contry, my box, my jar, my contrariness, my monosyllable – and he used words, words sexual, I did not understand.'[52] Here, her brother-in-law speaks to her, about her own body, using language that she does not understand in order to disorientate and intimidate her. Middle Sister frames this clearly in the language of power relations and entitlement: 'So he made his remarks and felt entitled to make his remarks and I did not speak because I did not know how to respond to this person.'[53] In the novel, there is usually either an abundance or a lack of words. Middle Sister is virtually silent in public, but Burns gives her a rich inner monologue which showcases someone trying to make sense of their own place in both an immediate political situation and also the way that context interacts with the politics of gender. Not only is Middle Sister largely silent because she does not feel she can speak but also because she does not have access to a lexicon that might describe her experience: 'You might not have used that word for it; you might not have the words for it; you might not be able to put your finger on it.'[54] Her experiences are not privileged within her society and, as a result, she is unable to fully express them.

'People got "moods"': The trouble with mental health

In addition to this silence, Middle Sister relates the process of closing down and shutting off emotionally in order to cope with the threat of civil and sexual violence: 'There was the disconnection of thoughts and feelings ... I think that was my way of coping. I didn't want to know, basically. I wasn't alone in that.'[55] Ahmed discusses this process as a safety mechanism: 'Not to be assaulted: maybe you might try to close yourself off, to withdraw from proximity, from proximity to a potential.'[56] While Middle Sister seeks to create an inner detached space of her own, she is unable to break the thrall of the attachments which are part of her community. This, therefore, demonstrates the subtle ways in which control exercises itself despite her best attempts to break free. The moments of optimism, such as maybe-boyfriend's attempts at actually doing something, or the sunset with her teacher, are initially undercut by the cycle beginning again. She is unable to become 'shiny', despite being drawn to those who exhibit hope and purpose. This regulation of affective displays is due to the perception of being continually watched and scrutinized for any signs of political or sexual aberrance that might leave Middle Sister vulnerable. Elmer Kennedy-Andrews, using Foucault in his discussion of the Troubles novel *Cal*, discusses how the Catholic father and son of the novel have internalized the norms of the dominant culture in which they live: 'Through this technique of surveillance, assessment, supervision and correction, the individual feels that he is being continually watched – regardless of whether or not he really is – and so eventually comes to regulate his own behaviour in accordance with the demands of the dominant society.'[57] Unlike

Cal and his father, however, Middle Sister and her family live within their 'own' religious community, but this sense of the regulation of behaviour is no less palpable. As we have seen, there are two dominant regulatory regimes within the community: the paramilitary 'renouncers' and Catholicism. On the fringes, there is also the presence of British Army surveillance: 'Already within a week of that first click, I'd been clicked again four times.'[58] Essentially this means that there are omnipresent and overlapping kinds of surveillance depicted in the novel that measure everything from perceived adherence to Catholic morality to signs of being either too sympathetic to the renouncer cause or not sympathetic enough. Against these demands, it is understandable why Middle Sister chooses to remain passive. However, as Lorde notes, passivity and silence have a cumulative effect on physical and mental health.

As noted at the beginning of this chapter, Middle Sister uses the term 'moods' to discuss depressive episodes. Throughout the novel, there is a suspicion of medical treatment in general and hospitals in particular, and this extends to the treatment of mental health. The novel examines a variety of mental health issues, despite Middle Sister and the community often lacking both a precise vocabulary and treatment options. The clearest depiction of the community's experience of mental health is in this passage:

> She meant depressions, for da had had them: big, massive, scudding, whopping, black-cloud, infectious, crow, raven, jackdaw, coffin-upon-coffin, catacomb-upon-catacomb, skeletons-upon-skulls-upon-bones crawling along the ground to the grave type of depressions. Ma herself didn't get depressions, didn't either, tolerate depressions and, as with lots of people here who didn't get them and didn't tolerate them, she wanted to shake those who did until they caught themselves on. Of course at that time they weren't called depressions. They were 'moods'.[59]

Middle Sister begins this passage with a macabre description of depression which emphasizes the deathly serious nature of chronic, persistent mental ill health. She also goes on to describe her own mother's attitude to the condition and how a depressive affect is seen as contagious. Both family members with depression are described as 'emanating atmospheres of monotonal extended sameness'.[60] The novel examines the complex effects of a build-up of anhedonia in a society where voicing your emotional state is taboo. It is clear from Middle Sister's comment here that depression is a persistent factor within a community during a prolonged violent conflict, but, as it is barely spoken about, there is no mechanism for these states to be mediated. In the novel, we see mental health issues in a variety of settings but rarely with a diagnosis attached. We see people living with chronic ill health and dying by suicide, while the community denies or invalidates their conditions. As we will see later, in the analysis of Middle Sister's physical responses to sustained trauma, Burns represents the interrelation of body and mind and, critically, what happens when it becomes more than we can bear.

Psychologists, sociologists and historians have examined the prevalence of mental ill health in Northern Ireland. C. C. Kelleher noted that the 'prevalence of violent crime, particularly related to firearms, has been associated with increased mistrust, personal vulnerability, and increased rates of mental ill health'.[61] Exposure to a dangerous conflict is a risk factor throughout the world. Cvetkovich reminds us, 'Epidemics of depression can be related (both as symptom and as obfuscation) to long-term histories of violence that have ongoing impacts at the level of everyday emotional experience.'[62] The community establishes a 'hierarchy of suffering'[63] but also which complaints can be tolerated and which cannot. Only briefly does Middle Sister directly discuss her own issues, with the brief marker of 'before my own depressions started'.[64] While the novel features frequent depictions of mental ill health and the troubles, the deepest expression of emotional life comes from a letter written by a woman who is accused of regularly poisoning members of the community. Where Middle Sister often has to resort to euphemism, it is rich with the language of emotion, the poisoner names feelings clearly:

> It is incumbent upon us to list you your fears lest you forget them: that of being needy; of being clingy; of being odd; of being invisible; of being visible; of being shamed; of being shunned; of being deceived; of being bullied, of being abandoned; of being hit; of being talked about; of being pitied; of being mocked; of being thought both 'child' and at the same time 'old woman'; of anger; of others; of making mistakes; of knowing instinctively; of sadness; of loneliness; of failure; of loss; of love; of death.[65]

As emotions are so repressed in the novel through silence and passivity, these rich, kaleidoscopic feelings pouring out are striking. The person who most clearly vocalizes the complexity of their mental ill health in the novel is a homicidal poisoner. Instead of being orientated towards an emotional life that prioritizes the goals of the 'struggle' and being either active or quietly compliant, Burns showcases an awareness of injustice, misogyny and bodily needs that serves to emphasize the stoicism and repression that the rest of the novel presents.

While the novel primarily focuses on the emotional states of Middle Sister and other women in the narrative, Burns also offers some valuable commentary on the difficulty of living through a conflict as a man. She states, 'I think in my book it's sexually dangerous to be female, but I think it's much more fatally dangerous to be male … I think neither females nor males are treated very well. But I think for females you could slip under the radar more than if you were male.'[66] In the novel, men are shown as vulnerable to violence. This can be directly due to the conflict, or in ways that have a complex relationship to it, such as serious issues of mental or physical health. Where women in the novel often have communities of solidarity, no such groupings exist for men outside of the hyper-masculine paramilitary structures. These have their own affective politics: a performance which blends stoicism and aggression, and does not allow for displays of emotion outside of this narrow range. There are intensified taboos around mental health care in Northern Ireland, but this process is detailed in *Milkman* as even more taboo for men:

> But it was mental hospitals, and it was mental breakdowns, which meant cover – up, which meant shame, which meant even more shame in his case because he was a man … Do you bear witness, even if, in the process, you cause more suffering and prolonged humiliation for your son or your brother or your husband or your father? Or do you go away, back inside, abandoning your son or your brother or your husband or your father to these people?[67]

Indeed, this demonstrates how mental health and shame function not just for the sufferer but also the ramifications for their family. Throughout the novel, we see that Middle Sister has internalized the rigid construction of masculinity in Northern Irish society: 'Secretly I had a worry that maybe-boyfriend might not be a proper man. This thought came in the darker moments, in my complex, unbidden moments, swiftly coming, swiftly going and which I wouldn't admit – especially to myself – to having had.'[68] Ideologies of masculinity limit the expression of feeling in many contexts, but this repression is particularly acute in Northern Ireland. However, just as there are divisions between different kinds of women in Middle Sister's community, there are also demarcations of men with attendant expectations:

> Ma's understanding of the nice wee boys was that they were the right religion, that they were devout, single, preferably not paramilitaries, overall more stable and durable than those – as she put it – 'fast, breathtaking, fantastically exhilarating, but all the same, daughter, early-to-death rebel men'. 'Nothing stops them,' she said, 'till death stops them. You'll regret it, daughter, finding

yourself ensnared in the underbelly of all that alluring, mind – altering, unruly paramilitary nightlife.'[69]

Here, men are associated with producing two different, affective states in women: either the agitated excitement of the renouncers or the more sedate mood of a 'pious' man. Middle Sister's home and family is overwhelmingly female, with male presences in her life limited to her brothers-in-law and maybe-boyfriend's circle. Her father is only fully present in the narrative during some disturbing deathbed revelations:

'I was raped many times as a boy,' he said. 'Did I ever tell you that?' At the time all I could think to reply was, 'No.' 'Yes,' he said. 'Many times. Many, many times he did me – me, a boy, and him, in his suit and hat, opening his buttons, pulling me back to him, in that back shed, that black shed, over and over and giving me pennies after.'[70]

This assault took place before the Troubles, and here Burns complicates the sexual harassment narrative by offering us the experience of a male victim. She also clearly sets out the disparities in power: the vulnerable young boy and the wealthy man in a suit. The Northern Ireland Historical Abuses Inquiry focuses on institutional abuse, and the Chairman Sir Anthony Hart found 'shocking levels of sexual, physical and emotional abuse in the period 1922 to 1995'.[71] Burns here is drawing attention to the repression of abuse in the post-partition pre-Troubles period to demonstrate the varied occasions for trauma and how large-scale trauma can be set against more intimate, personal family trauma. The naming process that her father develops during this difficult time mirrors the way in which Middle Sister relates to her family throughout the novel: 'Even that though, became too much and so, after a bit, he dropped the mental catalogue, opting instead for "son" or "daughter" which was easier. And he was right. It was easier which was how the rest of us came to substitute "brother" and "sister" and so on ourselves.'[72] The tactic of retreating when faced with danger is not the exclusive preserve of women, Middle Sister's father also offers it as a strategy when faced with sexual abuse: 'All shut down. Get it over with. Not going freshly into that place of terror, which was why, wife, it never felt right between me and you.'[73]While the novel has been lauded for offering a glimpse into the emotional lives of teenage girls in Northern Ireland, it is important to note that Burns examines the complexity of these 'force-relations' for men and how this influences their interactions. The atmosphere of 'bad feeling', then, is not just produced by the Troubles but is a multifaceted force which encompasses family trauma and sexual harassment.

In addition to the management of negative feelings that we've discussed, Middle Sister lacks the cultural cues to deal with positive feelings. She refers to people and situations which inspire hope or positivity as 'shiny'. Burns depicts a society that is unable to tolerate 'good feeling', and those who exhibit 'shiny tendencies' are often misunderstood or punished by the community. Part of Middle Sister's attraction to maybe-boyfriend is his upbeat practicality around difficult situations: ' "Well, it might work, I think it will work, so how about we try?" and even if it didn't work at least he didn't downgrade himself to misery before having a go.'[74] In a society with a pervasive depressive affect, the mere attempt of trying to defy the pervasive sense of anhedonia becomes a radical act. Burns carefully articulates this mood in her discussion of the dark/shiny dichotomy in 1970s Belfast:

> The very physical environment then, in collusion with, or as a result of, the human darkness discharging within it, didn't itself encourage light. Instead the place was sunk in one long, melancholic story to the extent that the truly shining person coming into this darkness ran the risk of not outliving it, of having their own shininess subsumed into it and, in some cases – if the person was viewed as intolerably extra – bright and extra – shiny – it might even reach the point of that individual having to lose his or her physical life.[75]

This passage describes the acute politics of performing the affective state deemed appropriate during violent conflict. It also unravels the problems of hope and the tenuousness of orientating oneself towards a positive object. What Burns begins by noting is the stultifying climate of negative affect in 1970s Belfast and relates it to place – she examines how these feelings are both 'caught' and maintained to the extent that they are considered the dominant landscape of feeling. Once such a climate has been established, then, any attempt to transgress the downbeat mood is viewed with initial suspicion and eventual threat. Burns examines here, then, how a mood goes from being part of the prevailing climate to causing danger to the body. Her characters are acutely aware about how they should present their emotional lives – they must not have the persona of the fully depressive but yet they must not be 'shiny'. These attempts to contort oneself into the shape required by society leave long-lasting profound impacts.

Middle Sister quickly learns that any outward displays of inappropriate emotions are unacceptable without ever being explicitly told. The coercive affective structures make her label certain emotional states as negative: 'So shiny was bad, and "too sad" was bad, and "too joyous" was bad, which meant you had to go around not being anything; also not thinking, least not at top level, which was why everybody kept their private thoughts safe and sound in those recesses underneath.'[76] During a time of conflict, to outwardly perform happiness is dangerous. Despite this, moments of joy regularly occurred, whether after the birth of a longed-for child or in everyday moments of humour. But, as discussed in Chapter 3, to feel any sort of pleasure during the Troubles might be read as perverse by the community at large. Middle Sister, however, seeks out and values these small moments, whether in maybe-boyfriend or her French teacher, who offers her small moments of possibility: 'I'd enjoyed it, as always I enjoyed it – the eccentricity of teacher, her talk of that "still, small voice," of "living in the moment", of "abandoning what you think should happen for what then might happen".'[77] This class offers Middle Sister an escape from her life that 'felt valuable, and I didn't want to lose that feeling'.[78] This is experienced as a glimpse at opening up to the world beyond her narrow neighbourhood. It also opens up the smallest glimpses at hope, possibility and optimism:

> If what she was saying was true, that the sky – out there – not out there – whatever – could be any colour, that meant anything could be any colour, that anything could be anything, that anything could happen, at any time, in any place, in the whole of the world, and to anybody – probably had too, only we just hadn't noticed. So no. After generation upon generation, fathers upon forefathers, mothers upon foremothers, centuries and millennia of being one colour officially and three colours unofficially, a colourful sky, just like that, could not be allowed to be.[79]

This is one of the most significant moments in the novel: where something potent shifts. It is so powerful to Middle Sister that she notes that 'the truth hit my senses'.[80] Here sensuality acts as a kind of knowledge, and we see multiple different kinds of emotional responses – incredulity, wonder, hope. This realization allows her to trouble the existing categories of identity that have been foisted upon her and her community. It is one of the pockets of lightness in a novel that otherwise hums with the frequency of 'human darkness'. Colour is also used, as we shall see, by Wee Sisters, in their play and dancing. Bright colour is something which is pleasurable but is also dangerous – it makes the subject who wears it stand out, and, indeed, the acknowledgement of pleasure is also affectively difficult in Northern Ireland. While saying that you receive pleasure from the colours changing in the sky and that things are not fixed is hazardous in this environment, in this moment it provides a sense of hope that pleasure and humanity endures in the most impossible times.

This hope is realized during the early stages of her relationship with maybe-boyfriend. There is one particular distinct moment of her as a desiring subject: 'That was why standing there, looking at him looking at his car, doing his out-loud wondering and pondering, I was getting wet and ...'.[81] The reason for her arousal is seeing maybe-boyfriend actively doing something rather than being passive. Middle Sister wants to orientate herself away from the predominant negative affect in her community and is drawn to anyone who exhibits a hopeful movement towards activity and futurity. Initially, her relationship offers her a glimpse at a life beyond the confines of her home. In a novel where negative affect predominates, it is striking to see Middle Sister lose herself in erotic reverie as maybe-boyfriend gently massages her head: 'At that point my mind would fall behind owing to deliciousness and to muddles with chronology ... I'd go to jelly which meant he'd have to put his arms around me to stop me from falling which meant I'd have to let him.'[82] Here, sensual pleasure has the ability to disrupt established scripts of memory and identity that have been handed down from her community. As Chapter 2 noted, moments of eroticism have great potential in Northern Ireland to unravel the politics of both society and self. In a novel of coercion here is a moment of genuine, active desire. Indeed, she goes on to discuss the power of sensual touch to her sexuality: 'Before the milkman, maybe-boyfriend's touch, those fingers, his hands, had been the best, the most, the absolute of lovely.'[83] For Middle Sister, sexuality without violence or coercion is 'the absolute of lovely': a feeling that mitigates against the shudders and 'sudden erotic alarm' of a sexuality that has been affected by violence. Touch, as we saw in Chapter 3, is an important portal for connection within Northern Irish fiction. In these small gestures, these moments where the self is 'lost' we see glimpses of a future beyond the conflict.

One of the survival strategies that Middle Sister uses throughout the novel to escape from this climate of negative affect is reading. Burns revealed in an interview that she was similarly notable for her pastime: 'I'd go into a shop or a cafe or a pub and someone would say: "Oh, you're that girl who walks and reads." '[84] While her novels firmly focus on Belfast, you can see the influence of this wide-ranging reading throughout. Middle Sister's reading is a small but powerful act of transgression, although it isn't until a pivotal conversation with her longest friend that she realizes just how transgressive this act is. Her choice of reading matter is always political, and writers have taken a particularly active role in the history of Irish nationalism. Therefore, to choose to immerse oneself in a different world is threatening to a sense of community cohesion which relies on shared myths expressed in literature. In Sara Ahmed's feminist toolkit, she asserts that 'your feminist books need to be handy. You need to take them with you; make them with you. Words can pick you up when you are down.'[85] Middle Sister carries books with her everywhere, she both reads while walking and also regularly retreats to her bedroom with a book, seeking the same sort of solace Ahmed identifies. But where Ahmed turns to feminist classics, Middle Sister turns towards classic fiction ('I was walking along reading Ivanhoe'[86]) and her Wee Sisters similarly show an eclectic reading. For Ahmed, the 'figures of the feminist killjoy and willful subject are studious'.[87] Middle Sister clearly articulates that she prefers classic literature, and does not engage with Irish texts: 'I myself spent most of my time with my back turned in the nineteenth century, even the eighteenth century, sometimes the seventeenth and sixteenth centuries, yet even then, I couldn't stop having a view.'[88] Her reading focus is on realist fiction. One can think of realist fiction as offering specific, comforting features: often featuring the development of a central protagonist who not only progresses through their own journey and charts a changing society but also offers features which make the novel legible: chapters, paragraphs, clear plotting. She is clear that a focus on classic fiction is an attempt to escape the present: 'So yes, keep the lid on, buy old books, read old books, seriously consider those scrolls and clay tablets. … This would be a nineteenth-century book because I did not like twentieth-century books because I did not like the twentieth century.'[89] The absurdity of reading being taboo is set against the deep pleasure that Middle Sister gets from 'relaxing' or 'sinking' into a book:

> That experience of relaxing into it, of walking out the door and slipping the book out of the pocket, of sinking into the paragraph coming up after the recently left-off paragraph, had changed since the stalking, also since the rumouring, since even the state forces had got suspicious and were stopping me to take Martin Chuzzlewit for state-security purposes out of my hands.[90]

Reading is not just reading but also 'reading': making oneself legible. In reading, she has actually made herself less readable, less understandable to her local community. She baulks at the absurdity of this: ' "Hold on a minute," I said. "Are you saying it's okay for him to go around with Semtex but not okay for me to read Jane Eyre in public?" '[91] Middle Sister's escapism, here, is outside of the proscribed norms of her community and marks her out as an 'affect alien'. Not only is she imaginatively venturing outside the bounds, she is also doing so, vitally, in public and while moving. However, reading alone only goes so far in the novel. Trauma is experienced primarily through strong bodily sensations, and it is only by reclaiming the body that any sort of small freedom is possible.

Moving through *Milkman*: Reclaiming the body

Before we discuss the ways in which Middle Sister copes with the restrictions placed on her by Northern Irish society, I want to consider the nadir of her relationship with her body. In the novel, physical symptoms of anxiety abound, and it is often hard to locate precisely which parts of the body are affected by which stimuli. This shows how affect can disrupt a settled understanding of the body. One of the clearest examples of this is when the district poisoner directs her attention to Middle Sister, who experiences the sensation in her guts as a consequence of her ongoing harassment: 'I was being sick because of Milkman stalking me, Milkman tracking me, Milkman knowing everything about me, biding his time, closing in on me, and because of the perniciousness of the secrecy, gawking and gossip that existed in this place.'[92] Burns represents a young woman fundamentally alienated from her own body. Ahmed talks about the power of gut feeling in her manifesto: 'We vomit; we vomit out what we have been asked to take in … Our guts become our feminist friends the more we are sickened.'[93] But Middle Sister is not attuned enough to her body to appreciate the true locus of her distress. Also, this episode reveals the extent to which her bodily autonomy is mediated by women: not only is it a woman who poisons her but it is also the women of the community who act to offer her medical care ('Therefore, purging and guts out it became'[94]). The body in this novel acts as a bellwether of the intangible force relations of negative affect.

As we have seen, men and women in the novel are both susceptible to the physical symptoms of anxiety, stress and trauma. It was written while Burns was in severe pain following a back surgery: 'But it's not just the physical pain. It's the whole emotional stress that goes with it.'[95] Following her interactions with the Milkman, Middle Sister recoils into what she describes as an 'anti-orgasm'. If an orgasm can be described as a release of tension in the body, this process is the reverse. As opposed to a post-orgasmic relaxed affect, this is a tense rigidity that affects her whole body but with the epicentre being her tailbone, which sits just below the sacrum and behind the pelvic cavity. Burns offers a vivid description of this sensation:

> At the same time, I dismissed a strange bodily sensation that had run the lower back half of my body, during which the base of my spine had seemed to move. … This had been a movement unnatural, an omen of warning, originating in the coccyx, with its vibration then setting off ripples – ugly, rapid, threatening ripples – travelling into my buttocks, gathering speed into my hamstrings from where, inside a moment, they sped to the dark recesses behind my knees and disappeared. This took one second, just one second, and my first thought – unbidden, unchecked – was that this was the underside of an orgasm, how one might imagine some creepy, back-of-body, partially convulsive shadow of an orgasm – an anti-orgasm.[96]

Middle Sister is attuned enough to her body to realize the sensation of orgasm and also to read this sensation as its opposite. Where the female orgasm tends to operate from the front of the body and radiate outwards, here we have something that draws the body into itself in a contracting motion: the anti-orgasm originates from a bone (the coccyx) which has no specific medical use but which is connected to muscles, tendons and ligaments in the pelvic region. Here we also see the influence of Burns's yoga practice, which will be discussed in the next session, that Middle Sister is aware that her spine can move on several planes. Burns uses the word 'ripple' ten times and the word 'shudder' twelve times in the text. A shudder is a kind of trembling convulsion, an involuntary contraction of motion. This sensation is not exclusive to Middle Sister, though, as her father details how his own painful experiences came to be located in the body: 'Always terrible, those sensations, nothing ridded me of them, those trembles, those shudders, those tiny persistent ripples. They just kept coming, kept repeating, kept being awful, my whole life through.'[97] Here we see the generational legacy of different kinds of trauma. The poisoner also refers to this feeling as 'then the shudders, the ripples, our legs turning to pulp because of those shudders and ripples',[98] and Middle Sister has similar feelings: 'After that came the leg shudders, those hamstring currents, all those neural, rippling dreads and permeations around my thighs and backside.'[99] The sensation of the 'anti-orgasm' is so physically specific and frequently discussed in *Milkman* that if offers a way to think about how trauma is stored in the body.

When asked by *Vanity Fair* to recommend the books that had influenced them and their work, Anna Burns chose *Light on Yoga* by B. K. S. Iyengar. Any initial surprise at this choice is ameliorated by a consideration of *Milkman* as a text centred around a certain kind of relationship to the body and, in particular, the dichotomy it presents between rigidity and softness. Burns has noted in interview that 'I had always been quite fit – yoga and hiking'.[100] There is a growing body of work, both academic and related to movement practice, that examines the relationship of stress and trauma to specific physical areas. Where some of this might be dismissed by medical practitioners, a focus on the hips and pelvic region as a site of tension is explored across mainstream medicine and alternative body work. In particular, the specific rippling/shuddering sensation that Burns details has been examined in the work of Peter A. Levine and David Berceli as a mechanism for confronting the effects of deep-seated trauma. They essentially advocate for a controlled practice of these sensations that Burns details in her traumatized characters. Berceli describes them thusly: 'Musculoskeletal tremors are a common neuro-physiological phenomena experienced before, during, or following stressful events.'[101] He advocates for these shudders/tremors within a 'safe' context under supervision as 'uncharacterized tremors might be a natural neurophysiological response to mitigate excess stress.'[102] This draws attention to the vitality of this area: a tightness in the hips is often characterized as part of the build-up of responses to the fight/flight/freeze instinct, and the pelvic region is vital in stabilizing the body and contains many muscles, ligaments and tendons which facilitate movement. To have it paralysed by fear affects the whole body's mobility. In *Milkman*, through the representation of these involuntary tremors, we see bodies trying to cope with the effects of extreme stress and the inability to move freely. These specific movements direct us not just towards Burns's understanding of the body but also towards a calmative for years of cumulative stress and tension during prolonged violent conflict – the movement of the whole body. Bad feeling is located via a tension in the pelvis and hips, but the body is also a route towards a different kind of future.

The school of movement that Burns was drawn to, Iyengar yoga, focuses on the precision of meticulous alignment in traditional yoga poses. There is an emphasis on breath and posture. Posture is also critical to *Milkman*, whether in running, ballroom dance or the curling up of the 'anti-orgasm'. Burns refers to Iyengar's approach as 'possibly the toughest, most "take no nonsense" yoga guy of them all'.[103] He was a student of Krishnamacharya, who is often referred to as the father of modern yoga. While the majority of Iyengar's book details the postures in great detail, focusing on alignment and technique, the beginning sets out in broad terms the values and virtues of the yogic lifestyle. The asana (movement) practice is only one of the eight limbs of yoga, which derive from the sutras of Patanjali. For a 9-year-old girl, living in Ardoyne, the language used by Iyengar and the principles he espouses must have seemed very far away, and she notes that she immediately engaged with it: 'Instantly I was entranced … I brought it home that day, knowing it was something different from anything in my whole nine years of life up until that point.'[104] This is a powerful image, of a young girl who finds a moment of revelation from a source outside her community. Burns's yoga also defies the Catholic Church: a Priest from Derry stated his belief that the practice would open one up to 'Satan and The Fallen Angels' and the Vatican's chief exorcist referred to it as 'satanic, it leads to evil just like reading Harry Potter'.[105] It offers, through the six limbs, an alternative way of living to the dictates of the Catholic Church. Yoga, as practised by Iyengar, offered Burns a clear system and routine amid the chaotic world of the Troubles. It is a self-sufficient practice which allows for independence, and, crucially, the home practice of yoga enables an acute awareness of the body. Although Middle Sister is never shown practising yoga, some of the sensations she notes towards the end of the novel (a lightness, ease of movement, a reclaiming of her own body) have much in common with the language of yoga.

This transformative introduction occurred in 1971, a year when four British soldiers and nine Catholics were shot dead in Ardoyne, and the area continued to be a flashpoint for violence throughout the Troubles. The rapidly changing political climate at this time was particularly pronounced in a year which saw the introduction of Operation Demetrius, or the mass arrest and internment of young men with suspected paramilitary involvement. In particular, Ardoyne is a Republican enclave that sits against predominantly Loyalist areas of Woodvale and Crumlin. Burns was raised in this area, and the novel presents a similar, if not explicitly named, locale. The novel regularly engages with the spatial limitations living at interface areas can produce, as Middle Sister struggles to find a run that does not place her in danger. Yoga offers something different to running. While both can be practised alone or with others and they rely on a sense of awareness of the whole body, yoga offers a way to transcend these geographical limitations as it can take place in the smallest of spaces yet allow the body to move in several different planes. At the beginning of *Light on Yoga*, Iyengar reminds his readers that yoga comes from the 'Sanskrit root yuj meaning to bind, join, attach and yoke, to direct and concentrate one's attention on, to use and apply'.[106] This coming together offers a way to reorientate a scattered identity. Iyengar's prescriptive approach appealed to the young Burns: 'My anxious child mind decided everything had to be done just so.'[107] The strictures of yoga would have appealed to someone who feels like they are not in control of their own body. The movement in the asana practice is designed to bring about comprehensive changes in both the physical body but is also designed to facilitate meditation which might be described as a very particular affective state, denoted by calmness and steadiness. In the repetition, the anxious young Burns found a kind of calmness. In the book, Iyengar describes the awareness that he wishes his practice to bring to yoginis 'the expression of the texture of the skin, co-ordination in the physical, chemical and energy metabolism, the rhythmic balance of the five elements in the body, the use of direction and gravitational pressure, the spacing of limbs and muscles, the elegance, shape, form, grave, beauty, power, strength, compactness of mind and intelligence'.[108] We witness the same sense of joy that Middle Sister finds in the French teacher and the shiny people in her yoga practice: 'I did go to it in the initial early child days with wonder, eagerness and love'.[109] In the way that Burns writes about the body in *Milkman*, we can directly see the influence of someone who has practised yoga since the age of 9 and has modified their practice throughout their life. Burns describes a softening of her practice against the rigid discipline of her punishing earlier routines: 'Looking back at it now, what was important and influential about this book – despite my growing gung-ho attitude towards it – was that it brought yoga to me. That yoga came to me. It was just I had to learn through the decades how to approach my practice better, how to begin to understand, really, what it might be all about'.[110] *Milkman* has a relationship to both elements of Burns's practice: both the punishing routines and the attempt to approach herself with what we might call self-compassion.

'The joy that was to be had': Running and dancing through *Milkman*

I want to move towards an analysis of the different kinds of physical activity within the novel and consider how this activity can serve as a temporary release from the inertia of living within a geographically confined area during a violent conflict. Throughout the novel, bodies are constrained by the spatial and behavioural limits placed by both gender norms and violent conflict. As Middle Sister moves through the city, she is acutely aware of which areas are dangerous and plans her walking and running routes carefully to avoid both unwanted male attention and also straying into 'no go' areas. Pleasure is meditated through the circumscribed movement patterns of the community. In the novel, the three main kinds of physical activity represented are walking, running and dancing. These all involve the full body and, critically, the pelvis and hip flexors. Dance is explored through the depiction of maybe-boyfriend's parents, who left their young family for their 'professional ballroom – dancing careers'.[111] They had to escape the rigid moral climate of Northern Ireland in order to fulfil their ambitions. Middle Sister muses on certain categories of people that are able to transcend the sectarian binary in Northern Ireland due to their talent: 'This meant they were one of those exceptions – as with the musicians here, the artists here, the stage and screen people and also the sportspeople, all those in the public eye who managed to rise above winning the complete approval of one community whilst bringing down upon themselves the disapprobation and death threats of the other community.'[112] All of these activities involve physical prowess and stamina: it seems the exceptional body is afforded a kind of other space due to the emotional effects they produce in people. Sports, dance and entertainment are designed to stoke emotions and fuel empathy: here the body is a conduit to something beyond the present.

In particular, Burns emphasizes the physicality of their chosen profession: 'with those eyes, that face, that body, the mobility, the confidence, the sensuality.'[113] This seems at direct odds with the cowed, small stance of the anti-orgasm. Dancers emphasize posture, as do runners as we will see below. Within the narrative, the discussion of the dancers offers movement, colour and rhythm which functions in the narrative to disturb the relentless grind of negativity. Middle Sister's younger siblings are captivated by their performance: 'And now wee sisters were explaining the joy that was to be had from playing Mr and Mrs International.'[114] To dance can be an avowedly political act, particularly in a society where movement is so rigorously policed. Dance has a variety of cultural meanings: it can be a collective act of solidarity, or one of individual defiance. In 2001, Ian Paisley declared that dance was sinful: 'The dancing of the world, hugging the other sex, set to music, is sensual and clearly caters to the lust of the flesh. Line dancing is as sinful as any other type of dancing, with its sexual gestures and touchings. It is sensual, not a crucifying of lust, but an excitement of lust. It is a war against the soul.'[115] This taboo over movement is explored in an essay by Jan Carson, 'No Dancing', where she examines her complex relationship with the Presbyterian faith of her youth and how this influenced her relationship with her body in motion. She identifies a 'tightness' in her body that she describes as the legacy of an upbringing where there was a huge taboo around moving for pleasure: 'Every time I dance I feel constrained. I feel as if every part of me is ludicrous and I need to sit down. I feel as if I'm veering dangerously close to being out of control and I can't cope with this feeling.'[116] Carson links her experience of feeling the vestiges of shame that she was raised with as a limitation on the movement of her body. This shame has constrained her spatially: she is acutely self-conscious. This explores the legacy of a religious upbringing in

Northern Ireland and how this affects even those who have moved away from this tradition: 'It is possible to both say, and actually believe, that something is no longer wrong and yet find yourself so programmed to abstain that you simply cannot get your body in gear.'[117] The body has been set, it has kept the score. Like Middle Sister, there are areas of pressure and tension which are directly related to experiences of constraint. However, like *Milkman*, Carson's piece ends with a renegotiated relationship with movement: 'The tightness is slowly losing its hold. I can't dance yet, but I'm getting there.'[118] Textual clues indicate that the novel is not set in the same community that Paisley is ministering to and Carson details, taken together they establish a climate of restricted movement within Northern Irish culture that is not the sole preserve of either community. Within the 'renouncer' community in *Milkman*, women are often particularly spatially confined and aberrations from prescribed movement regimes are met with prohibitions and punishment.

Sara Ahmed, in discussing Emma Goldman's famous assertion that 'I won't join your revolution if I cannot dance', sets out the affective politics of choosing to dance when your body is coded as victim or perpetrator:

> Goldman affirms at this moment dance as an affective rebellion against the requirement to be mournful; against the requirement not to live in her body through joyful abandon. This is what I call an affect alien moment. A killjoy survival kit is also about allowing your body to be the site of a rebellion, including a rebellion against the demand to give your body over to a cause or to make your body a cause.[119]

Throughout *Milkman*, we see small moments of rebellion through the body. In the final scene of Series 1 of the television programme *Derry Girls*, there is a poignant scene as the main characters dance with abandon to Madonna's 'Like a Prayer' while news of a terrorist attack reaches their families. The gut-wrenching affective power of this scene comes in the juxtaposition of fear with the joy that comes from fully inhabiting your own body. In a similar way, Wee Sisters find joy and pleasure in unselfconscious dancing against the backdrop of sustained violent conflict:

> This explained the colour – for there had been an explosion of colour – plus fabric, accessories, make-up, feathers, plumes, tiaras, beads, sparkles, tassels, lace, ribbons, ruffles, layered petticoats, lipsticks, eyeshadows, even fur – I had glimpsed fringed fur – high heels too, which belonged to the little girls' big sisters and which didn't fit which was why periodically the little girls fell over,

sustaining injuries. 'But the thing is,' reiterated wee sisters, 'and you don't seem overjoyed by this, middle sister, you get to be her every time!'[120]

The dancing body refuses, even for a short while, to participate in violent conflict. This performance is for the girls alone: both dancers dress as Mrs International and do not participate in the heteronormative codes of ballroom dancing. In this style of dancing, one partner takes the lead and the other shadows their movements. However, the performance they create is an almost drag pageantry of femininity where everyone wants to be the woman and roles are easily reversed. In their childish play, they present a movement that is unavailable to many of the adults in the novel. Ahmed discusses the 'bodies that prance; bodies that dance; "bodies that matter", to borrow Judith Butler's terms; bodies that have to wiggle about to create space'.[121] To move your body out of pleasure is to assert that you think your body matters. That *you* matter. It is an assertion of pleasure, of pride and of autonomy.

Throughout the novel, Middle Sister's emotional state can be linked with her running activity. She curtails this when faced with Milkman's unwanted attentions and seeks solace and recovery in it after she has been freed from them. Running bookends the novel, and we can trace her state of mind against her physical activity. As she becomes more intimidated by the Milkman, her relationship to her own body changes as does her relationship to the local area: 'I was finding myself more and more circumscribed into an incoherent, debilitated place.'[122] This identifies how a coercive affect changes the body and mental state. A combination of sexual and ethno-sectarian violence causes the world to become smaller for Middle Sister. Physical activity offers her a way to shake out of a heavy, dense affect and create some space. Runners often aim for lightness of stroke and a feeling of buoyancy – a very different sensation to the mood of 'human darkness' Burns describes. It also requires a great deal of self-knowledge and awareness to manage everything from gait to timings to ward off injury: an acute sense of proprioception. Her appetite for long distance running also offers her the same kind of escapism that she finds in reading. As one running magazine declared, 'The steady, repetitive movement of distance running triggers one's intellectual autopilot, freeing room for creative thought. Neuroscientists describe this experience as a feeling of timelessness, where attention drifts and imagination thrive.'[123] Running allows Middle Sister both the physical and imaginative space she needs to live outside the narrow confines of Northern Irish society.

Running, like yoga and walking, is a whole-body workout. In addition to the cardiovascular and mental health benefits, running also offers a different viewpoint on one's local area. Middle Sister does not just have the mental maps of sectarian geography in her head, she mingles this spatial awareness with planning her runs. There, she must balance caution with a desire to traverse as much of the city as she can. Middle Sister plots out her running route carefully for her long-distance run, with the pressures of routing around the sectarian geography of 1970s North Belfast: 'If you didn't, you were left with a curtailed route owing to religious geography, which meant repeatedly going round a much smaller area in order to get a comparable effect.'[124] She is determined, however, to keep moving despite the difficulties which face her every day. The magazine *Runner's World* carefully explains to its international readership that, unlike rugby, cricket, or football, 'running is a neutral sport in Belfast, devoid of sectarianism'.[125] But while the act of a body running may be seen as politically neutral, routing is clearly not a neutral act. To add to this, running as a woman carries additional pressures and the risks of sexual harassment. It means having your body visible in public in a simultaneous show of strength and vulnerability. These two contexts directly influence her relationship to the city: her gender and her religious identity. In an extension of the process that caused the 'anti-orgasm', Middle Sister's process of body recoil prevents her from doing physical activity:

> Then my legs hurt, so that bit by bit I pulled out of my runs with third brother-in-law. First it was the odd run, then more and more cancellations as the pain continued and a lack of coordination overtook me. It came that I couldn't anymore relax and feel myself in flow, couldn't breathe properly whereas before, the act of running brought breath through me, kept me in touch, filled me up.[126]

As Middle Sister notes here, running 'brought breath through' her, something Burns would have been acutely aware of with the pranayama practice of Iyengar yoga. Rather than depleting, a run enervates her. She spends so much of the novel mute and still, where the running body is fast and breathes heavily. For Middle Sister, movement becomes a kind of meditation. The most vital muscles from running are the hip flexors, which are engaged every time the knee raises and is also proximate to the location of her anti-orgasm. Running offers a different kind of engagement with the pelvic region: rather than the dark shudders of recoil, the pelvis should be strong, engaged, neutral and stable. This offers an alternative to these tremors – reclaiming this region as somewhere where momentum and power are located. The very last paragraph of the novel is, for many readers, the one which offers a sense of hope:

So that was that settled. We fell back to stretching which was when the others, amused by our little passage until they were bored by our little passage, pushed us out of this stretching … Meanwhile, we two resumed our stretching then brother-in-law said, 'Right? Are ye right?' and I said, 'Aye, come on, we'll do it.' As we jumped the tiny hedge because we couldn't be bothered with the tiny gate to set off on our running, I inhaled the early evening light and realised this was softening, what others might term a little softening. Then, landing on the pavement in the direction of the parks & reservoirs, I exhaled this light and for a moment, just a moment, I almost nearly laughed.[127]

Here we see Middle Sister coming back to her body. I don't want to replicate the language of trauma that this book has a complicated relationship with – Burns's novel refuses easy readings. It is clear that the conflict will continue to rage for decades after the close of the novel and lead to a huge loss of life and the deteriorating mental and physical health of her community. Sexual violence is still endemic. This is not a novel of healing and recovery. It is a novel of moments of possibility and pleasure that live alongside the worst days. It is a novel of intimate partner violence, the problems of intimacy and ways in which kinship can form and reform in unexpected places. Before Middle Sister's sustained harassment, she had an instinctual, natural relationship to her own body and emotional life. What we see here is a sort of homecoming, a return to herself through a relationship with the body in motion. What does it mean, then to come back to the body after a time spent under duress? How does it feel? Although he was writing about capitalism and the economic crash, Mark Fisher's comment is useful here: 'From a situation in which nothing can happen, suddenly everything is possible again.'[128] Through Middle Sister's body we can chart the cumulative effect of sectarian violence and sexual harassment to make the world smaller. The reader can clearly see how, in being ground down, we can lose our relationship with what we know to be true. As Middle Sister runs towards the parks and reservoirs, almost nearly laughing, we see glimmer and glints of hope. While we know, from our vantage point, that the violence of the Troubles will continue for decades after the novel's close, something in her exhalation offers the reader a chance to breathe out. Everything is possible again, and anything can be rewritten.

Open endings

When you frame a book project on contemporary writing, several practical considerations emerge. Firstly, you must be flexible about the thematic parameters shifting as new books are published during the course of writing. For example, I had not expected to write a chapter on skin and touch, but the more I read, the more I saw this preoccupation in Northern Irish writing. Also, although Anna Burns's earlier fiction was well respected in discerning quarters, few expected the stratospheric success of *Milkman*, which profoundly tied together the ideas of how the body can mediate between the past and the present. The second significant issue is that at some point you have to stop writing, therefore excluding any novels and short stories published after your imposed deadline. You reluctantly accept that authors will continue to publish texts that will speak to the themes and ideas you are interested in after you hit 'send'. I was nearly at that point in this project that I received two proof copies – Lucy Caldwell's *Intimacies* (which after a Covid-19 delay in publishing may well arrive around the same time as this book) and Susannah Dickey's *Tennis Lessons*. The chapter on intimacy was already in train when I received Caldwell's book, and I could barely believe my good fortune at reading a book that was so engaged with precisely what it means to be in relationship with others. The latter book, however, was more difficult to place in my schema. Like *Milkman*, it stood out as a different kind of Northern Irish novel, and its arrival made me think about which direction Northern Irish fiction might go in the coming years. I want to conclude with this novel for two reasons: because it explores themes that are central to this study but also that it offers a particular kind of intimacy that is further untethered from the conflict. As the youngest writer featured in this study, Dickey's work points towards how the coming generation might intertwine the representation of intimacy, pleasure and the body with a different sense of the past.

Susannah Dickey's *Tennis Lessons*, published in 2020, is a different kind of Northern Irish novel. The nameless protagonist experiences a great deal of trauma over the course of the novel – from her father's infidelity and her uncle's death following his diagnosis with HIV to a brutal sexual assault at 17. Dickey's narrative is unsparing about her protagonist's body, from detailing her bowel movements and menstrual blood clots and also examines the physical and mental after-effects of rape. A careful reader might spot some clues to the novel's location in contemporary Northern Ireland but these are not foregrounded. As with *Milkman*, the novel does not offer a meticulous description of specific Northern Irish geography, but instead, the names and reported speech are largely neutral until this context is woven into the later stages of the novel. The protagonist's mother references the 'irregular war',[1] and there are brief references to punishment shootings and Loyalists. If the protagonist is 28 in the present day, their experiences of being born into Northern Ireland in the 1990s would have been one of relative distance from the worst of the violence of the conflict and to have experienced it through the conversation of older people or reading. However, it is clear that, even as a child, she wants to move beyond the narrative of conflict: 'You wish your class could read books about something other than war and the children of war: you want to read about normal people trying to do normal things.'[2] Despite this context, however, the central narrative drivers are not this historical framework but rather the central, bodily traumas which inform her youth and adolescence. Dickey stated, 'I don't want to speak to any ostensible uniqueness of becoming a person in Northern Ireland, because I never tried to become a person somewhere else, but it seems to me that so much was, and is, going unsaid.'[3] The novel begins to pick apart some of this unsaid intimacy, and one hopes that Dickey will explore this vital concern further in her fiction and poetry.

Like other fiction in this study, Dickey deals with a range of small, intimate encounters. The novel opens with a picture of security with the protagonist and her mother: 'She would kiss your head and rock you back and forth.'[4] Her youth is marked by her mother's depression after the death of her uncle. He is depicted as an outgoing, funny character who can relax her uptight mother: 'Your mother is more like a rag doll when her twin brother is around; she is malleable, easily coaxed into some posture of relaxation.'[5] As her mother's depression intensifies, her father seeks out an extramarital affair which eventually breaks up the family. She eventually has an affair with a married man that Rachel refers to as a 'daddy issue starter kit.'[6] Her template for relationships, then, is defined by her uncle's condition and suicide, her father's infidelity and her teenage sexual assault. The context of the Troubles is far from this narrative of young women navigating their bodily autonomy.

One of the novel's most powerful aspects is how Dickey charts a young woman coming to terms with her own sexual pleasure. In Chapter 2, we discussed the role of pleasure as a destabilizing agent within Northern Irish fiction but something subtly different is happening here. Our protagonist's experiences of sexuality in the novel are, for the most part, not pleasurable for her. She also is firmly situated in the internet age, where she seeks to find out more about her body online: 'Your new year's resolution is to be normal, to be knowing, to be sexual. The vulva has promised you the keys to the kingdom of adult pleasure.'[7] As she looks at the 'anthropomorphised vulva' on screen and looks at her own genitals using a hand-mirror, she finds her own body curious and her vulva the 'colour of a squalling newborn's face'. Her subsequent attempts at masturbation fail for what appears to be two reasons: her focus on the anatomical nature of her genitals and her focus on 'being normal' rather than her own pleasure. This is 'being sexual' as opposed to 'having pleasure'. Her complicated history affects her sexual present. Her encounters are marked by a lack of arousal on her part: 'It feels wrong … Your insides feel arid and tight and like there's no give.'[8] A recurring event in the novel is the inability of penetrative intercourse due to her displeasure, which she codes as her own failure. Her partners respond to this in a variety of different ways, from awkwardness to rejection to comparing her to other women. One man cannot tell the difference between urine and vaginal lubrication, another resents her attempts to explain what has happened: 'You think he looks slightly put out by your having spoken, and you wonder if his arousal is dependent on your silence.'[9] She often imagines a future that involves a social life with her lovers, but this does not materialize and her encounters often dent her self-esteem, until she finally runs away from a potential encounter in a nightclub alleyway. Agency can come from the refusal of intimacy.

There are only two pleasurable sexual moments in this novel, which is full of painful and traumatic sex, and both of them relate to non-heterosexual stimuli. After she sees a gay male couple on the train, she masturbates to orgasm: 'You keep going. After a while your body tenses. A constructed hotness starts to build deep inside you – patches of pink appear on your thighs.'[10] This is one of the most sensual moments in the novel, a world away from her stilted encounters with straight men. She also only briefly expresses same-sex desires: 'She's kind to you, and so you can't help imagining having sex with her. You think sex with Andrea would be nice. There would be laughter – you can picture the two of you waking up and her playing with the soft water balloons of your breasts.'[11]

This joyous, soft intimacy is reminiscent of the lovers in Caldwell's 'Here We Are'. There is kindness, laughter and playfulness, a world away from the other, more transactional encounters she depicts. Indeed, the central love story in the novel is between the protagonist and her best friend Rachel. While they are not physically intimate, it is clear that their intimacy sustains the protagonist during the most difficult moments in her young life and is, eventually, the only person she tells about her rape. Years after the assault, she is tested for HIV and feels something 'akin to lightness, freedom: there is a newly vacant place in your mind for new thoughts to grow'.[12] However tempting, it would be ultimately reductive to read this novel as a young woman eventually moving towards some kind of recovery from a core traumatic event. What Dickey presents us with is much more complex than that as she examines the way in which traumatic events are absorbed into the protagonist's sense of self: 'You also think it would be too easy for her to attribute all your failings to this one event, and you don't want to be absolved in that way – you know you were strange and wrong from the beginning'.[13] This internalized shame begins to break down towards the end of the novel, but the questions are never fully resolved or answered, a testament to the difficult path of recovery. The novel ends with a clearing out of digital intimacy as she deletes the number of her married lover and his messages and thinks, 'You wonder what happens now.'[14] It is this open-endedness in the face of repeated trauma that I want to focus on at the close of this study. There is nothing resolved at the end of the novel, no grand plan that orientates the protagonist towards the future. This open-endedness appears to be a feature of recent fiction from Northern Ireland but particularly pronounced in the fiction of younger writers, such as Dickey. In her poem 'In Belfast', Sinéad Morrissey describes her return to the city and a sense of 'the future unspoken and the past/unencountered and unaccounted for'.[15] In new writing from Northern Ireland, this 'future unspoken' begins to find expression. As critics who have 'skin in the game', we must move away from centring the voices that we know and respond to because their experiences mirror our own and pay attention to the new writers who will reshape the cultural landscape – whether they have a different relationship to trauma in their work like Dickey, illuminate the scourge of racism in Northern Irish society like Shannon Yee or enlighten us on LGBTQ+ life like the writers championed by the Outburst Queer Arts Festival.

It is impossible to make predictions about the themes and ideas that will preoccupy authors at the best of times and feels like a wild goose chase now. All of our creative and critical work is shaped by practical considerations but this feels heightened at the time of writing – those with caring responsibilities have fewer opportunities to write, and all our domestic lives are bleeding into our writing and teaching careers. I taught a seminar in May 2020 on intimacy in Lucy Caldwell's writing with my house plants and sofa in full view, the domestic barriers broken as my partner handed me a cup of coffee. Most urgently, the creative profession is under threat from cancelled income, as Rosemary Jenkinson put it,: 'Like most writers, "send an invoice" are my three favourite words in the English language, but my income from festival readings and commissions has been decimated.'[16] The Arts Council of Northern Ireland was able to offer some funding to writers and other artists, but it is clear that the next few years will be challenging. However, Jenkinson goes on to note how the pandemic has fed her imagination:

> The past weeks have been a time of new sights and sounds – the blast of the shipyard horn in praise of key workers; the nocturnal loners brandishing their eccentric walks by daylight; the fevered dreams through the night of being caught up in vast inescapable crowds. All these will feed into our imaginations and, ultimately, our experience of this strange reality will usher in a new creative sensibility.[17]

Of the writers featured in the study, Jenkinson's stories features characters whose intimate lives would be most constrained by the current situation – travellers, revellers and 'serial sleeper[s]'.[18] But, so much of the fiction in the study has been outward-looking in the search for intimacy. These are profoundly social texts – about relationships with others, whether pleasurable or coercive, committed or casual. While this fiction has showcased an array of thematic preoccupations, genres and subject matter, this privileging of intimacy has emerged as a common thread. Taken together, this acts as a ballast against traditional political narratives and orientates us towards the vitally important small moments of intimacy that make up a life against the sweep of history. When I am asked about my own upbringing during the Troubles, reeling off historical events is not enough on its own. Talking about my own family and intimate relationships is not enough on its own. Considering the music I listened to, books I read and television I watched is not enough on its own. All these things – history, intimacy and culture – need to be woven together to produce an account of Northern Irish life which *feels* all-encompassing. For example, when Maxine in *The Rest Just Follows* is listening to Magazine and falling in lust while the violence in 1970s Belfast rages outside. This is what fiction can do. It can also be attentive to the ways that past hurts can resonate in the fibres of the body. It can offer comfort that life can go on, that the impulse for pleasure can endure regardless of the past.

I have two hopes for the future. Firstly, that some of the models of thinking about intimacy, pleasure and the body will be useful to critics in the years to come both to examine newer writing and to re-evaluate the intimate history of Northern Ireland. Secondly, that writers continue to explore intimacy and sexuality in ways that challenge received orthodoxy about what it means to live in a Northern Irish body. The writers in this study have interwoven the personal and the political in subtler ways than previous fiction – this is not fiction *about* Northern Ireland in the same way as previous writing that engaged with the conflict and its aftermath. For decades, writers have used intimacy as a way to subvert expectations of Northern Irish fiction, however, the fiction that was presented in this study *feels* different to earlier writing. These writers privilege the body as a place to unmake and remake the world. They dwell on small, tender moments of intimate connection. They allow women to be unashamedly sexual. The self can be lost in sensation or found in the surface of the skin. Things are not fixed. Pleasure and generosity are valuable. The body yearns to be touched. But most of all, they share an interest in intimacy – both the desire to be close and the pressures of that closeness. These novels and short stories are complex meditations on what it means to be with and for each other, both in a universal sense but they also consider the complex social and personal histories of their Northern Irish protagonists. These texts often feature a close examination of what it means to be truly vulnerable. The 'moments' featured in this study, when taken together, are not blithely optimistic but offer kernels of hope alongside a recognition of the forces that shape lives in a society with a history of violent conflict. At a time when we are reconsidering what it means to be together and apart, they are a vital reminder of what is important.

Manchester, November 2020

On intimacy: Reflections from writers

Author's note: with the exception of Phil Harrison's piece, all of these were written before the Covid-19 lockdown of 2020.

Lucy Caldwell

When Faber acquired my second collection of stories, they did so on the basis of a manuscript of six stories called, well, *Six Stories*. Shortly afterwards I was in the Faber offices discussing something *Being Various* – related with my editor, Angus Cargill. As he walked me to the door, he said, 'Oh by the way, any idea what you'll call the new collection?'

And I found myself saying, 'It's called *Intimacies*.'

I hadn't known I knew, but as soon as I said the word, it was perfect.

I wanted a title that was akin to *Multitudes*, my first book of stories. I'd published *Multitudes* after the birth of my son, and dedicated it to him. *Intimacies* was to be a sister-volume, in both senses of that word, dedicated to my daughter. Both collections were to have eleven stories (indeed, in a nod to Richard Yates' *Eleven Kinds of Loneliness*, a title, and collection, that Angus and I both love, we gave *Multitudes* the subtitle *Eleven Stories* and *Intimacies* will be subtitled *Eleven More Stories*), all narrated by or from the point of view of girls and young women, all of whom were unnamed – for although superficial and occasionally fundamental details differed, I wanted the sense that each collection could be a cubist portrait of childhood, young womanhood, motherhood.

But if *Multitudes* celebrated plurality and possibility, the overcoming of difficulty, the myriad ways a life could take, *Intimacies* was tauter, more tightly controlled, more inward-looking.

To intimate means to imply, to communicate something urgent or delicate or otherwise impossible to articulate with the most sparing of signs: and this seemed as good a definition as any of what these short stories were trying to do, this form where every sentence, every word, every punctuation mark needs to be pulling its weight, playing its part; this art of conjuring into being something greater than itself.

Intimate in its noun-form comes from the Latin *intimus* meaning innermost, from *intus* meaning within. I wanted to write about the greatest intimacies I've known: what it means to conceive and to carry a child inside of you, and then realise that the real work is in learning to let them go. And from the inside-out to the outside-in: I wanted to write, too, about desire, about desiring someone so much you want to be not just inside their clothes, but inside *them*, beyond the boundary of skin. The Biblical euphemism for physical intimacy carries a sense of knowledge ('she knew no man', 'he knew her again no more', 'they knew her') and I wanted to write about how close it is possible to come to another, how possible it is to ever truly know another.

Because if *intimacy* suggests proximity, I wanted to write, too, about distances. The stories marked a tipping point, for me – as much time spent living away from Belfast as I'd ever spent living there – and I wanted to write about the distance between where we come from and where we end up; between who we think we are and who we turn out to be. Between what we dream, and what we do. The distance – and here I return to the short story form, and its intensity, its sense of things distilled, its power of ellipsis – between words said and not said, or thought but not said.

Most of all, I wanted to continue to find a way to write *truthfully*. That doesn't mean that all the things I was writing about had to have actually happened: it's more to do with a pitch of emotional truthfulness, an openness, a vulnerability. Something not confessed so much as confided, shared; the possibility of a new closeness forged. I thought of those beautiful lines of Katherine Mansfield's, which Yiyun Li took as the title of her 2017 memoir: 'Dear friend, from my life I write to you in your life'. 'What a long way it is', Li writes, 'from one life to another, yet why write if not for that distance?'

That would have been a good epigraph for *Intimacies*. But I chose, finally, the lines towards the end of Frank O'Hara's 'A True Account of Talking to the Sun on Fire Island', the sun's injunction to the poet about always embracing things 'freely and with / an appropriate sense of space'.

That *and* could almost be a *but*, I always think, yet it's not: and so becomes not a warning but a possibility, the lines suddenly offering a way of living, of being in the world. A way of reconciling the impossible tensions between holding close and letting go, a promise of no more distance from loved ones, or places, than is bearable, but just what is enough, in order to be in this world, to live your own life truly.

Jan Carson

I've been living in East Belfast for the better part of a decade now. During this period the scope and focus of my writing seems to have narrowed. I've moved away from the abstract, generalities of my early short stories and first novel to focus upon the Northern Irish experience, followed by the Belfast experience and, of late, a tight and oftentimes uncomfortably intimate portrayal of East Belfast, the part of the city I now call home. This pattern, apparent within my writing, mirrors a strange period of readjustment to life here in Northern Ireland. Ten years ago I reluctantly moved back from America, and whilst I resented this move and could see nothing positive in Belfast, the city gradually and persistently wore me down until I came to love this wee part of the world, warts and all. For me, looking back over the body of work I've produced in the last decade, this period of transition and gradual intimacy with the city, can be traced through the trajectory of my stories as I wrestle with questions around national, political and religious identity; as I slowly try to decipher what it means to be a Protestant, Northern Irish woman in both real life and fiction.

East Belfast is now home to me. I work here as a community arts facilitator and the greater part of my fiction is also set in this neighbourhood. It can sometimes feel as if the walls are coming in. However, there's something about the forced intimacy of the architecture (both physical and social) in this part of the city which seems to be exactly the kind of creative constraint I like to push against and challenge. I'm increasingly fascinated by small, enclosed spaces (I've lost track of how many stories I've recently written which are set in cars, caravans and buses) and how they throw people together, exposing both the best and worst of their personalities. I live in a terraced house where I can hear much of my neighbours comings and goings on either side. My neighbours are equally 'intrigued' by me. They peer out through their venetian blinds as I enter and leave my house. They squint through my front window as they walk past, trailing reluctant Jack Russells and grandchildren.

I watch them. They watch me. I watch them watching me. I scurry off to a coffee shop and write down all my observations. It somehow seems to help that I am both the watcher and the watched in this dynamic. I'm fascinated by the blurring of the public and the private; how the geography of the East pitches us all together. My life is, quite literally, sandwiched to my neighbours, separated only by the thinnest of walls and a polite, front garden kind of standoffishness which keeps us from mounting an all out interrogation. It's intriguing to write about a community with such an active level of intimacy. I often feel like I have very little distance from my subject matter. I don't necessarily think this is a bad thing. In some strange way it helps me to be a more measured writer. I think carefully about what I'm going to write about this community because I am part of it. I am complicit in both its triumphs and failures. I have to take responsibility for my words because there's so little distance between them and myself. On the simplest level, I want to do this place justice when I sit down to write about it.

Billy Cowan

When I read a novel or a short story, I'm looking to develop an intimate relationship with the writer where I allow myself to be impacted in some way by the story, the characters and the words I encounter on the page; by the things the writer has created. I am not necessarily looking for the representation of intimate relationships in the plot or between the fictional characters – it's the intimate relationship I'm going to have with the work itself that interests me most: Will it make me cry, laugh? Will I learn something? Will my belief systems be challenged? Will I fall in love with it or hate it? Will I be changed in some way through reading it?

As a writer, I'm therefore concerned with how I engender this kind of relationship with my readers. Writing about fictional intimate relationships between characters they can understand and relate to may be one way of doing it, but for me the best way to create intimacy is to make my readers *feel* that what they are reading has come from a place of truth; that it's a kind of secret I have decided to share with them. This doesn't mean that everything I write is autobiographical, that my stories are always true, that would be limiting, but the use of autobiographical detail is, for me at any rate, a crucial component in fostering this sense of intimacy.

By autobiographical detail, I mean the specific experiences I've actually had, the specific things I've seen and heard, the people and situations I've encountered – these are the things that ground the work in truth. By using them, I feel a sense of intimacy as I write which transfers to my readers when they read the work. Of course, it can be argued that all writers use these autobiographical details, so every piece of writing is, in a way, intimate, but it's all about degrees.

There's no doubt that a work that is totally autobiographical has the potential to be an intensely intimate experience for the reader, and for the writer, and this is why I write about my own life a lot. However, I would argue that grounding your fictional work heavily in these personal details can also have the same effect. For example, I recently entered a flash fiction competition with a story entitled *Big Strong Giant* which was placed second and then nominated for a Pushcart Prize. From the judge's comments and from the response I got from readers, I knew this short piece had been emotionally impactful. Alison Moore, the judge, said 'it brought tears to my eyes.' I have no doubt that people responded emotionally because of the sense of intimacy they felt when reading it. The story itself isn't autobiographical. It is about an abusive father who comes back from the dead to ask his son's forgiveness. My father wasn't abusive in any way, in fact he was a gentle, passive man. Yet, all the details I use to flesh out the father in the story are true of my own dad. He's a golfer, he wears a linen cap, he eats marmalade sandwiches, he did take me to the cinema to see *The Aristocats* when I was a child. All these specific details give the story a sense of truthfulness, which the readers pick up on. The fact that the story is also written in the first person heightens this sense of intimacy because it gives the impression that the writer is writing about his own relationship with his father.

In many ways, what I'm doing is similar to an actor using the Stanislavskian technique of 'emotion method' or what Lee Strasberg calls 'affective memory' when the actor recalls experiences from their own lives to bring them closer to the emotional experience of their characters. Recalling and using details of things I have experienced personally provokes an emotional, intimate experience during the writing process that develops a vividly imagined and intimate experience for the reader when they read that work.

Reading fiction without truth, and therefore intimacy, is like having a fling with a stranger you've just met at a party then realising, in the cold light of morning, you don't actually like them.

Big Strong Giant

I open the door and there he is. Sitting in my armchair with his linen cap on as if he belongs there, as if it's his home.

'I've got ten minutes son,' he says. And all I can think of is Flash Gordon and his ten minutes to save the universe. Has he got ten minutes to save me? Is this why he's come back?

'I could make you some marmalade sandwiches and a cup a tay,' I say. 'That's doable.'

He smiles. I don't remember him ever smiling except in that one photograph taken on the 14th green after his hole-in-one, which I now keep secretly tucked into the back of a drawer, along with his linen cap.

'I have one memory,' he says. 'We're coming back from the Tonic and yer on my shoulders. Yer singing *Everybody wants to be a Cat* and I'm holding onto yer ankles so you don't fall. Suddenly you stop singing and say, Da … you and me are like one big strong giant.'

I want to spit in his face, tell him about my memories, about the many terrible memories I keep – a wet towel dropped on a bedroom floor, a calloused hand squeezing my throat, a skelp that burns my skin red – but before I have a chance he speaks.

'And we were, son. Weren't we? One big strong giant?'

His eyes fill with water and I realise he hasn't come back to save me, he wants me to save him. I hesitate. But then I feel his hands holding my ankles and hear a child's voice singing *Everybody wants to be a Cat.*

I walk over to him, sit down on the arm of the chair. I take off his cap and kiss the top of his head.

Grease smears my lips.

(First Published by Reflex Fiction, reprinted with permission of the author)

Susannah Dickey

Are we treating intimacy as a synonym for closeness? If we are then I think the self is always going to be an impediment. Here I'm thinking of the self as the internal soliloquy; the silent voice that exists distinct from our external presentation (words and actions and how the world perceives us). I'm picturing two teenagers, forced to hold a balloon between their pelvises while they dance.

A nun or priest or minister or some other paragon of piety stands guard. If the balloon pops, you know their genitals were itching too close. That balloon seems to me to be representative of the self in matters of intimacy. If we could just get rid of it, our groins could truly know each other; curl around each other like otters.

I don't want to speak to any ostensible uniqueness of becoming a person in Northern Ireland, because I never tried to become a person somewhere else, but it seems to me that so much was, and is, going unsaid. What develops in its place is an interiority that belies a kind of intimacy. There's something to be said (ha) for verbalizing, for communication, and yet I still have an inbuilt suspicion of anyone who can vocalise what they're thinking at any given time and then stand by it, not spend a lifetime ruminating over it. Has this got anything to do with intimacy? I'm not sure. If I were to posit the question as to any closeness I have with my protagonist – and here I guess intimacy becomes a synonym for autobiography – then I would say she has the misfortune of sharing my communicative constipation.

The novel for me is a bit about memory, how it is both mutable and fallible. When you're forever cultivating and nurturing the vapours of your own thoughts without ever saying to someone, 'Hey, what if I told you I've been thinking this,' then I think it becomes dangerous. It's a false approximation of intimacy. Maybe that's why the book is written in the second person: a cacophony of 'you's has the potential to create an alarming and internalized hall of mirrors. Ideas and notions and recriminations and fears, all liable to gain new limbs with each reverberation, are just bouncing and bouncing. I think the second person most adequately captures the potential dissociative impact of not communicating with anyone other than yourself. It achieves the necessary simultaneous distancing and closeness for writing trauma – the attached fears and stoicisms. It asks of both its reader and its character: 'You. Yeah, you: are you complicit?'

I owe a huge debt to books like *Rape: A Love Story*, and the short stories of Lorrie Moore ('How to be an Other Woman': 'It sounds dumb. It makes no sense. But it is how you meet'). Obviously *Citizen*, by Claudia Rankine. A book I wish had existed prior to my writing *Tennis Lessons* is *Brass* by Xhenet Aliu. I also owe a debt to Zadie Smith's *NW* for its embedded bildungsroman – a series of vignettes toying with the notion of Kierkegaard's 'moment' and the idea of formative experience, generally. Spiritual eureka and manly valour are replaced with sexual selfactualization, both crucial and bathetic. So much happens in the swathes between text, but what the reader is given are these concentrated moments of intense exposure. It's a piece of writing that achieves a greater intimacy for its sparsity – Natalie's interiority goes subjugated, so we can get closer to her.

In a *Paris Review* interview with Lorrie Moore, following her describing her youth, watching her parents put on amateur productions of plays, the interviewer asks, 'Did you ever act yourself?' The question, I guess, is meant to be, 'Did you ever act, yourself?' and that's how Moore interprets it, but it's a question that maybe risks an examination of the distance between the person and the self.

I think the points at which you can find intimacy with a character change. Vulnerability is a $y = \sin x$ curve with the variables always shifting, the points of contact, shifting. With that in mind *Tennis Lessons* will probably become more and less recognizable to me over time. Tomorrow I might need to read about a character crying at a swan. Who knows?

Wendy Erskine

In real life I am less interested in the couple on the bus having a happy and prolonged kiss than in the two heterosexual men in the gym, one gently touching the other – 'spotting' him – as he struggles to lift a heavy weight. And so, my sad, funny and complicated fictive worlds are rarely demonstrating ecstatic, issue-free, physical contact. Nor are they too interested in the comfortable and repeated physical acts of a couple who have been together for years. In my stories intimacy is nuanced, contingent, absent but desired, perhaps unwanted. I am often drawn to locales – real and fictional – where intimacy between relative strangers is legitimised, such as the beauty salon. Within minutes of meeting, one woman can be tenderly touching the skin of another, skin rarely seen, private skin. I travel a lot by taxi and regard this often as an intimate experience akin to a confessional: the hermetic little space, the talk without being able to look at each other. The stories that unknown drivers have told me, and the ones that I have told them, although usually commonplace, have sometimes been strange, heartfelt and revealing.

The semi-autonomous city state of the home fascinates me: the rules, regulations and customs of the place and the way in which individuals living in close proximity negotiate space and privacy. In one of my stories a teenage girl, Cath, enjoys spending time at her friend's house so that she can observe the complex lives of her friend, her friend's mother, and her friend's mother's boyfriend. She considers the way in which they, in the confined space of the house, are physically: 'Those things in the light were motes and, rarer than rainbows, you only got to see them now and again: fibres from Lauren's jumpers, Kim Cassells' hoodies, flakes of skin, tiny particles of paper, the white dust of dry shampoo, the icing sugar from the buns they ate one time, all moving slowly in the narrow beam of morning light between the curtains. This house was full of the stuff and they all bathed in it.' The story is called 'Observation' and Cath is a sublimated version of me I suppose, since I too am watchful, noticing the tiny ways in which people try to establish connections with others, the light little touch on an arm. I too peer into bedrooms, see the duvet cover that has been chosen, the pyjamas on the floor.

Phil Harrison

Of all the ways we've created to avoid intimacy, sex might be the best.

I write this during the two great turmoils of our present moment: the Coronavirus pandemic and the TV adaptation of Sally Rooney's *Normal People*. Questions of intimacy have been drawn in starker relief; I watch a film and think, 'Those two people are standing too close togeth … oh yeah.' Intimacy has always been our measure. Freud recognised that our desire to be close enough to somebody else, but not too close, was our great struggle, failures of which lay at the heart of most modern anxiety, even most modern illness. Rooney's book, and Lenny Abrahamson's adaptation, brilliantly dramatise the relentlessness with which questions about intimacy – mostly questions which can't quite find expression in words – take up root in us, occupy us, overwhelm us. This is perhaps what makes the sex scenes so visceral – there is both an attempt to connect and the refusal of connection. There is something indefinably sexy about the abandonment of words to actions. Many of the problems people have with sex stem from not being able to 'get out of their own heads', to lose, one might otherwise say, the commentary, the endless narrativising we do in ourselves, to ourselves. It seems to me that in sex – in *Normal People* sex, anyway – there is both a commitment to one's own desire and a commitment to the other. And the question, or the balance, is never quite decidable; it is always, dangerously, swaying. Some of this can be spoken, and is; some cannot. But Rooney's wisdom is in allowing her characters a very real measure of ambivalence – towards themselves, and each other – and this ambivalence fuels, literally – provides energy for – their relationships. Paul Goodman said 'there is no sex without love or its refusal'; Marianne and Connell experience both sides of this equation. But both sides are truthful, necessary even; intimacy depends on it. 'Kindness entails the acknowledgement of hatred', as Barbara Taylor and Adam Phillips put it. 'It is kind to see people as they are, and not as one would like them to be.'

Inevitably, we are in the territory of shame. Shame shatters intimacy, as does its concealment. Shame, of course, must be one of the truest things about us, given its remarkable hold. But it may not be true in the way it claims. Both Marianne's and Connell's shame trap them throughout. But they are wonderfully suspicious of each other's sources. Shame is a sort of tyranny. (Phillips, again: 'Shame is a figure for the mind colonised.') They cannot fix one another (who can?), but they each refuse to credit the part of the other convinced of their own shamefulness. And so, their intimacy, moving back and forth between words and bodies. Writers – good writers, anyway – must wrestle with this contradiction, the necessity to get into words what must necessarily escape them. The hope is that the reader perhaps can bring enough of themselves to keep it moving, to catch the fleeting moment as it bolts. As must lovers.

Michael Hughes

In July 2016, a 31-year-old man called Mohamed Lahouaiej-Bouhlel drove a truck into a crowd celebrating Bastille Day in Nice, killing eighty-six people and injuring hundreds more. My own way to deal with this kind of horror has always been to put myself in the position of the attacker: to sit in the cab of that truck with him and run the events through his eyes, to try to understand what it feels like, what it means, what sense it could possibly make. This time, I didn't get very far.

Talking to a friend who was deeply disturbed by the news, I found myself reaching even further, and invoking my own upbringing, as a Catholic living near the border in Co. Armagh during the seventies and eighties, to help them understand how someone could end up believing that savage, indiscriminate violence against civilians is a proper tactic to adopt in defense of a political ideal. But I walked away from that conversation feeling disturbed. I grew up in a quiet town, in a moderate Nationalist family, and I had never witnessed any of the violence that defined the Northern Ireland conflict. Was I really claiming I could understand what drove members of the IRA to kill, just because I grew up in the same part of the world?

Country was my attempt to answer that question: to see the violence I only knew second-hand through the eyes of those taking part, using the structure of the *Iliad* to dodge the queasiness of fictionalizing real events. And it was very important to me the book presented the intimacy of person-to-person close-quarter violence, as the *Iliad* so graphically does. But *Country* is set in the mid-nineties, and by that stage, the IRA was largely concentrating on commercial and prestige targets, often city centre bombs with prior warnings given. So I allowed the narrative to include a few reflections by the central characters on their past activity, significantly in Dog's abducting of an undercover army intelligence officer, and in the section which details Pig's history as an active IRA member, responsible for the deaths of local police and army reservists. In the latter section I was consciously influenced by my reading of *Lost Lives*, which I found by far the most powerful source I consulted in the writing of the novel. I wanted to catch something of that book's unblinking, uninflected tone, stating the facts concisely, without straining for drama or sensation, and letting any emotion arise in the reader.

Even so, the single incident of violence that seems to produce the strongest reaction from readers isn't even a lethal one: it's the kneecapping of Thirsty. I wonder if what strikes people here is the presence of an audience, the local hangers-on who crowd around to watch. I have no evidence this ever happened – though it wouldn't totally surprise me – but I wanted to gesture towards the reality that this kind of summary justice is impossible without the tolerance and collusion of many in the local community.

Aside from violence, I think of the intimacy presented in the initial relationship between Nellie and Brian (Dog), and in particular their first sex scene. For Nellie, sex is often a tactic. It's clear she wants a relationship with Brian, but her decision to have sex for the first time is strategic, not impulsive. When she makes a similar decision later, to get back together, it's even more explicitly calculated. In this section, I was after a sense that the landscape of intimate relationships was used instrumentally, on all sides: by the RUC in blackmailing Nellie, by Theresa and Achill in their dealings with each other. I wanted to suggest that, in this time and place, you use whatever you have available to your advantage, and equally, that any sentimentality around intimate relationships is a likely to prove a weakness. In fact it's the men who are more likely to fall into sentimentality, about politics, or sex, or their own pride, and that's often at the heart of the violence they inflict, and it's often what leads to their own downfall.

Rosemary Jenkinson

'What do you mean by "To have sex with someone is akin to knowing their genetic blueprint"?' an academic asked me recently.

I immediately realized that the academic in question hadn't slept with many people because, if she had, she would have known that no two people are the same in bed and that every individual is perceptibly unique in word, sigh, touch and mind. For me, sex with a stranger is a mysterious, unpredictable act; it's like unlocking a person's being, just like you unlock DNA. It's a mad rush of blood, saliva, hair and cells, all examined under a writer's microscope. During this act, I'm part animal, part forensic scientist, part chronicler.

The best sexual experience is not just corporeosexual but sapiosexual and spiritosexual, a fusion of body, mind and spirit. I don't need to write about sex, however, to depict intimacy. For instance, in my story *Revival* the narrator forges a mental and spiritual connection with ex-snooker star, Alex Higgins. When I write I often think of Colette's exhortation to look closely at what gives you pleasure in life and look even more closely at what gives you pain. Intimacy is at its most piquant when physical proximity contrasts with an underlying inner loneliness. However, as a writer, it's not so much intimacy I experience as extimacy, as I'm partially in the moment and partially outside observing.

One of the big problems I have is a need for quietness when I write. I'm almost as obsessed by silence as Kafka who said, 'I need solitude for my writing; not 'like a hermit' – that wouldn't be enough – but like a dead man.' Because of it, I prefer to live by myself, and my intimate moments with friends are shorter and more intense now. My parents are dead, so my family intimacies have shrunk too, but the effect is that I'm on closer terms with myself now.

I'm particularly keen on writing first-person narratives which combine storytelling with the writer's own liveliness, humour and reader-wooing charm. Over the years I've found Belfast taxi drivers to be among the greatest storytellers around, as there is something about the movement of travel that equates to the narrative drive of a story; a roadtrip is a mindtrip. My BBC Radio 4 story, *Two People Shorten the Road*, was based on a conversation I had with a taxi driver. Even though the journey was over, I stayed in his taxi listening to the story of one of his passengers who had died and, during those huge, heart-shivering moments, I felt like his soulmate.

Theatre, of course, is a much less intimate medium than prose given that a play is experienced collectively in a large space. That's why I aim for a more political, global dimension in my plays and a more human, local dimension in my stories. As I've now branched out into memoir, I have come to realise that the hardest thing to write of all is self-intimacy.

Bernie McGill

I don't begin a story knowing what's going to happen. For me the starting point is often a voice speaking in a particular place, and nearly always that speaker is a woman. I'm interested in hearing what those characters will say when they are given voice to say it and I'm interested, too, in the language they use, in the codes they construct, in how they translate themselves. The process, to begin with, feels tentative, almost an act of listening. It feels important to gain the trust of the speaker: 'I'm here. Tell me. What is it you want to say?' It's the intimacy of the encounter that draws me in.

I grew up in a rural, working class, Nationalist community in Northern Ireland and that is often the background for the stories I write. I'd say there's always something of me, to a greater or lesser degree, in the fictional women I create. It's even possible, in some cases, to think of their stories as being alternative versions of mine (or of each other's), fictional manifestations of sliding doors moments, 'There but for the grace of God, go I'. Of all the stories I've written, 'The Language Thing' is the one that relates most closely to an experience of my own. Like the first person narrator, I studied Italian (with English) and spent a year in Italy. In March 1988, a friend and Irish speaker who was studying in Germany travelled down to meet me at a time when Northern Ireland featured heavily in the international press. Two plain clothes British soldiers had been brutally killed at the funeral in West Belfast of a man who had himself been killed by a loyalist gunman at the burial of three IRA members in Milltown cemetery who had been shot dead by British forces in Gibraltar, and all within a period of two weeks. From that distance – from any distance – the cycle of violence was dizzying, incomprehensible. It was a difficult time to be away from home, to find ourselves nominated unwilling spokespersons for the situation, to try to answer the questions that were being put to us, about language, about identity, about allegiances, about where we stood. We spent a lot of time insisting that our experiences of growing up in Northern Ireland in the seventies and eighties were normal and, for a long time, I did believe that. I see things with a little more clarity now. There was nothing normal about it.

When I started writing, I wasn't particularly drawn to write about the conflict but more recently, that period in history has occupied my thinking. My story 'There is More Than One Word', anthologised in *Belfast Stories,* centres on a woman who has returned to Belfast having lived abroad and worked for years as a language teacher. She has been drawn back by news of the possible discovery of the remains of her older brother who was 'disappeared' forty-seven years earlier. In some ways, this story could be viewed as a sequel to 'The Language Thing', the reluctant spokesperson thirty odd years on, a linguistic exile returned. It could even be viewed as the fictional consequence of a sliding doors moment for the narrator of another story, 'No Angel', in which a family is traumatised by the death of a young man in a suspected sectarian killing.

It is only with time, a little distance, a certain degree of objectivity that it is possible for me to identify patterns in the stories, hesitant connections to my own experiences. Recently I've been reading Philip Pullman's book *Daemon Voices: Essays on Storytelling* in which he writes about writing (exam-hall style) with the hunched shoulder and the encircling arm in an attempt to protect the work from prying eyes. 'There's something fragile there,' he writes, 'something fugitive'; something which isn't yet strong enough or formed enough to withstand the scrutiny of a stranger. That impulse to guard the work persists. It's still unnerving, even after a story has been published, to relax the arm, to prepare to expose the writing to the reader's analytical gaze.

Roisín O'Donnell

As the saying goes, the body doesn't lie. In writing fiction, I find the most profound intimacy is to step completely into a character's skin and speak through their bodily senses. The truth of a story can often be found in how the character is physically feeling. I see this as developing a true sense of intimacy in my work.

This realisation came to me relatively recently. Perhaps like all beginners, I initially wrote from an external point of view. Even when writing in the first person, my early forays into fiction were mainly focused on describing what the characters saw and heard. I dwelt on dialogue and passages of visual description, without much thought for the characters as physical beings. I was at a workshop taught by Claire Keegan in 2015 when I first heard the idea of writing through the senses, allowing the character's sensory experience to guide your narrative. Keegan gave a beautiful example from her story 'Night of the Quicken Trees'. As with most good advice I've been given in my life, initially I rejected it. Resistant to change, I didn't see how this physically intimate form of writing could make much difference to my prose. But the idea stayed with me, and once I began to employ it, my fiction really began to *work*; which is to say, I began to feel I was crafting stories that felt very real to me, and might potentially feel real to other people too.

The first story I ever wrote with this type of sensory intimacy was 'On Cosmology'. In it, a professor of science at Trinity College has a rather disastrous sexual encounter with an American stranger, and suspects she may have become pregnant. The story follows twenty-four hours of crisis in her life, as she tries to wrap her head around a possible pregnancy. She is honed-in on her physical sensations to a heightened degree, and I allowed her bodily experience to guide the narrative. I didn't plan for her to climb a mountain at the end of the story, but this is what her body wanted to do, as a way of working through her stress and frustration. I didn't know that reaching the summit, hot and breathless, would bring back a childhood memory of loving motherhood that ultimately leaves her feeling calm, having regained control of her racing mind. Writing this story was an entirely new experience. It went on to be shortlisted for a Hennessy award, and featured in my collection *Wild Quiet* (it was one of the last stories I wrote in the collection, and I have kept using this technique for everything I have written since then, including my IBA-winning story 'How to Build a Space Rocket').

As I write this, beside me in bed, my fourteen month old daughter snores. There is no division between my writing and my life at this point. I write from within the rich sensory tapestry of motherhood, my physical sensations spilling onto the page. And at times when I am getting too wordy, too wrapped up in a piece of dialogue or description of a beautiful landscape, I think to myself, *Shut up. What is the character feeling? What is their physical sensation right now?* Perhaps it's a strange kind of beacon, but I let that physical intimacy guide me through.

·

David Park

I spent my childhood and much of my teenage years on the hard pews of a Baptist church. The weaknesses and failures of evangelical religion are well-documented and I subscribe to most of them, but one new thought has struck me recently. In the essence of its theology it's actually an intensely intimate experience. The soul's salvation is achieved not through good works or piety but by asking Jesus into your heart. Into your heart. No priestly hierarchy is required to intercede on your behalf – you have a direct communication with God, personal, intimate and shared with other believers.

However, what ultimately also accompanied my experience of this particular religion was an enduring sense of loneliness. The prevailing idea that the saved were of the world, but not in it, has stayed with me even when I travelled far beyond the boundaries of that faith. At times it felt as if I existed in a kind of limbo world, not belonging to a spiritual world or fully to a secular one. I know now that much of my writing has been about the search for the connection between these two worlds and the profound desire for the intimacy of human connection.

Human intimacy might take a sexual form but equally it can be found in a momentary glance, the slightest of touches, the briefest exchange of words. I think I am always searching for such intimate moments in my writing. Sometimes it is achieved, sometimes it falls short. There is always sadness in failure. In the short story 'Gecko' a married couple celebrate an anniversary by hoping to see the Northern Lights. Although they both love each other there is an undisclosed lie at the heart of their relationship. On the night they hope to see the Lights they are housed in a glass igloo sleeping in single beds. The story ends:

> She rubbed her eyes and asked him if she had missed anything. He said no then stretched out his hand and she stretched hers, the distance between allowing them only to touch at the tips of their fingers.

In intimacy there is often a falling short of the fullness of the heart's desire.

In my writing there are many things that come unasked into the heart – grief as in 'Travelling in a Strange Land' and 'Swallowing the Sun'; parental love as in 'The Light of Amsterdam' and the mystery of the universe itself in 'The Big Snow'. I am also increasingly seeking to find a spiritual image in a secular world, something to which our eyes can be lifted in hope of healing.

I also carry an enduring image from my own childhood that I incorporated into 'The Light of Amsterdam'. Boys who live close in adjoining Belfast streets arrange to signal each other: 'At precisely eleven o'clock when they were supposed to be fast asleep they had flashed their torches in the darkness, thrilled briefly by the returning signals … but then both realised they had no code, no way of actually talking to each other.'

The image of the torches flashing secretly and mysteriously through the Belfast darkness is imbued with a momentary sense of human connection, of the powerful mystery of intimacy however ephemeral and unconsummated it ultimately proves.

Glenn Patterson

The jacket for the paperback of my fifth novel, *Number 5*, featured ripped wallpaper. It was apt: the novel was about a single house and the five families who inhabited it over a fifty-year period. One of the prompts to writing it (aside from the friend who used to refer his novels simply by the order in which they had been written, including the unfortunate Number 2) was the handwriting I found after stripping the paper from the living-room wall of the house I had recently moved into in the late 1990s: 'Leatham Edwards papered this, 19 November 1935'. Which happened to be my Mum's first birthday.

For my next book, *That Which Was*, I actually suggested a jacket image to my publishers and – miraculously – got my way. It was (I only realised later) a variation on the Plastic Ono Band Live Peace in Toronto album cover, though where the former consisted of a single white cloud in one corner of a 12' x 12' square of bright blue sky, my sky – I nearly said book (and might not have been too far wrong) – was a little cloudier, and, unlike the text-free Live Peace image, carried both the title and my name against it in white and orange lettering respectively. I still thought it looked great, and entirely in keeping with a novel whose central character was a Presbyterian minister – 'sky pilot'.

I don't know how many copies the hardback sold, but it was many fewer, clearly, than the publishers had been hoping. They didn't say it was the cover's fault, but for the paperback, and prompted perhaps by reviews referencing attunement to the 'intimacies of local and domestic life', they reverted to ripped wallpaper.

So much for cosmic.

I was already in the habit then of saying I wrote about people living ordinary lives in extraordinary circumstances. Suddenly I thought, no, it wasn't the lives that were ordinary, it was the mayhem of the world that was: wars, financial crises, pandemics … few generations managed to escaped one or other (or other) of them. What was extraordinary was the ability of people to find one another.

Which for some reason reminded me of the *Girona*.

In 1967 divers discovered the wreck of the Spanish Armada-era warship off the coast of Northern Ireland. By the mid 70s, an exhibition of artifacts from the wreck was on display in the Ulster Museum, just across the road from my school. (The Ulster Museum to which my class had been taken one day to hear Seamus Heaney read, by an English teacher who knew him.) The *Girona* exhibition was housed in a specially built display case, at the centre of a dimly (my memory is *barely*) lit circular annex. At the rear of the display, halfway in either direction from the entrance, you were effectively out of sight, and light. It was the point to which every single person I knew – no, wait, every person who was going out, or hoping to go out, with another person – made a beeline, giving the Museum staff the slip (we worked on the wildebeest principle: there were so many of us they couldn't catch is all), as soon as the bell rang to let us out of school for lunch.

> We would stand, looking through the glass, at that centuries' old treasure,
>   letting our fingers point out this thing (a ring with the message 'I have
>   nothing more to give thee') or that thing – look: there … and there …
>   and there … – until – how did that happen? – they touched, and all of
>   recorded history seemed merely
> the
> pre-
> amble
> to that.

Notes

Intimacies, affects, pleasures: An introduction

1 I will, more often than not, use the terms Northern Ireland, Northern Irish and the North, while recognizing that these are loaded, political terms that do not reflect everyone's identity and experiences. I will use these in offhand, absent-minded ways during this book. I may occasionally slip into 'the North of Ireland' but probably not 'the Occupied Six' or 'Carsonia' (with thanks to Stephen O'Neill for all our conversations about this, do make further enquiries to him for a complete list of terms).

2 Whenever I think about writing through the contemporary, I hear Sarah Clancy's poem of this title from *The Truth and Other Stories* (Co. Clare: Salmon, 2014), which deals with the aftermath of the financial crash of 2008 and the policies of economic austerity in the Republic. This poem highlight what it means to *live* despite chronic injustice. Walt Hunter traces Clancy's influences for this poem to Adrienne Rich in *Forms of a World: Contemporary Poetry and the Making of Globalization* (New York: Fordham University Press, 2019).

3 Jocelyn Evans and Jonathan Tonge, 'Partisan and religious drivers of moral conservatism: Same-sex marriage and abortion in Northern Ireland', *Party Politics* 24, no. 4 (2018): 335–46; Lisa Smyth, 'The cultural politics of sexuality and reproduction in Northern Ireland', *Sociology* 40, no. 4 (2006): 663–80.

4 Ann Marie Gray, 'Attitudes to abortion in Northern Ireland', *ARK Research Update* 115 (2017): 1–8; Bernadette Hayes and Andrew McKinnon, 'Belonging without believing: Religion and attitudes towards gay marriage and abortion rights in Northern Ireland', *Religion, State & Society* 46, no. 4 (2018): 351–66.

5 Leanne Calvert, '"He came to her bed pretending courtship": Sex, courtship and the making of marriage in Ulster, 1750–1844', *Irish Historical Studies* 42, no. 162 (2018): 244–64.

6 Sean Brady, 'Why examine men, masculinities and religion in Northern Ireland?', in *Men, Masculinities and Religious Change in Twentieth-Century Britain*, ed. Sue Morgan and Lucy Delap (London: Macmillan, 2013): 218–51.

7 Fiona McCann, *A Poetics of Dissensus: Confronting Violence in Contemporary Prose Writing from the North of Ireland* (Oxford: Peter Lang AG, 2014).

8 Stefanie Lehner, ' "Parallel games" and queer memories: Performing LGBT testimonies in Northern Ireland', *Irish University Review* 47, no. 1 (2017): 103–18.

9 Alison Garden, 'Girlhood, desire, memory, and Northern Ireland in Lucy Caldwell's short fiction', *Contemporary Women's Writing* 12, no. 3 (2018): 306–21.

10 Eli Davies, 'Domestic space and memory: Remembering Deirdre Madden's *One by One in the Darkness* and the Belfast Agreement', *Open Library of Humanities* 4, no. 2 (2018).

11 Sara Ahmed, *Living a Feminist Life* (Durham, NC: Duke University Press, 2017).

12 Anne Mulhall, 'The ends of Irish studies? On whiteness, academia, and activism', *Irish University Review* 50, no. 1 (2020): 94–111.

13 bell hooks, *Feminist Theory: From Margin to Center* (London: Pluto Press, 2000).

14 Audre Lorde, *Your Silence Will Not Protect You* (London: Silver Press, 2017): 22–30.

15 Ahmed, *Living a Feminist Life.*

16 Judith Butler, 'Interview with George Yancy: Mourning is A political act amid the pandemic and its disparities', *Truthout*, 2020, accessed 1 May 2020, https://truthout.org/articles/judith-butler-mourning-is-a-political-act-amid-the-pandemic-and-its-disparities/.

17 Thanks to Stephanie Barnes for our discussions on the disgusting woman in the age of contagion during the writing of her MA dissertation.

18 Thanks to Eli Davies for all the conversations online and in person about the politics of the domestic in Northern Ireland and beyond, particularly over messaging apps during lockdown in spring 2020.

19 This is a term used on social media for the period preceding the Covid-19 pandemic.

20 Rowena Mason, 'Boris Johnson boasted of shaking hands on day sage warned not to', *The Guardian*, 2020, accessed 1 June 2020, https://www.theguardian.com/politics/2020/may/05/boris-johnson-boasted-of-shaking-hands-on-day-sage-warned-not-to.

21 Kimberley Barchard, Stephen Benning and Brian Labus, 'How to stop touching your face to minimize spread of coronavirus and other germs', *The Conversation*, 2020, accessed 1 June 2020, https://theconversation.com/how-to-stop-touching-your-face-to-minimize-spread-of-coronavirus-and-other-germs-133683.

22 Dominic Penna, 'Britons switched from "pleasure-seeking" to "pain-avoiding" mentality during coronavirus pandemic', *The Telegraph*, 2020, accessed 1 June 2020, https://www.telegraph.co.uk/news/2020/05/09/britons-switched-pleasure-seeking-pain-avoiding-mentality-coronavirus/.

23 adrienne maree brown, *Pleasure Activism* (Chico: AK Press, 2019).

1 Intimacy

1 Jennifer Cooke, *Scenes of Intimacy* (London: Bloomsbury, 2013): 3.

2 Appendix.

3 Cooke, *Scenes of Intimacy*, 12.

4 Lauren Berlant, 'Intimacy: A special issue', *Critical Inquiry* 24, no. 2 (1998): 281.

5 Lauren Berlant and Michael Warner, 'Sex in public', *Critical Inquiry* 24, no. 2 (1998): 547–66.

6 Quoted in Eli Davies, 'Domestic space and memory', *Open Library of Humanities* 4, no. 2 (2018).

7 Adam Hanna, *Northern Irish Poetry and Domestic Space* (Basingstoke: Palgrave, 2015): 6.

8 In Davies's forthcoming PhD thesis, her interviews with women about domestic space during the Troubles will provide an invaluable resource for thinking through the politics of domestic and the intimate.

9 Davies, 'Domestic space and memory'.

10 Michael Hughes, *Country* (London: John Murray, 2018), Kindle Edition.

11 Dawn Miranda Sherratt-Bado, 'Keep her country: An interview with Michael Hughes', *Honest Ulsterman*, 2019, accessed 26 July 2019, https://humag.co/features/keep-her-country.

12 Eoin McNamee, '*Country* by Michael Hughes: A hard, rigorous and necessary book', *Irish Times*, 2018, accessed 26 July 2019, https://www.irishtimes.com/culture/books/country-by-michael-hughes-a-hard-rigorous-and-necessary-book-1.3580957.

13 Hughes, *Country*.

14 Appendix.

15 David Roy, 'Co Armagh author Michael Hughes on new Troubles novel *Country*', *Irish News*, 2018, accessed 26 July 2019, https://www.irishnews.com/arts/2018/08/16/news/co-armagh-author-michael-hughes-on-new-troubles-novel-country-1407922/.

16 Florence Impens, *Classical Presences in Irish Poetry after 1960* (Basingstoke: Palgrave, 2018): 106.

17 Personal communication with author.

18 Impens, *Classical Presences in Irish Poetry after 1960*, 104.

19 Kalliopi Nikolopoulou, 'Deserting Achilles reflections on intimacy and disinheritance', *European Journal of English Studies* 9, no. 3 (2005): 231.

20 McNamee, '*Country* by Michael Hughes: A hard, rigorous and necessary book'.

21 Hughes, *Country*.

22 Hughes, *Country*.

23 Hughes, *Country*.

24 Hughes, *Country*.

25 Jayne Steel, *Demons, Hamlets and Femme Fatales: Representations of Irish Republicanism in Popular Fiction* (Bern: Peter Lang, 2007).

26 Hughes, *Country*.

27 Hughes, *Country*.

28 Margaret Ward, *The Missing Sex: Putting Women into History* (Dublin: Attic Press, 1991): 7.

29 Hughes, *Country*.

30 Hughes, *Country*.

31 Hughes, *Country*.

32 Hughes, *Country*.

33 Hughes, *Country*.

34 Hughes, *Country*.

35 Joachim DK Uys and Raymond JM Niesink, 'Pharmacological aspects of the combined use of 3, 4-methylenedioxymethamphetamine (MDMA, ecstasy) and gamma-hydroxybutyric acid (GHB): A review of the literature', *Drug and Alcohol Review* 24, no. 4 (2005): 359–68.

36 Hughes, *Country*.

37 Hughes, *Country*.

38 Hughes, *Country*.

39 Hughes, *Country*.

40 William M. Clarke, 'Achilles and Patroclus in love', *Hermes* 106, no. 3 (1978): 381–96; David M. Halperin, *One Hundred Years of Homosexuality: And Other Essays on Greek Love* (Hove: Psychology Press, 1990).

41 Hughes, *Country*.

42 Hughes, *Country*.

43 Hughes, *Country*.

44 Hughes, *Country*.

45 Michael Longley, *Collected Poems* (London: Jonathan Cape, 2006): 225.

46 Hughes, *Country*.

47 Hughes, *Country*.

48 Nikolopoulou, 'Deserting Achilles Reflections On Intimacy And Disinheritance', 247.

49 Wendy Erskine, *Sweet Home* (Dublin: Stinging Fly, 2018): 154.

50 Joanne Hayden, '"I want to deal with the biggest themes possible" – interview with Wendy Erskine', *Irish Independent*, 2018, accessed 26 July 2019, https://www.independent.ie/entertainment/books/book-news/i-want-to-deal-with-the-biggest-themes-possible-wendy-erskine-37314614.html.

51 Wendy Erskine, 'How a teacher's book of short stories, all set in her native East Belfast and inspired by the likes of smash hits, is already one of the year's standout

debuts', *Belfast Telegraph*, 2018, accessed 26 July 2019, https://www.belfasttelegraph. co.uk/life/books/how-a-teachers-book-of-short-stories-all-set-in-her-native-east-belfast-and-inspired-by-the-likes-of-smash-hits-is-already-one-of-the-years-stand-out-debuts-37301518.html.

52 Hayden, ' "I want to deal with the biggest themes possible" – interview with Wendy Erskine'.

53 Kelly McAllister, 'Belfast's Wendy Erskine on debut short stories collection sweet home', *Irish News*, 2018, accessed 26 July 2019, https://www.irishnews.com/arts/2018/10/18/news/belfast-s-wendy-erskine-on-debut-short-stories-collection-sweet-home-1459153/.

54 Erskine, *Sweet Home*, 201.

55 Erskine, *Sweet Home*, 68.

56 Erskine, *Sweet Home*, 70.

57 Erskine, *Sweet Home*, 141.

58 Erskine, *Sweet Home*, 125.

59 Paula Black, *The Beauty Industry: Gender, Culture, Pleasure* (London: Routledge, 2004): 4.

60 Black, *The Beauty Industry*, 8.

61 Erskine, *Sweet Home*, 7.

62 Black, *The Beauty Industry*, 11.

63 Erskine, *Sweet Home*, 9.

64 Appendix.

65 Erskine, *Sweet Home*, 19.

66 Erskine, *Sweet Home*, 21.

67 Erskine, *Sweet Home*, 26.

68 Erskine, *Sweet Home*, 30.

69 Erskine, *Sweet Home*, 30.

70 Erskine, *Sweet Home*, 35.

71 Erskine, *Sweet Home*, 33.

72 Erskine, *Sweet Home*, 34.

73 Erskine, *Sweet Home*, 75.

74 Erskine, *Sweet Home*, 75.

75 Erskine, *Sweet Home*, 83.

76 Erskine, *Sweet Home*, 76.

77 Erskine, *Sweet Home*, 86.

78 Erskine, *Sweet Home*, 88.

79 Erskine, *Sweet Home*, 92.

80 Erskine, *Sweet Home*, 103.

81 Erskine, *Sweet Home*, 114.

82 Erskine, *Sweet Home*, 89.

83 Wendy Erskine, 'NOTES FOR THE ATTENTION OF THOSE WORKING IN
    THE XANADU NIGHTCLUB, THE HENNESSY COURT HOTEL, BELFAST,
    1983, Found in the pocket of an old handbag when clearing a roof space, 2018', in
    Still Worlds Turning, ed. Emma Warnock (Belfast: No Alibis Press, 2019): 13.

84 Erskine, NOTES FOR THE ATTENTION, 15.

85 Erskine, NOTES FOR THE ATTENTION, 16.

86 Erskine, NOTES FOR THE ATTENTION, 20.

87 Jan Carson, *The Fire Starters* (Dublin: Doubleday Ireland, 2019): 39.

88 Jan Carson, '…Ten years later', *Jan Carson Writes*, 2018, accessed 26 July 2019,
    https://jancarsonwrites.wordpress.com/2018/07/12/ten-years-later/.

89 Carson, *The Fire Starters*, 15.

90 Carson, *The Fire Starters*, 16.

91 Colin Graham, 'Luxury, peace and photography in Northern Ireland', *Visual
    Culture In Britain* 10, no. 2 (2009): 139–54. doi:10.1080/14714780902925077.

92 Greg McLaughlin and Stephen Baker, 'The media, the peace dividend and "bread
    and butter" politics', *Political Quarterly* 83, no. 2 (2012): 292–8.

93 Carson, *The Fire Starters*, 7.

94 Carson, *The Fire Starters*, 9.

95 Lee Henry, 'Jan Carson, keeper of the flames', *The Times*, 2019, accessed 26 July
    2019, https://www.thetimes.co.uk/article/jan-carson-keeper-of-the-flames-
    r8v59gnjf.

96 Carson, *The Fire Starters*, 27.

97 Carson, *The Fire Starters*, 10.

98 Judith Butler, *Gender Trouble* (New York: Routledge, 1990).

99 Carson, 'Writing home', *Kin*, accessed 26 July 2019, https://kinmagazine.co.uk/
    writing-home/.

100 Carson, *The Fire Starters*, 248.

101 Carson, 'Writing home'.

102 Appendix.

103 Henry, 'Jan Carson, keeper of the flames'.

104 Jenny Lee, 'Arts Q&A', *Irish News*, 2019, accessed 26 July 2019,
     https://www.irishnews.com/arts/2019/04/11/news/arts-q-a-belfast-author-jan-
     carson-on-flannery-o-connor-elliott-smith-alfred-hitchcock-1592911/.

105 Irish Times, 'Ep 302 Jan Carson on magic realism, women's voices & politics in the
     North', *Irish Times Women's Podcast*, 2019, accessed 26 July 2019,
     https://soundcloud.com/irishtimes-women/ep-302-optimistic-but-tired-
     is-what-we-all-are-in-the-north-jan-carson.

106 Irish Times, 'Ep 302 Jan Carson on magic realism, women's voices & politics in the
     North'.

107 Dawn Miranda Sherratt-Bado, ' "Things we'd rather forget": Trauma, the troubles, and magical realism in post-agreement Northern Irish women's short stories', *Open Library of Humanities* 4, no. 2 (2018), doi:10.16995/olh.247.

108 Carson, *The Fire Starters*, 65.

109 Carson, *The Fire Starters*, 87.

110 Carson, *The Fire Starters*, 87.

111 Carson, *The Fire Starters*, 85.

112 Deirdre Nuttall and Críostóir MacCarthaigh, 'A 'Protestant folk?" – history Ireland', *History Ireland*, 2017, accessed 26 July 2019, https://www.historyireland. com/volume-25/a-protestant-folk/.

113 Andrew Sneddon and John Privilege, 'The supernatural in Ulster scots literature and folklore reader', Centre for Ulster Scots Studies, University of Ulster, accessed 7 May 2019, https://www.ulster.ac.uk/__data/assets/pdf_file/0011/226595/MAGUS.pdf.

114 Carson, *The Fire Starters*, 246.

115 Maev Kennedy, 'Carthaginians sacrificed own children, archaeologists say', *The Guardian*, 2014, accessed 26 July 2019, https://www.theguardian.com/ science/2014/jan/21/carthaginians-sacrificed-own-children-study.

116 N. Scott Amos, ' "Do to me according to what has gone out of your mouth": A reformation debate on the tragedy of Jephthah and his daughter', *Reformation & Renaissance Review* 21, no. 1 (2019): 3–26, doi:10.1080/14622459.2019.1568369.

117 Carson, *The Fire Starters*, 218.

118 Within the novel, mothers play a secondary role. Sammy's wife is kind and benign but does not take an active role in dealing with their son. The mother of Jonathan's daughter leaves as soon as she has given birth. However, in the novel, action is not necessarily a positive step. Carson notes 'a theme of women being silenced' in the novel but argues that they are actually the 'most balanced, nice characters'.

119 This has been explored by Fidelma Farley in 'In the name of the family: Masculinity and fatherhood in contemporary Northern Irish films', *Irish Studies Review* 9, no. 2 (2001): 203–13.

120 Christopher Vardy, 'Happier days for all of us? Childhood and abuse in death of a murderer', in *Rupert Thomson: Critical Essays*, ed. Rebecca Pohl and Christopher Vardy (London: Gylphi, 2016): 68.

121 This is explored in Ed Cairns, *Caught in Crossfire: Children and the Northern Ireland Conflict* (Syracuse, NY: Syracuse University Press, 1987).

122 Clive Limpkin, *The Battle of Bogside* (Harmondsworth: Penguin, 1972).

123 Alex Thomson, 'Lyra Mckee's partner: Theresa May "derelict in her duties to Northern Ireland" ', *Channel 4 News*, 2019, accessed 26 July 2019, https://www. channel4.com/news/lyra-mckees-partner-theresa-may-derelict-in-her- duties-to-northern-ireland.

124 Henry McDonald, 'Northern Ireland "punishment" attacks rise 60% in four years', *The Guardian*, 2018, accessed 26 July 2019, https://www.theguardian.com/uk-news/2018/mar/12/northern-ireland-punishment-attacks-rise-60-in-four-years.

125 Carson, *The Fire Starters*, 142.

126 Lyra McKee, 'Suicide of the Ceasefire Babies', *Mosaic*, 2016, accessed 26 July 2019, https://mosaicscience.com/story/conflict-suicide-northern-ireland/.

127 Carson, *The Fire Starters*, 37.

128 Hanna, *Northern Irish Poetry and Domestic Space*, 1.

129 Hanna, *Northern Irish Poetry and Domestic Space*, 2.

130 Carson, *The Fire Starters*, 224.

131 Carson, *The Fire Starters*, 202.

132 Carson, *The Fire Starters*, 203.

133 Carson, *The Fire Starters*, 47.

134 Carson, *The Fire Starters*, 269.

135 Carson, *The Fire Starters*, 29.

136 Carson, *The Fire Starters*, 31.

137 Carson, *The Fire Starters*, 31.

138 Carson, *The Fire Starters*, 9.

139 Carson, *The Fire Starters*, 33.

140 Carson, *The Fire Starters*, 34.

141 Carson, *The Fire Starters*, 60.

142 Carson, *The Fire Starters*, 88.

143 Carson, *The Fire Starters*, 66.

144 Carson, *The Fire Starters*, 282.

145 Carson, *The Fire Starters*, 3.

146 Carson, *The Fire Starters*, 161.

147 Carson, *The Fire Starters*, 162.

148 Carson, *The Fire Starters*, 276.

149 Carson, *The Fire Starters*, 288–9.

150 Carson, 'Writing home'.

151 Phil Harrison, *The First Day* (London: Little, Brown Book Group, 2017). Kindle Edition.

152 Harrison, *The First Day*.

153 Harrison, *The First Day*.

154 Harrison, *The First Day*.

155 Harrison, *The First Day*.

156 Brendan Dowling, 'Phil Harrison on finding the joy in the darkness of his new novel', *Public Libraries Online*, 2017, accessed 26 July 2019, http://publiclibrariesonline.org/2017/11/phil-harrison-on-finding-the-joy-in-the-darkness-of-his-new-novel.

157 Harrison, *The First Day*.

158 Peter Hallward, 'Desire – cahiers pour l'analyse (An electronic edition)', *Cahiers. Kingston.Ac.Uk*, accessed 2 July 2019, http://cahiers.kingston.ac.uk/concepts/ desire.html.

159 Harrison, *The First Day*.

160 Harrison, *The First Day*.

161 Harrison, *The First Day*.

162 Harrison, *The First Day*.

163 Harrison, *The First Day*.

164 Harrison, *The First Day*.

165 Harrison, *The First Day*.

166 Harrison, *The First Day*.

167 Camillus John, 'Interview with Phil Harrison: Author of the first day and staunch pats fan', *Litro.Co.Uk*, 2017, accessed 2 July 2019, https://www.litro.co.uk/2017/10/ interview-phil-harrison-author-first-day-staunch-pats-fan/.

168 Rob Kitchin and Karen Lysaght, 'Sexual citizenship in Belfast, Northern Ireland', *Gender, Place & Culture* 11, no. 1 (2004): 86.

169 Harrison, *The First Day*.

170 Harrison, *The First Day*.

171 Harrison, *The First Day*.

172 Harrison, *The First Day*.

173 Harrison, *The First Day*.

174 Lauren Berlant, *Desire/Love* (New York: Punctum Books, 2012): 6.

175 Harrison, *The First Day*.

176 Harrison, *The First Day*.

177 Harrison, *The First Day*.

178 Harrison, *The First Day*.

179 Harrison, *The First Day*.

180 Harrison, *The First Day*.

181 Harrison, *The First Day*.

182 Harrison, *The First Day*.

183 Harrison, *The First Day*.

184 Harrison, *The First Day*.

185 Harrison, *The First Day*.

186 Harrison, *The First Day*.

187 Harrison, *The First Day*.

188 Harrison, *The First Day*.

189 Harrison, *The First Day*.

190 Harrison, *The First Day*.

191 Harrison, *The First Day*.

192 Harrison, *The First Day.*
193 Harrison, *The First Day.*
194 Harrison, *The First Day.*
195 Harrison, *The First Day.*
196 Harrison, *The First Day.*
197 Roland Barthes, 'The metaphor of the eye', *Critical Essays* (1982): 239–48.
198 Sigmund Freud, 'The uncanny', *Standard Edition of the Complete Psychological Works of Sigmund Freud* 17 (1976): 217–56.
199 Harrison, *The First Day.*
200 Harrison, *The First Day.*
201 Harrison, *The First Day.*
202 Harrison, *The First Day.*
203 Harrison, *The First Day.*
204 Harrison, *The First Day.*
205 Harrison, *The First Day.*
206 Harrison, *The First Day.*
207 Harrison, *The First Day.*
208 Harrison, *The First Day.*
209 Harrison, *The First Day.*
210 Harrison, *The First Day.*
211 Harrison, *The First Day.*
212 Harrison, *The First Day.*
213 Lucy Caldwell, *Intimacies* (London: Faber, 2021). Proof copy.
214 Appendix.
215 Caldwell, *Intimacies.*
216 Caldwell, *Intimacies.*
217 Caldwell, *Intimacies.*
218 Caldwell, *Intimacies.*
219 Caldwell, *Intimacies.*
220 Caldwell, *Intimacies.*
221 Caldwell, *Intimacies.*
222 Caldwell, *Intimacies.*
223 Caldwell, *Intimacies.*
224 Caldwell, *Intimacies.*
225 Caldwell, *Intimacies.*
226 Caldwell, *Intimacies.*
227 Caldwell, *Intimacies.*
228 Caldwell, *Intimacies.*
229 Caldwell, *Intimacies.*
230 Caldwell, *Intimacies.*

231 Caldwell, *Intimacies*.

232 Caldwell, *Intimacies*.

233 Caldwell, *Intimacies*.

234 Caldwell, *Intimacies*.

235 Caldwell, *Intimacies*.

236 Caldwell, *Intimacies*.

237 Caldwell, *Intimacies*.

238 Caldwell, *Intimacies*.

239 Caldwell, *Intimacies*.

240 Caldwell, *Intimacies*.

241 Caldwell, *Intimacies*.

242 Caldwell, *Intimacies*.

243 Caldwell, *Intimacies*.

244 Berlant, 'Intimacy: A special issue', 286.

2 Pleasure

1 Laura Frost, *The Problem with Pleasure: Modernism and its Discontents* (New York: Colombia University Press, 2013): 8.

2 Bill Rolston, 'Dealing with the past in Northern Ireland: The current state of play', *Estudios Irlandeses* 8 (2013): 143–9; John D. Brewer and Bernadette C. Hayes, 'Victimhood and attitudes towards dealing with the legacy of a violent past: Northern Ireland as a case study', *British Journal of Politics & International Relations* 17, no. 3 (2015): 512–30.

3 Alexander Beaumont, *Contemporary British Fiction and the Cultural Politics of Disenfranchisement* (Basingstoke: Palgrave, 2015): 2.

4 Eve Sedgwick, *Touching, Feeling: Affect, Pedagogy, Performativity* (Durham: Duke University Press, 2003): 123–53.

5 Robyn Wiegman, 'The times we're in: Queer feminist criticism and the reparative "Turn"', *Feminist Theory* 15 (2014): 11.

6 Frost, *The Problem with Pleasure*, 12.

7 Elizabeth Freeman, *Time Binds: Queer Temporalities, Queer Histories* (Durham, NC: Duke University Press, 2010): xvi.

8 Virginia Woolf, *Mrs Dalloway* (Oxford: Oxford World's Classics, 2000): 27.

9 Lauren Berlant, *Desire/Love* (New York: Punctum Books, 2012): 5.

10 Roland Barthes, *The Pleasure of the Text* (New York: Hill and Wang, 1975): 19.

11 Berlant, *Desire/Love*, 59.

12 Frost, *The Problem with Pleasure*, 7.

13 Heather Love, *Feeling Backward* (Cambridge: Harvard University Press, 2007): 1.

14 Fintan Walsh, 'Saving Ulster from Sodomy and hysteria: Sex, politics and performance', *Contemporary Theatre Review* 23, no. 3 (2013): 292.

15 Tim Hume, 'Farmer orders Rihanna to cover up during risqué video shoot', *The Independent*, 28 September 2011.

16 Clair Wills, *Improprieties: Politics and Sexuality in Northern Irish Poetry* (Oxford: Clarendon Press, 1993): 3.

17 I address the history of sexual violence against women in Northern Ireland in ' "That's not so comfortable for you, is it?": The spectre of misogyny in "The Fall" ', in Fionnaula Dillane, Naomi McAreavey and Emilie Pine (eds), *The Body in Pain in Irish Culture* (Basingstoke: Palgrave, 2016).

18 Appendix.

19 Billy Cowan, *Smilin' Through & Still Ill* (Portsmouth: Playdead Press, 2014): 138.

20 Cowan, *Still Ill*, 158.

21 Cowan, *Still Ill*, 82.

22 Sean Brady, 'Ian Paisley (1926–2014) and the "Save Ulster from Sodomy!" campaign', *Notches Blog*, 2014, accessed 8 April 2016, http://notchesblog.com/2014/09/16/ian-paisley-1926-2014-and-the-save-ulster-from-sodomy-campaign/.

23 Cowan, *Still Ill*, 171.

24 Cowan, *Still Ill*, 196.

25 Cowan, *Still Ill*, 202.

26 Cowan, *Still Ill*, 227.

27 Laura Pelaschiar, 'Transforming Belfast: The evolving role of the city in Northern Irish fiction', *Irish University Review* 30, no. 1 (2000): 117–31.

28 Glenn Patterson, *The Rest Just Follows* (London: Faber, 2014): 58.

29 Patterson, *The Rest Just Follows*, 57.

30 Patterson, *The Rest Just Follows*, 119.

31 Lucy Caldwell, *Multitudes* (London: Faber, 2016): 113.

32 Lucy Caldwell, *Multitudes*, 129.

33 Alison Garden, 'Girlhood, desire, memory, and Northern Ireland in Lucy Caldwell's short fiction', *Contemporary Women's Writing* 12, no. 3 (2018): 315.

34 Lucy Caldwell, *Multitudes*, 126.

35 Rosemary Jenkinson, *Catholic Boy* (Galway: Doire Press, 2018): 127.

36 Clive Everton, 'Alex Higgins, snooker's anti-hero, dies aged 61', *The Guardian*, 2010, accessed 1 December 2019, https://www.theguardian.com/sport/2010/jul/25/alex-higgins-dies-aged-61.

37 Jenkinson, *Catholic Boy*, 7.

38 Jenkinson, *Catholic Boy*, 11.

39 Jenkinson, *Catholic Boy*, 11.

40 Jenkinson, *Catholic Boy*, 67.

41 Jenkinson, *Catholic Boy*, 67.

42 Jenkinson, *Catholic Boy*, 68.

43 Brian Hollywood, 'Dancing in the dark: Ecstasy, the dance culture, and moral panic in post ceasefire Northern Ireland', *Critical Criminology* 8, no. 1 (1997): 62–77.

44 Jenkinson, *Catholic Boy*, 68.

45 Jenkinson, *Catholic Boy*, 69.

46 Jenkinson, *Catholic Boy*, 70.

47 Jenkinson, *Catholic Boy*, 75.

48 Cited in Christian Klesse, 'Bisexual women, non-monogamy and differentialist anti-promiscuity discourses', *Sexualities* 8, no. 4 (2005): 445.

49 Jenkinson, *Catholic Boy*, 15.

50 Jenkinson, *Catholic Boy*, 16.

51 Jenkinson, *Catholic Boy*, 16.

52 Jenkinson, *Catholic Boy*, 19.

53 Jenkinson, *Catholic Boy*, 20.

54 Jenkinson, *Catholic Boy*, 25.

55 Jenkinson, *Catholic Boy*, 27.

56 Jenkinson, *Catholic Boy*, 41.

57 Jenkinson, *Catholic Boy*, 42.

58 Jenkinson, *Catholic Boy*, 78.

59 Jenkinson, *Catholic Boy*, 80.

60 Jenkinson, *Catholic Boy*, 102.

61 Jenkinson, *Catholic Boy*, 105.

62 Jenkinson, *Catholic Boy*, 106.

63 Jenkinson, *Catholic Boy*, 107.

64 Jenkinson, *Catholic Boy*, 111.

65 Jenkinson, *Catholic Boy*, 111.

66 Jenkinson, *Catholic Boy*, 114.

67 Jenkinson, *Catholic Boy*, 118.

68 Jenkinson, *Catholic Boy*, 121.

69 Rosemary Jenkinson, 'Banter and Booze – you can't write about Belfast without them', *Irish Times*, 2016, accessed 2 July 2019, https://www.irishtimes.com/culture/books/rosemary-jenkinson-banter-and-booze-you-can-t-write-about-belfast-without-them-1.2698502.

70 Rosemary Jenkinson, *Lifestyle Choice 10mg* (Galway: Doire Press, 2020): 88.

71 Jenkinson, *Lifestyle Choice 10mg*, 5.

72 I would like to again thank Stephanie Barnes, for her conversations during our supervision meetings on the figure of the 'disgusting woman' in contemporary women's writing.

73 Jenkinson, *Lifestyle Choice 10mg*, 188.

74 Jenkinson, *Lifestyle Choice 10mg*, 7.

75 Jenkinson, *Lifestyle Choice 10mg*, 9.

76 Jenkinson, *Lifestyle Choice 10mg*, 12.
77 Jenkinson, *Lifestyle Choice 10mg*, 12.
78 Jenkinson, *Lifestyle Choice 10mg*, 55.
79 Jenkinson, *Lifestyle Choice 10mg*, 66.
80 Jenkinson, *Lifestyle Choice 10mg*, 57.
81 Jenkinson, *Lifestyle Choice 10mg*, 58.
82 Jenkinson, *Lifestyle Choice 10mg*, 58.
83 Jenkinson, *Lifestyle Choice 10mg*, 69.
84 Jenkinson, *Lifestyle Choice 10mg*, 61.
85 Jenkinson, *Lifestyle Choice 10mg*, 75.
86 Jenkinson, *Lifestyle Choice 10mg*, 112.
87 Jenkinson, *Lifestyle Choice 10mg*, 123.
88 Jenkinson, *Lifestyle Choice 10mg*, 118.
89 Jenkinson, *Lifestyle Choice 10mg*, 111.
90 Jenkinson, *Lifestyle Choice 10mg*, 115.
91 Jenkinson, *Lifestyle Choice 10mg*, 129.
92 Jenkinson, *Lifestyle Choice 10mg*, 132.
93 Jenkinson, *Lifestyle Choice 10mg*, 83.
94 Jenkinson, *Lifestyle Choice 10mg*, 135.
95 Jenkinson, *Lifestyle Choice 10mg*, 139.
96 Jenkinson, *Lifestyle Choice 10mg*, 141.
97 Jenkinson, *Lifestyle Choice 10mg*, 143.
98 Jenkinson, *Lifestyle Choice 10mg*, 145.
99 Jenkinson, *Lifestyle Choice 10mg*, 165.
100 Jenkinson, *Lifestyle Choice 10mg*, 166.
101 Jenkinson, *Lifestyle Choice 10mg*, 170.
102 Jenkinson, *Lifestyle Choice 10mg*, 172.
103 Leanne Byrne, 'Sharp rise in use of overdose-reversing drug', *BBC News*, 2020, accessed 1 April 2020, https://www.bbc.co.uk/news/uk-northern-ireland-51179028.
104 Jenkinson, *Lifestyle Choice 10mg*, 103.
105 Jenkinson, *Lifestyle Choice 10mg*, 105.
106 Jenkinson, *Lifestyle Choice 10mg*, 106.
107 Berlant, *Desire/Love*, 43.

3 Skin

1 Robert McLiam Wilson, *Eureka Street* (London: Vintage, 1997): 20.
2 Abbie Garrington, *Haptic Modernism* (Edinburgh: Edinburgh University Press, 2015): 16.

3 Garrington, *Haptic Modernism*, 47.

4 Constance Classen, *The Book of Touch* (Oxford: Berg, 2005).

5 Marc LaFrance, 'Skin studies', *Body & Society* 24, nos 1–2 (2018): 3–32. doi:10.1177/1357034x18763065.

6 Sara Ahmed and Jackie Stacey, *Thinking through the Skin* (London: Routledge, 2005).

7 Ahmed and Stacey, *Thinking through the Skin*, 1.

8 Ahmed and Stacey, *Thinking through the Skin*, 1.

9 Steven Connor, *The Book of Skin* (London: Reaktion Books, 2009): 27.

10 Ben Allen, 'Fans moved to tears by powerful ending of derry girls finale', *Radio Times*, 2018, accessed 16 July 2019, https://www.radiotimes.com/news/tv/2018-02-09/derry-girls-series-1-finale-viewer-reviews/.

11 Bessel A. Van der Kolk, *The Body Keeps the Score: Brain, Mind, and Body in the Healing of Trauma* (London: Penguin Books, 2015): 99.

12 Van der Kolk, *The Body Keeps the Score*, 53

13 Van der Kolk, *The Body Keeps the Score*, 79.

14 Jackie Stacey, *Teratologies: A Cultural Study of Cancer* (London: Routledge, 2013): 84.

15 Jay Prosser, 'Skin memories', in *Thinking through the Skin*, ed. Sara Ahmed and Jackie Stacey (London: Routledge, 2001): 67.

16 Prosser, 'Skin memories', 52.

17 Richard Haslam, ' "The pose arranged and lingered over": Visualizing the "Troubles"', in *Contemporary Irish Fiction: Themes, Tropes, Theories*, ed. Liam Harte and Michael Parker (Basingstoke: Macmillan, 2000); Elmer Kennedy-Andrews, *Fiction and the Northern Ireland Troubles since 1969: (De-) Constructing the North* (Dublin: Four Courts, 2002).

18 David Park, *Gods and Angels* (London: Bloomsbury, 2016). Kindle Edition.

19 Allen Feldman, *Formations of Violence* (Chicago: University of Chicago Press, 1991): 176.

20 Scott Brewster, 'Rites of defilement: Abjection and the body politic in Northern Irish poetry', *Irish University Review* 35, no. 2 (2004): 304.

21 Gloria Anzaldúa, *Borderlands/La frontera: The New Mestiza* (San Francisco: Aunt Lute, 1987); Wendy Brown, 'Wounded attachments', *Political Theory* 21, no. 3 (1993): 390–410; Mark Seltzer, *Serial Killers: Death and Life in America's Wound Culture* (London: Routledge, 2013); Gilles Deleuze, *Logic of Sense* (London: Bloomsbury, 2004).

22 My thinking of the body as a site of unmaking and remaking was informed by Elaine Scarry's *The Body in Pain: The Making and Unmaking of the World* (USA: Oxford University Press).

23 Ahmed and Stacey, *Thinking through the Skin*, 3.

24 David McKittrick, Seamus Kelters, Brian Feeney, Chris Thornton and David McVea, *Lost Lives: The Stories of the Men, Women and Children Who Died as a Result of the Northern Ireland Troubles* (London: Random House, 2001).

25 Connor, *The Book of Skin*, 51.

26 Connor, *The Book of Skin*, 52.

27 David Runciman, 'I could fix that: Clinton', *London Review of Books* 31, no. 24 (2009), accessed 16 July 2019, https://www.lrb.co.uk/v31/n24/david-runciman/i-could-fix-that.

28 Lewis Perry Curtis, *Apes and Angels* (Washington, DC.: Smithsonian Institution Press, 1971); R. F. Foster, *Paddy and Mr Punch* (London: Penguin Books, 1995).

29 Richard Dyer, *White: Essays on Race and Culture* (London: Routledge, 1997).

30 Michael Walker, 'Northern Ireland's increasing problem with racism', *Amnesty International*, 2018, accessed 13 August 2019, https://www.amnesty.org.uk/blogs/belfast-and-beyond/northern-irelands-increasing-problem-racism.

31 Ruth Gilligan, 'Eimear McBride's Ireland: A case for periodisation and the dangers of marketing modernism', *English Studies* 99, no. 7 (2018): 775–92.

32 Shannon Yee, 'The brightening up side', in *Belfast Stories*, ed. Lisa Frank and Paul McVeigh (Galway: Doire Press, 2019): 148.

33 Yee, 'The brightening up side', 152.

34 Yee, 'The brightening up side', 152.

35 Yee, 'The brightening up side', 155.

36 Yee, 'The brightening up side', 155.

37 Yee, 'The brightening up side', 156.

38 Una Brankin, 'David Park: "I thought it would be easier to write short stories than a novel, but found it a surprisingly difficult change"', *Belfast Telegraph*, 2016, accessed 1 March 2019, https://www.belfasttelegraph.co.uk/life/books/author-david-park-i-thought-it-would-be-easier-to-write-short-stories-than-a-novel-but-found-it-a-surprisingly-difficult-change-34780519.html.

39 Appendix.

40 Park, *Gods and Angels*.

41 Park, *Gods and Angels*.

42 Park, *Gods and Angels*.

43 Park, *Gods and Angels*.

44 Park, *Gods and Angels*.

45 Joanne Sweeney, 'David Park: I wanted to try to delve as deeply as I could into a man's heart and soul"', *Irish News*, 2018, accessed 2 March 2019, http://www.irishnews.com/arts/2018/03/31/news/david-park-i-wanted-to-try-to-delve-as-deeply-as-i-could-into-a-man-s-heart-and-soul-1288709/.

46 Brankin, 'David Park: "I thought it would be easier to write short stories than a novel, but found it a surprisingly difficult change"'.

47 Park, *Gods and Angels*.

48 Park, *Gods and Angels*.

49 Park, *Gods and Angels*.

50 Achsah Guibbory, 'Erotic poetry', in *The Cambridge Companion To John Donne*, ed. Achsah Guibbory (Cambridge: Cambridge University Press, 2006): 142.

51 Park, *Gods and Angels*.

52 Connor, *The Book of Skin*, 99.

53 Park, *Gods and Angels*.

54 Sean O'Connell, 'Violence and social memory in twentieth-century Belfast: Stories of Buck Alec Robinson', *Journal of British Studies* 53, no. 3 (2014): 734–56. doi:10.1017/jbr.2014.76.

55 Park, *Gods and Angels*.

56 Park, *Gods and Angels*.

57 Park, *Gods and Angels*.

58 Park, *Gods and Angels*.

59 Church of England Archbishop's Council, *Common Worship: Services and Prayers for the Church of England* (London: Church House, 2000): 116.

60 National Gallery Online, 'Tenebrism', accessed 16 July 2019, https://www. nationalgallery.org.uk/paintings/glossary/tenebrism.

61 Connor, *The Book of Skin*, 156.

62 Dyer, *White: Essays on Race and Culture*, 13.

63 Park, *Gods and Angels*.

64 Connor, *The Book of Skin*, 160.

65 Park, *Gods and Angels*.

66 Park, *Gods and Angels*.

67 Park, *Gods and Angels*.

68 Park, *Gods and Angels*.

69 Park, *Gods and Angels*.

70 Park, *Gods and Angels*.

71 Park, *Gods and Angels*.

72 Park, *Gods and Angels*.

73 Park, *Gods and Angels*.

74 Park, *Gods and Angels*.

75 Park, *Gods and Angels*.

76 Park, *Gods and Angels*.

77 Park, *Gods and Angels*.

78 Connor, *The Book of Skin*, 24.

79 Park, *Gods and Angels*.

80 Park, *Gods and Angels*.

81 Park, *Gods and Angels*.

82 Park, *Gods and Angels*.

83 Park, *Gods and Angels*.

84 Park, *Gods and Angels*.

85 Park, *Gods and Angels*.

86 Park, *Gods and Angels*.

87 Park, *Gods and Angels*.

88 Park, *Gods and Angels*.

89 Park, *Gods and Angels*.

90 Park, *Gods and Angels*.

91 Park, *Gods and Angels*.

92 Park, *Gods and Angels*.

93 Park, *Gods and Angels*.

94 Park, *Gods and Angels*.

95 Park, *Gods and Angels*.

96 Park, *Gods and Angels*.

97 Ahmed and Stacey, *Thinking through the Skin*, 2.

98 Park, *Gods and Angels*.

99 Park, *Gods and Angels*.

100 Park, *Gods and Angels*.

101 Park, *Gods and Angels*.

102 Ahmed and Stacey, *Thinking through the Skin*, 7.

103 Appendix.

104 Personal correspondence.

105 Rosemary Jenkinson, 'Banter and Booze – you can't write about Belfast without them', *Irish Times*, 2016, accessed 2 July 2019, https://www.irishtimes.com/culture/books/rosemary-jenkinson-banter-and-booze-you-can-t-write-about-belfast-without-them-1.2698502.

106 Rosemary Jenkinson, 'Coronavirus: I feel half between house arrest and solitary confinement', *Irish Times*, 2020, accessed 1 September 2020, https://www.irishtimes.com/culture/books/coronavirus-i-feel-half-between-house-arrest-and-solitary-confinement-1.4340412.

107 Roland Barthes, *A Lover's Discourse: Fragments* (London: Macmillan, 1978): 73.

108 Penelope Deutscher, 'Three touches to the skin and one look', in *Thinking through the Skin*, ed. Sara Ahmed and Jackie Stacey (London: Routledge, 2001): 145.

109 Deutscher, 'Three Touches to the Skin and One Look', 17.

110 Rosemary Jenkinson, *Aphrodite's Kiss and Further Stories* (Limavady: Whittrick, 2016). Kindle Edition.

111 Jenkinson, 'Banter and Booze – you can't write about Belfast without them'.

112 Jenkinson, *Aphrodite's Kiss*.

113 Jenkinson, *Aphrodite's Kiss*.

114 Jenkinson, *Aphrodite's Kiss*.

115 Sinéad Morrissey, *Between Here and There* (Manchester: Carcanet, 2002): 14.

116 Jenkinson, *Aphrodite's Kiss*.

117 Jenkinson, *Aphrodite's Kiss*.

118 Jenkinson, *Aphrodite's Kiss*.

119 Jenkinson, *Aphrodite's Kiss*.

120 Jenkinson, *Aphrodite's Kiss*.

121 Jenkinson, *Aphrodite's Kiss*.

122 Jenkinson, *Aphrodite's Kiss*.

123 Jenkinson, *Aphrodite's Kiss*.

124 Jenkinson, *Aphrodite's Kiss*.

125 Jenkinson, *Aphrodite's Kiss*.

126 Jenkinson, *Aphrodite's Kiss*.

127 Jenkinson, *Aphrodite's Kiss*.

128 Jenkinson, *Aphrodite's Kiss*.

129 Jenkinson, *Aphrodite's Kiss*.

130 Jenkinson, *Aphrodite's Kiss*.

131 Jenkinson, *Aphrodite's Kiss*.

132 Jenkinson, *Aphrodite's Kiss*.

133 Jenkinson, *Aphrodite's Kiss*.

134 Jenkinson, *Aphrodite's Kiss*.

135 Jenkinson, *Aphrodite's Kiss*.

136 Jenkinson, *Aphrodite's Kiss*.

137 Jenkinson, *Aphrodite's Kiss*.

138 Jenkinson, *Aphrodite's Kiss*.

139 Jenkinson, *Aphrodite's Kiss*.

140 Jenkinson, *Aphrodite's Kiss*.

141 Jenkinson, *Aphrodite's Kiss*.

142 Jenkinson, *Aphrodite's Kiss*.

143 Jenkinson, *Aphrodite's Kiss*.

144 Jenkinson, *Aphrodite's Kiss*.

145 Jenkinson, *Aphrodite's Kiss*.

146 Jenkinson, *Aphrodite's Kiss*.

147 Jenkinson, *Aphrodite's Kiss*.

148 Jenkinson, *Aphrodite's Kiss*.

149 Jenkinson, *Aphrodite's Kiss*.

150 Jenkinson, *Aphrodite's Kiss*.

151 Jenkinson, *Aphrodite's Kiss*.

152 Jenkinson, *Aphrodite's Kiss*.

153 Appendix.

154 Bernie McGill, 'Dropping your gaze: A day of mindfulness and writing with Michelle Gibb and Bernie McGill', 2018, accessed 16 July 2019, http://berniemcgill. co.uk/event/dropping-your-gaze-a-day-of-mindfulness-and-writing-with-michelle-gibb-and-bernie-mcgill-at-flowerfield-arts-centre-portstewart/.

155 Bernie McGill, *Sleepwalkers and Other Stories* (Limavady: Whittrick, 2013). Kindle Edition.

156 McGill, *Sleepwalkers*.

157 McGill, *Sleepwalkers*.

158 McGill, *Sleepwalkers*.

159 McGill, *Sleepwalkers*.

160 McGill, *Sleepwalkers*.

161 McGill, *Sleepwalkers*.

162 McGill, *Sleepwalkers*.

163 McGill, *Sleepwalkers*.

164 Prosser, 'Skin memories', 52.

165 McGill, *Sleepwalkers*.

166 McGill, *Sleepwalkers*.

167 McGill, *Sleepwalkers*.

168 Sara Ahmed, *The Promise of Happiness* (Durham: Duke University Press, 2010). Kindle Edition

169 McGill, *Sleepwalkers*.

170 Seamus Heaney, *Opened Ground: Selected Poems, 1966–1996* (London: Macmillan, 1999). Kindle Edition.

171 McGill, *Sleepwalkers*.

172 Ahmed, *The Promise of Happiness*.

173 McGill, *Sleepwalkers*.

174 McGill, *Sleepwalkers*.

175 McGill, *Sleepwalkers*.

176 McGill, *Sleepwalkers*.

177 McGill, *Sleepwalkers*.

178 McGill, *Sleepwalkers*.

179 McGill, *Sleepwalkers*.

180 McGill, *Sleepwalkers*.

181 McGill, *Sleepwalkers*.

182 McGill, *Sleepwalkers*.

183 McGill, *Sleepwalkers*.

184 McGill, *Sleepwalkers*.

185 McGill, *Sleepwalkers*.

186 McGill, *Sleepwalkers*.

187 McGill, *Sleepwalkers*.

188 McGill, *Sleepwalkers*.

189 McGill, *Sleepwalkers*.

190 McGill, *Sleepwalkers*.

191 McGill, *Sleepwalkers*.

192 Appendix.

193 Dawn Miranda Sherratt-Bado, ' "Things we'd rather forget": Trauma, the Troubles, and magical realism in post-Agreement Northern Irish women's short stories', *Open Library of Humanities* 4, no. 2 (2018).

194 Roisín O'Donnell, *Wild Quiet* (Dublin: New Island Books, 2016). Kindle Edition.

195 O'Donnell, *Wild Quiet*.

196 O'Donnell, *Wild Quiet*.

197 O'Donnell, *Wild Quiet*.

198 O'Donnell, *Wild Quiet*.

199 O'Donnell, *Wild Quiet*.

200 O'Donnell, *Wild Quiet*.

201 O'Donnell, *Wild Quiet*.

202 Michiko Iwasaka and Barre Toelken, *Ghosts and the Japanese* (Logan: Utah State University Press, 1994): 13.

203 O'Donnell, *Wild Quiet*.

204 O'Donnell, *Wild Quiet*.

205 O'Donnell, *Wild Quiet*.

206 O'Donnell, *Wild Quiet*.

207 O'Donnell, *Wild Quiet*.

208 Napier, *The Fantastic in Modern Japanese Literature*, 11.

209 O'Donnell, *Wild Quiet*.

210 O'Donnell, *Wild Quiet*.

211 O'Donnell, *Wild Quiet*.

212 O'Donnell, *Wild Quiet*.

213 O'Donnell, *Wild Quiet*.

214 O'Donnell, *Wild Quiet*.

215 O'Donnell, *Wild Quiet*.

216 O'Donnell, *Wild Quiet*.

217 O'Donnell, *Wild Quiet*.

218 O'Donnell, *Wild Quiet*.

219 O'Donnell, *Wild Quiet*.

220 O'Donnell, *Wild Quiet*.

221 O'Donnell, *Wild Quiet*.

222 O'Donnell, *Wild Quiet*.

223 O'Donnell, *Wild Quiet*.

224 O'Donnell, *Wild Quiet.*

225 O'Donnell, *Wild Quiet.*

226 O'Donnell, *Wild Quiet.*

227 O'Donnell, *Wild Quiet.*

228 O'Donnell, *Wild Quiet.*

229 O'Donnell, *Wild Quiet.*

230 O'Donnell, *Wild Quiet.*

231 O'Donnell, *Wild Quiet.*

232 O'Donnell, *Wild Quiet.*

233 O'Donnell, *Wild Quiet.*

234 Virginia Braun, '"Proper sex without annoying things": Anti-condom discourse and the "nature" of (hetero) sex', *Sexualities* 16, nos 3–4 (2013): 361–82.

235 O'Donnell, *Wild Quiet.*

236 Ahmed and Stacey, *Thinking through the Skin*, 15.

4 *Milkman*

1 Burns's earlier writing is particularly well explored in the work of Fiona McCann, particularly 'The good terrorist(s)'? Interrogating gender and violence in Ann Devlin's 'Naming the Names' and Anna Burns' No Bones', *Estudios Irlandeses* 7 (2012): 69–78.

2 Seán Hewitt, 'Anna Burns's first two novels: Bold, terrifying, funny, profound', *Irish Times*, 2018, accessed 14 September 2019, https://www.irishtimes.com/culture/books/anna-burns-s-first-two-novels-bold-terrifying-funny-profound-1.3729146.

3 Alison Flood, 'Booker winner *Milkman* defies "challenging" reputation to become bestseller', *The Guardian*, 2018, accessed 14 September 2019, https://www.theguardian.com/books/2018/oct/23/booker-winner-milkman-defies-challenging-bestseller-anna-burns.

4 Claire Kilroy, '*Milkman* review – creepy invention at heart of an original, funny novel', *The Guardian*, 2018, accessed 14 September 2019, https://www.theguardian.com/books/2018/may/31/milkman-anna-burns-review-northern-ireland.

5 Ron Charles, '"Milkman" – one of the most challenging books of the year – is also one of the most rewarding', *Washington Post*, 2018, accessed 14 September 2019, https://www.washingtonpost.com/entertainment/books/milkman--one-of-the-most-challenging-books-of-the-year--is-also-one-of-the-most-rewarding/2018/12/04/c3be904c-f764-11e8-8c9a-860ce2a8148f_story.html?noredirect=on&utm_term=.004d58a4d771.

6 Laura Miller, 'A novel about coming of age amid the Troubles', *New Yorker*, 2018, accessed 14 September 2019, https://www.newyorker.com/magazine/2018/12/10/a-novel-about-coming-of-age-amid-the-troubles.

7 Dwight Garner, ' "Milkman" slogs through political and cultural tensions in Northern Ireland', *New York Times*, 2018, accessed 14 September 2019, https://www.nytimes.com/2018/12/03/books/review-milkman-anna-burns-man-booker-prize-winner.html.

8 Flood, 'Booker winner *Milkman* defies "challenging" reputation to become bestseller'.

9 Ruth Gilligan, 'Eimear McBride's Ireland: A case for periodisation and the dangers of marketing modernism', *English Studies* 99, no. 7 (2018): 776.

10 In this chapter, Middle Sister's name will be capitalized to reflect her status as the novel's protagonist. In the novel, none of the terms used to refer to the characters are capitalized, except for Milkman.

11 Anna Burns, *Milkman* (London: Faber & Faber, 2018). Kindle Edition.

12 Sara Ahmed, *Living a Feminist Life* (Durham, NC: Duke University Press, 2017). Kindle Edition.

13 Eve Kosofsky Sedgwick, Adam Frank, and Irving E. Alexander, eds. *Shame and Its Sisters* (Durham, NC: Duke University Press, 1995).

14 Ann Cvetkovich, *Depression: A Public Feeling* (Durham, NC: Duke University Press, 2012): 5.

15 Cvetkovich, *Depression: A Public Feeling*, 4.

16 Melissa Gregg and Gregory J. Seigworth, *The Affect Theory Reader* (Durham, NC: Duke University Press, 2011): 1.

17 Cvetkovich, *Depression: A Public Feeling*, 2.

18 Lisa Allardice, ' "It's nice to feel I'm solvent. That's a huge gift": Anna Burns on her life-changing Booker win', *The Guardian*, 2018, accessed 14 September 2019, https://www.theguardian.com/books/2018/oct/17/anna-burns-booker-prize-winner-life-changing-interview.

19 Richard Martin, ' "Non specific threat (production still) 2003", Willie Doherty, 2007', *Tate*, accessed 14 September 2019, https://www.tate.org.uk/art/artworks/doherty-non-specific-threat-production-still-2003-p79361.

20 Burns, *Milkman*.

21 Burns, *Milkman*.

22 Burns, *Milkman*.

23 Burns, *Milkman*.

24 Kaye Mitchell, 'Cleaving to the scene of shame: Stigmatized childhoods in *The End of Alice* and *Two Girls, Fat and Thin*', *Contemporary Women's Writing* 7, no. 3 (2012): 311.

25 Media Mole, 'Will Self knocks "simple" Sally Rooney – in interview plugging his promotional macarons', *New Statesman*, 2019, accessed 14 September 2019, https://www.newstatesman.com/politics/media/2019/02/will-self-knocks-simple-sally-rooney-interview-plugging-his-promotional.

26 Burns, *Milkman*.

27 Ahmed, *Living a Feminist Life*.

28 Burns, *Milkman*.

29 Ahmed, *Living a Feminist Life*.

30 Lauren Berlant, *Cruel Optimism* (Durham, NC: Duke University Press, 2012): 49

31 Burns, *Milkman*.

32 Ahmed, *The Promise of Happiness*.

33 Burns, *Milkman*.

34 Claire Henry, *Revisionist Rape-Revenge: Redefining a Film Genre* (London: Palgrave Macmillan, 2016).

35 Burns, *Milkman*.

36 Burns, *Milkman*.

37 Burns, *Milkman*.

38 Ahmed, *Living a Feminist Life*.

39 Burns, *Milkman*.

40 Katie Markham, 'Touring the post-conflict city', *Emotion, Affective Practices, and the Past in the Present*, ed. Gary Campbell, Laurajane Smith and Margaret Wetherell (London: Routledge, 2018): 17.

41 Ahmed, *The Promise of Happiness*.

42 Ahmed, *Living a Feminist Life*.

43 Burns, *Milkman*.

44 Burns, *Milkman*.

45 Burns, *Milkman*.

46 Marisol Morales-Ladrón, '*Milkman* by Anna Burns: Silence as an architectural form of containment', *Irish Times*, 2019, accessed 14 September 2019, https://www.irishtimes.com/culture/books/milkman-by-anna-burns-silence-as-an-architectural-form-of-containment-1.3988554.

47 Audre Lorde, *Your Silence Will Not Protect You* (London: Silver Press, 2017): 2.

48 Lorde, *Your Silence Will Not Protect You*, 3.

49 Lorde, *Your Silence Will Not Protect You*, 3.

50 Burns, *Milkman*.

51 Burns, *Milkman*.

52 Burns, *Milkman*.

53 Burns, *Milkman*.

54 Ahmed, *Living a Feminist Life*.

55 Allardice, ' "It's nice to feel I'm solvent. That's a huge gift": Anna Burns on her life-changing Booker win'.

56 Ahmed, *Living a Feminist Life*.

57 Elmer Kennedy-Andrews, *Fiction and the Northern Ireland Troubles since 1969: (De-)Constructing the North* (Dublin: Four Courts, 2002): 89.

58 Burns, *Milkman*.

59 Burns, *Milkman*.

60 Burns, *Milkman*.

61 C. C. Kelleher, 'Mental health and "the Troubles" in Northern Ireland: Implications of civil unrest for health and wellbeing', *Journal of Epidemiology & Community Health* (2003): 474–5.

62 Cvetkovich, *Depression: A Public Feeling*, 7.

63 Burns, *Milkman*.

64 Burns, *Milkman*.

65 Burns, *Milkman*.

66 Frederick Studemann, 'Man Booker winner Anna Burns on lessons from the "powder keg"', *Financial Times*, 2018, accessed 14 September 2019, https://www. ft.com/content/67502218-d2b5-11e8-a9f2-7574db66bcd5.

67 Burns, *Milkman*.

68 Burns, *Milkman*.

69 Burns, *Milkman*.

70 Burns, *Milkman*.

71 RTÉ, 'Inquiry finds widespread abuse of children in care', *RTÉ*, 2017, accessed 14 September 2019, https://www.rte.ie/news/2017/0120/846364-inquiry-into-alleged-child-abuse-to-publish-report/.

72 Burns, *Milkman*.

73 Burns, *Milkman*.

74 Burns, *Milkman*.

75 Burns, *Milkman*.

76 Burns, *Milkman*.

77 Burns, *Milkman*.

78 Burns, *Milkman*.

79 Burns, *Milkman*.

80 Burns, *Milkman*.

81 Burns, *Milkman*.

82 Burns, *Milkman*.

83 Burns, *Milkman*.

84 Allardice, ' "It's nice to feel I'm solvent. That's a huge gift": Anna Burns on her life-changing Booker win'.

85 Ahmed, *Living a Feminist Life*.

86 Burns, *Milkman*.

87 Ahmed, *Living a Feminist Life*.

88 Burns, *Milkman*.

89 Burns, *Milkman*.

90 Burns, *Milkman*.

91 Burns, *Milkman*.

92 Burns, *Milkman*.

93 Ahmed, *Living a Feminist Life*.

94 Burns, *Milkman*.

95 Alex Marshall, 'Anna Burns: The new Booker Prize winner who may never write again', *The Independent*, 2019, accessed 14 September 2019, https://www.independent.co.uk/arts-entertainment/books/features/anna-burns-interview-milkman-booker-prize-winner-2018-next-book-writer-a8661321.html.

96 Burns, *Milkman*.

97 Burns, *Milkman*.

98 Burns, *Milkman*.

99 Burns, *Milkman*.

100 Paul McVeigh, 'Anna Burns: The Booker winner on why she is unable to write', *Irish Times*, 2018, accessed 14 September 2019, https://www.irishtimes.com/culture/books/anna-burns-the-booker-winner-on-why-she-is-unable-to-write-1.3726472.

101 David Berceli, Melanie Salmon, Robin Bonifas and Nkem Ndefo, 'Effects of self-induced unclassified therapeutic tremors on quality of life among non-professional caregivers: A pilot study', *Global Advances in Health and Medicine* 3, no. 5 (2014): 46.

102 Berceli, Salmon, Bonifas and Ndefo, 'Effects of self-induced unclassified therapeutic tremors on quality of life among non-professional caregivers: A pilot study', 48.

103 Anna Burns, 'Man Booker writers on the books that have inspired them', *Vanity Fair*, 2018, accessed 14 September 2019, https://www.vanityfair.com/london/2018/09/man-booker-writers-on-the-books-that-have-inspired-them-what-to-read.

104 Burns, 'Man Booker writers on the books that have inspired them'.

105 James Dunn, 'A Northern Irish priest says yoga is a surefire way to hell', *The Independent*, 2015, accessed 14 September 2019, https://www.independent.co.uk/news/uk/home-news/yoga-leads-to-satan-says-northern-ireland-priest-10061463.html.

106 B. K. S. Iyengar, *Light on Yoga* (London: HarperCollins, 2015): 1.

107 Burns, 'Man Booker writers on the books that have inspired them'.

108 Iyengar, *Light on Yoga*, xii.

109 Burns, 'Man Booker writers on the books that have inspired them'.

110 Burns, 'Man Booker writers on the books that have inspired them.'

111 Burns, *Milkman*.

112 Burns, *Milkman*.

113 Burns, *Milkman*.

114 Burns, *Milkman*.

115 Henry McDonald, 'Sober Mayor bans "lustful" charity ball', *The Guardian*, 2003, accessed 14 September 2019, https://www.theguardian.com/uk/2003/feb/23/ northernireland1.

116 Jan Carson, 'No dancing', in *Winter Papers 4*, ed. Ken Barry and Olivia Smith (Curlew: Sligo, 2018): 70–6.

117 Carson, 'No dancing', 75.

118 Carson, 'No dancing', 76.

119 Ahmed, *Living a Feminist Life*.

120 Burns, *Milkman*.

121 Ahmed, *Living a Feminist Life*.

122 Burns, *Milkman*.

123 Nick Ripatrazone, 'Why do so many writers love to run?', *The Atlantic*, 2015, accessed 14 September 2019, https://www.theatlantic.com/entertainment/ archive/2015/11/why-writers-run/415146/.

124 Burns, *Milkman*.

125 Nell Wulfhart, 'Running the world: Belfast', *Runner's World*, 2017, accessed 14 September 2019, https://www.runnersworld.com/races-places/g20848842/ running-the-world-belfast/.

126 Burns, *Milkman*.

127 Burns, *Milkman*.

128 Mark Fisher, *Capitalist Realism* (Winchester: Zero Books, 2010): 81.

Open endings

1 Suzannah Dickey, *Tennis Lessons* (London: Penguin, 2020): 137.

2 Dickey, *Tennis Lessons*, 35.

3 Appendix.

4 Dickey, *Tennis Lessons*, 1.

5 Dickey, *Tennis Lessons*, 11.

6 Dickey, *Tennis Lessons*, 229.

7 Dickey, *Tennis Lessons*, 51.

8 Dickey, *Tennis Lessons*, 67.

9 Dickey, *Tennis Lessons*, 67.

10 Dickey, *Tennis Lessons*, 165.

11 Dickey, *Tennis Lessons*, 103.

12 Dickey, *Tennis Lessons*, 222.

13 Dickey, *Tennis Lessons*, 183.

14 Dickey, *Tennis Lessons*, 237.

15 Morrissey, *Between Here and There*, 13.

16 Rosemary Jenkinson, 'Coronavirus: I feel half between house arrest and solitary confinement', *Irish Times* 2020, accessed 1 September 2020, https://www.irishtimes.com/culture/books/coronavirus-i-feel-half-between-house-arrest-and-solitary-confinement-1.4340412.

17 Rosemary Jenkinson, 'Coronavirus: I feel half between house arrest and solitary confinement'

18 Jenkinson, *Catholic Boy*, 27.

References

Ahmed, Sara. *Living a Feminist Life*. Durham, NC: Duke University Press, 2017. Kindle Edition.

Ahmed, Sara. *The Promise of Happiness*. Durham, NC: Duke University Press, 2010. Kindle Edition.

Ahmed, Sara, and Jackie Stacey. *Thinking through the Skin*. London: Routledge, 2005.

Alcobia-Murphy, Shane. '"Snared by words": Trauma and the shoah in the poetry of Medbh McGuckian'. *Études Irlandaises* 36, no. 1 (2011): 109–20.

Allardice, Lisa. '"It's nice to feel I'm solvent. That's a huge gift": Anna burns on her life changing Booker win'. *The Guardian*. 2018. Accessed 14 September 2019. https://www.theguardian.com/books/2018/oct/17/anna-burns-booker-prize-winner-life-changing-interview.

Allen, Ben. 'Fans moved to tears by powerful ending of derry girls finale'. *Radio Times*. 2018. Accessed 16 July 2019. https://www.radiotimes.com/news/tv/2018-02-09/derry-girls-series-1-finale-viewer-reviews/.

Amos, N. Scott. '"Do to me according to what has gone out of your mouth": A reformation debate on the tragedy of Jephthah and his daughter'. *Reformation & Renaissance Review* 21, no. 1 (2019): 3–26. doi:10.1080/14622459.2019.1568369.

Anzaldúa, Gloria. *Borderlands/La frontera: The New Mestiza*. San Francisco: Aunt Lute, 1987.

Barchard, Kimberly, Stephen Benning and Brian Labus. 'How to stop touching your face to minimize spread of coronavirus and other germs'. *The Conversation*. 2020. Accessed 1 June 2020. https://theconversation.com/how-to-stop-touching-your-face-to-minimize-spread-of coronavirus-and-other-germs-133683.

Barthes, Roland. *A Lover's Discourse: Fragments*. London: Macmillan, 1978.

Barthes, Roland. 'The metaphor of the eye'. *Critical Essays* (1982): 239–48.

Barthes, Roland. *The Pleasure of the Text*. New York: Hill and Wang, 1975.

Beaumont, Alexander. *Contemporary British Fiction and the Cultural Politics of Disenfranchisement*. Basingstoke: Palgrave, 2015.

Beckett, Mary. *Give Them Stones*. New York: Beech Tree Books, 1987.

Berceli, David, Melanie Salmon, Robin Bonifas and Nkem Ndefo. 'Effects of self-induced unclassified therapeutic tremors on quality of life among non-professional caregivers: A pilot study'. *Global Advances in Health and Medicine* 3, no. 5 (2014): 45–8.

Berlant, Lauren. *Cruel Optimism*. Durham: Duke University Press, 2012.

Berlant, Lauren. *Desire/Love*. New York: Punctum Books, 2012.

Berlant, Lauren. 'Intimacy: A special issue'. *Critical Inquiry* 24, no. 2 (1998): 281–8.

Berlant, Lauren, and Michael Warner. 'Sex in public'. *Critical Inquiry* 24, no. 2 (1998): 547–66.

Black, Paula. *The Beauty Industry: Gender, Culture, Pleasure*. London: Routledge, 2004.

Brady, Sean. 'Ian Paisley (1926–2014) and the "Save Ulster From Sodomy!" campaign'. *Notches Blog*. 2014. Accessed 8 April 2016. http://notchesblog.com/2014/09/16/ian-paisley-1926-2014-and-the-save-ulster-from-sodomy-campaign/.

Brady, Sean. 'Why examine men, masculinities and religion in Northern Ireland?' In *Men, Masculinities and Religious Change in Twentieth-Century Britain*. Ed. Lucy Delap and Sue Morgan. Basingstoke: Palgrave, 2013: 218–51.

Brankin, Una. 'David Park: "I thought it would be easier to write short stories than a novel, but found it a surprisingly difficult change"'. *Belfast Telegraph*. 2016. Accessed 1 March 2019. https://www.belfasttelegraph.co.uk/life/books/author-david-park-i-thought-it-would-be-easier-to-write-short-stories-than-a-novel-but-found-it-a-surprisingly-difficult-change-34780519.html.

Braun, Virginia. '"Proper sex without annoying things": Anti-condom discourse and the "nature" of (hetero) sex'. *Sexualities* 16, nos. 3–4 (2013): 361–82.

Brewer, John, and Bernadette C. Hayes, 'Victimhood and attitudes towards dealing with the legacy of a violent past: Northern Ireland as a case study'. *British Journal of Politics & International Relations* 17, no. 3 (2015): 512–30.

Brewster, Scott. 'Rites of defilement: Abjection and the body politic in Northern Irish poetry'. *Irish University Review* 35, no. 2 (2005): 304–19.

brown, adrienne maree. *Pleasure Activism*. Chico: AK Press, 2019.

Brown, Wendy. 'Wounded attachments'. *Political Theory* 21, no. 3 (1993): 390–410.

Burns, Anna. 'Man booker writers on the books that have inspired them'. *Vanity Fair*. 2018. Accessed 14 September 2019. https://www.vanityfair.com/london/2018/09/man-booker-writers-on-the-books-that-have-inspired-them-what-to-read.

Burns, Anna. *Milkman*. London: Faber & Faber, 2018. Kindle Edition.

Butler, Judith. *Gender Trouble*. New York: Routledge, 1990.

Butler, Judith. 'Interview with George Yancy: Mourning is a political act amid the pandemic and its disparities'. *Truthout*. 2020. Accessed 1 May 2020. https://truthout.org/articles/judith-butler-mourning-is-a-political-act-amid-the-pandemic-and-its-disparities/.

Byrne, Leanna. 'Sharp rise in use of overdose-reversing drug'. *BBC News*. 2020. Accessed 1 April 2020. https://www.bbc.com/news/uk-northern-ireland-51179028.

Cairns, Ed. *Caught in Crossfire: Children and the Northern Ireland Conflict*. Syracuse, NY: Syracuse University Press, 1987.

Caldwell, Lucy. *Intimacies*. London: Faber, 2021. Proof copy.

Caldwell, Lucy. *Multitudes*. London: Faber, 2016.

Calvert, Leanne. '"He came to her bed pretending courtship": Sex, courtship and the making of marriage in Ulster, 1750–1844'. *Irish Historical Studies* 42, no. 162 (2018): 244–64.

Carson, Jan. *The Fire Starters*. Dublin: Doubleday Ireland, 2019.

Carson, Jan. 'No dancing'. In *Winter Papers 4*. Ed. Ken Barry and Olivia Smith. Curlew: Sligo, 2018: 70–6.

Carson, Jan. '… Ten years later'. *Jan Carson Writes*. 2018. Accessed 26 July 2019. https://jancarsonwrites.wordpress.com/2018/07/12/ten-years-later/.

Carson, Jan. 'Writing home'. *Kin*. Accessed 26 July 2019. https://kinmagazine.co.uk/writing-home/.

Charles, Ron. '"Milkman" – one of the most challenging books of the year – is also one of the most rewarding'. *Washington Post*. 2018. Accessed 14 September 2019. https://www.washingtonpost.com/entertainment/books/milkman--one-of-the-most-challenging-books-of-the-year--is-also-one-of-the-most-rewarding/2018/12/04/c3be904c-f764-11e8-8c9a-860ce2a8148f_story.html.

Church of England Archbishop's Council. *Common Worship: Services and Prayers for the Church of England*. London: Church House, 2000.

Clancy, Sarah. *The Truth & Other Stories*. Co. Clare: Salmon, 2014.

Clarke, William M. 'Achilles and Patroclus in love'. *Hermes* 106, no. 3 (1978): 381–96.

Classen, Constance. *The Book of Touch*. Oxford: Berg, 2005.

Connor, Steven. *The Book of Skin*. London: Reaktion Books, 2009.

Cooke, Jennifer. *Scenes of Intimacy*. London: Bloomsbury, 2013.

Cowan, Billy. *Smilin' Through & Still Ill*. Portsmouth: Playdead Press, 2014.

Curtis, Lewis Perry. *Apes and Angels*. Washington: Smithsonian Institution Press, 1971.

Cvetkovich, Ann. *Depression: A Public Feeling*. Durham, NC: Duke, 2012.

Davies, Eli. 'Domestic space and memory: Remembering Deirdre Madden's *One by One in the Darkness* and the Belfast Agreement'. *Open Library of Humanities* 4, no. 2 (2018).

Deleuze, Gilles. *Logic of Sense*. London: Bloomsbury, 2004.

Deutscher, Penelope. 'Three touches to the skin and one look'. In *Thinking through the Skin*. Ed. Sara Ahmed and Jackie Stacey. London: Routledge, 2001: 143–59.

Dickey, Susannah. *Tennis Lessons*. London: Penguin, 2020. Proof copy.

Dowling, Brendan. 'Phil Harrison on finding the joy in the darkness of his new novel'. *Public Libraries Online*. 2017. Accessed 26 July 2019. http://publiclibrariesonline.org/2017/11/phil-harrison-on-finding-the-joy-in-the-darkness-of-his-new-novel/.

Dunn, James. 'A Northern Irish priest says yoga is a surefire way to hell'. *The Independent*. 2015. Accessed 14 September 2019. https://www.independent.co.uk/news/uk/home-news/yoga-leads-to-satan-says-northern-ireland-priest-10061463.html.

Dyer, Richard. *White: Essays on Race and Culture*. London: Routledge, 1997.

Erskine, Wendy. 'How a teacher's book of short stories, all set in her native East Belfast and inspired by the likes of smash hits, is already one of the year's standout debuts'. *Belfast Telegraph*. 2018. Accessed 26 July 2019. https://www.belfasttelegraph.co.uk/life/books/how-a-teachers-book-of-short-stories-all-set-in-her-native-east-belfast-

and-inspired-by-the-likes-of-smash-hits-is-already-one-of-the-years-standout-
    debuts-37301518.html.

Erskine, Wendy. 'NOTES FOR THE ATTENTION OF THOSE WORKING IN THE
    XANADU NIGHTCLUB, THE HENNESSY COURT HOTEL, BELFAST, 1983,
    found in the pocket of an old handbag when clearing a roof space, 2018'. In *Still
    Worlds Turning*. Ed. Emma Warnock. Belfast: No Alibis Press, 2019.

Erskine, Wendy. *Sweet Home*. Dublin: Stinging Fly, 2018.

Evans, Jocelyn, and Jonathan Tonge. 'Partisan and religious drivers of moral
    conservatism: Same-sex marriage and abortion in Northern Ireland'. *Party Politics*
    24, no. 4 (2018): 335–46.

Everton, Clive. 'Alex Higgins, snooker's anti-hero, dies aged 61'. *The Guardian*. 2010.
    Accessed 1 December 2019. https://www.theguardian.com/sport/2010/jul/25/
    alex-higgins-dies-aged-61.

Farley, Fidelma. 'In the name of the family: Masculinity and fatherhood in
    contemporary Northern Irish films'. *Irish Studies Review* 9, no. 2 (2001): 203–13.

Feldman, Allen. *Formations of Violence*. Chicago: University of Chicago Press, 1991.

Fisher, Mark. *Capitalist Realism*. Winchester: Zero Books, 2010.

Flatley, Jonathan. *Affective Mapping: Melancholia and the Politics of Modernism*.
    Cambridge: Harvard University Press, 2009.

Flood, Alison. 'Booker winner *Milkman* defies "challenging" reputation to become
    bestseller'. *The Guardian*. 2018. Accessed 14 September 2019. https:// www.
    theguardian.com/books/2018/oct/23/booker-winner-milkman-defies-
    challenging-bestseller-anna-burns.

Foster, R. F. *Paddy and Mr Punch*. London: Penguin Books, 1995.

Freeman, Elizabeth. *Time Binds: Queer Temporalities, Queer Histories*. Durham,
    NC: Duke, 2010.

Freud, Sigmund. 'The uncanny'. *The Standard Edition of the Complete Psychological
    Works of Sigmund Freud* 17 (1976): 217–56.

Frost, Laura. *The Problem with Pleasure*. New York: Colombia University Press, 2013.

Garden, Alison. 'Girlhood, desire, memory, and Northern Ireland in Lucy Caldwell's
    short fiction'. *Contemporary Women's Writing* 12, no. 3 (2018): 306–21.

Garner, Dwight. '"Milkman" slogs through political and cultural tensions in Northern
    Ireland'. *New York Times*. 2018. Accessed 14 September 2019. https://www.nytimes.
    com/2018/12/03/books/review-milkman-anna-burns-man-booker-prize-winner.
    html.

Garratt, Robert F. *Trauma and History in the Irish Novel: The Return of the Dead*.
    New York: Palgrave Macmillan, 2011.

Garrington, Abbie. *Haptic Modernism*. Edinburgh: Edinburgh University Press, 2015.

Gilligan, Chris. *Northern Ireland and the Crisis of Anti-racism: Rethinking Racism and
    Sectarianism*. Manchester: Manchester University Press, 2017.

Gilligan, Ruth. 'Eimear McBride's Ireland: A case for periodisation and the dangers of
    marketing modernism'. *English Studies* 99, no. 7 (2018): 775–92.

Graham, Colin. 'Luxury, peace and photography in Northern Ireland'. *Visual Culture in Britain* 10, no. 2 (2009): 139–54. doi:10.1080/14714780902925077.

Gray, Ann Marie. 'Attitudes to abortion in Northern Ireland'. *ARK Research Update* 115 (2017): 1–8.

Gregg, Melissa, and Gregory J. Seigworth. *The Affect Theory Reader*. Durham, NC: Duke University Press, 2011.

Guibbory, Achsah. 'Erotic poetry'. In *The Cambridge Companion to John Donne*. Ed. Achsah Guibbory, Cambridge Companions to Literature. Cambridge: Cambridge University Press, 2006: 133–48.

Hallward, Peter. 'Desire – Cahiers pour l'analyse (An electronic edition)'. Cahiers. Kingston.Ac.Uk. Accessed 2 July 2019. http://cahiers.kingston.ac.uk/concepts/desire. html.

Halperin, David M. *One Hundred Years of Homosexuality: And Other Essays on Greek Love*. Hove: Psychology Press, 1990.

Hanna, Adam. *Northern Irish Poetry and Domestic Space*. Basingstoke: Palgrave, 2015.

Harrison, Phil. *The First Day*. London: Little, Brown Book Group, 2017. Kindle Edition.

Haslam, Richard. '"The Pose Arranged and Lingered Over": Visualizing the 'Troubles'". *Contemporary Irish Fiction: Themes, Tropes, Theories*. Ed. Liam Harte and Michael Parker. Basingstoke: Macmillan, 2000: 192–212.

Hayden, Joanne. '"I want to deal with the biggest themes possible" – interview with Wendy Erskine'. *Irish Independent*. 2018. Accessed 26 July 2019. https://www. independent.ie/entertainment/books/book-news/i-want-to-deal-with-the-biggest-themes-possible-wendy-erskine-37314614.html.

Hayes, Bernadette C., and Andrew McKinnon. 'Belonging without believing: Religion and attitudes towards gay marriage and abortion rights in Northern Ireland'. *Religion, State & Society* 46, no. 4 (2018): 351–66.

Heaney, Seamus. *Opened Ground: Selected Poems, 1966–1996*. London: Macmillan, 1999. Kindle Edition.

Henry, Claire. *Revisionist Rape-Revenge: Redefining a Film Genre*. London: Palgrave Macmillan, 2016.

Henry, Lee. 'Jan Carson, keeper of the flames'. *The Times*. 2019. Accessed 26 July 2019. https://www.thetimes.co.uk/article/jan-carson-keeper-of-the-flames-r8v59gnjf.

Hewitt, Christopher. 'Catholic grievances, Catholic nationalism and violence in Northern Ireland during the civil rights period: A reconsideration'. *British Journal of Sociology* 32, no. 3 (1981): 362–80.

Hewitt, Seán. 'Anna Burns's first two novels: Bold, terrifying, funny, profound'. *Irish Times*. 2018. Accessed 14 September 2019. https://www.irishtimes.com/culture/books/anna-burns-s-first-two-novels-bold-terrifying-funny-profound-1.3729146.

Hollywood, Brian. 'Dancing in the dark: Ecstasy, the dance culture, and moral panic in post ceasefire Northern Ireland'. *Critical Criminology* 8, no. 1 (1997): 62–77.

hooks, bell. *Feminist Theory: From Margin to Center*. London: Pluto Press, 2000.

Hope, Anna. *Expectation*. London: Doubleday, 2019.

Hughes, Michael. *Country*. London: John Murray, 2018. Kindle Edition.

Hume, Tim. 'Farmer orders Rihanna to cover up during risqué video shoot', *The Independent*, 28 September 2011.

Hunter, Walt. *Forms of a World: Contemporary Poetry and the Making of Globalization*. New York: Fordham University Press, 2019.

Impens, Florence. *Classical Presences in Irish Poetry after 1960*. Basingstoke: Palgrave, 2018.

Irish Times, 'Ep 302 Jan Carson on magic realism, women's voices & politics in the North'. *Irish Times Women's Podcast*. 2019. Accessed 26 July 2019. https://soundcloud.com/irishtimes-women/ep-302-optimistic-but-tired-is-what-we-all-are-in-the-north-jan-carson.

Iwasaka, Michiko, and Barre Toelken. *Ghosts and the Japanese*. Logan: Utah State University Press, 1994.

Iyengar, B. K. S. *Light on Yoga*. London: Harper Collins, 2015.

Jenkinson, Rosemary. *Aphrodite's Kiss and Further Stories*. Limavady: Whittrick, 2016.

Jenkinson, Rosemary. 'Banter and Booze – you can't write about Belfast without them'. *Irish Times*. 2016. Accessed 2 July 2019. https://www.irishtimes.com/culture/books/rosemary-jenkinson-banter-and-booze-you-can-t-write-about-belfast-without-them-1.2698502.

Jenkinson, Rosemary. *Catholic Boy*. Galway: Doire Press, 2018.

Jenkinson, Rosemary. 'Coronavirus: I feel half between house arrest and solitary confinement'. *Irish Times*. 2020. Accessed 1 September 2020. https://www.irishtimes.com/culture/books/coronavirus-i-feel-half-between-house-arrest-and-solitary-confinement-1.4340412.

Jenkinson, Rosemary. *Lifestyle Choice 10mg*. Galway: Doire Press, 2020. Proof copy.

John, Camillus. 'Interview with Phil Harrison: Author of The First Day And Staunch Pats Fan'. Litro.Co.Uk. 2017. Accessed 2 July 2019. https://www.litro.co.uk/2017/10/interview-phil-harrison-author-first-day-staunch-pats-fan/.

Kelleher, C. C. 'Mental health and "the Troubles" in Northern Ireland: Implications of civil unrest for health and wellbeing'. *Journal of Epidemiology & Community Health* (2003): 474–5.

Kennedy, Maev. 'Carthaginians sacrificed own children, archaeologists say'. *The Guardian*. 2014. Accessed 26 July 2019. https://www.theguardian.com/science/2014/jan/21/carthaginians-sacrificed-own-children-study.

Kennedy-Andrews, Elmer. *Fiction and the Northern Ireland Troubles since 1969: (De-) Constructing the North*. Dublin: Four Courts, 2002.

Kilroy, Claire. '*Milkman* By Anna Burns review – creepy invention at heart of an original, funny novel'. *The Guardian*. 2018. Accessed 14 September 2019. https://www.theguardian.com/books/2018/may/31/milkman-anna-burns-review-northern-ireland.

Kitchin, Rob, and Karen Lysaght. 'Sexual citizenship in Belfast, Northern Ireland'. *Gender, Place & Culture* 11, no. 1 (2004): 83–103. doi:10.1080/0966369042000188567.

Klesse, Christian. 'Bisexual women, non-monogamy and differentialist anti-promiscuity discourses'. *Sexualities* 8, no. 4 (2005): 445–64.

Kristeva, Julia. *Powers of Horror*. New York: Columbia University Press, 1982.

Lafrance, Marc. 'Skin studies'. *Body & Society* 24, nos 1–2 (2018): 3–32. doi:10.1177/1357034x18763065.

Lee, Jenny. 'Arts Q&A: Belfast author Jan Carson on Flannery O'Connor, Elliott Smith & Alfred Hitchcock'. *Irish News*. 2019. Accessed 26 July 2019. https://www.irishnews.com/arts/2019/04/11/news/arts-q-a-belfast-author-jan-carson-on-flannery-o-connor-elliott-smith-alfred-hitchcock-1592911/.

Lehner, Stefanie. ' "Parallel games" and queer memories: Performing LGBT testimonies in Northern Ireland'. *Irish University Review* 47, no. 1 (2017): 103–18.

Limpkin, Clive. *The Battle of Bogside*. Harmondsworth: Penguin, 1972.

Longley, Michael. *Collected Poems*. London: Jonathan Cape, 2006.

Lorde, Audre. *Your Silence Will Not Protect You*. London: Silver Press, 2017.

Love, Heather. *Feeling Backward*. Cambridge: Harvard University Press, 2007.

Magennis, Caroline. ' "That's not so comfortable for you, is it?": The spectre of misogyny in The Fall'. In *The Body in Pain in Irish Culture*. Ed. Fionnuala Dillane, Naomi McAreavey and Emilie Pine. Basingstoke: Palgrave, 2016.

Magennis, Caroline. *Sons of Ulster: Masculinities in the Contemporary Northern Irish Novel*. Oxford: Peter Lang, 2010.

Markham, Katie. 'Touring the post-conflict city'. In *Emotion, Affective Practices, and the Past in the Present*. Ed. Gary Campbell, Laurajane Smith and Margaret Wetherell. London: Routledge, 2018.

Marshall, Alex. 'Anna Burns: The new Booker Prize winner who may never write again'. *The Independent*, 2019. https://www.independent.co.uk/arts-entertainment/books/features/anna-burns-interview-milkman-booker-prize-winner-2018-next-book-writer-a8661321.html.

Martin, Richard. ' "Non specific threat (production still) 2003", Willie Doherty, 2007'. *Tate*. Accessed 14 September 2019. https://www.tate.org.uk/art/artworks/doherty-non-specific-threat-production-still-2003-p79361.

Mason, Rowena. 'Boris Johnson boasted of shaking hands on day sage warned not to'. *The Guardian*. 2020. Accessed 1 June 2020. https://www. theguardian.com/politics/2020/may/05/boris-johnson-boasted-of-shaking-hands-on-day-sage-warned-not-to.

McAllister, Kelly. 'Belfast's Wendy Erskine on debut short stories collection *Sweet Home*'. *Irish News*. 2018. Accessed 26 July 2019. https://www.irishnews.com/arts/2018/10/18/news/belfast-s-wendy-erskine-on-debut-short-stories-collection-sweet-home-1459153/.

McCann, Fiona. '"The good terrorist (s)"? Interrogating gender and violence in Ann Devlin's' "Naming the Names" and Anna Burns' No Bones'. *Estudios Irlandeses* 7 (2012): 69–78.

McCann, Fiona. *A Poetics of Dissensus: Confronting Violence in Contemporary Prose Writing from the North of Ireland*. Oxford: Peter Lang, 2014.

McDonald, Henry. 'Northern Ireland "punishment" attacks rise 60% in four years'. *The Guardian*. 2018. Accessed 26 July 2019. https://www.theguardian.com/uk-news/2018/mar/12/northern-ireland-punishment-attacks-rise-60-in-four-years.

McDonald, Henry. 'Sober Mayor bans "lustful" charity ball'. *The Guardian*. 2003. Accessed 14 September 2019. https://www.theguardian.com/uk/2003/feb/23/northernireland1.

McGill, Bernie. 'Dropping your gaze: A day of mindfulness and writing with Michelle Gibb and Bernie McGill'. 2018. Accessed 16 July 2019. http://berniemcgill.com/event/dropping-your-gaze-a-day-of-mindfulness-and-writing-with-michelle-gibb-and-bernie-mcgill-at-flowerfield-arts-centre-portstewart/.

McGill, Bernie. *Sleepwalkers and Other Stories*. Limavady: Whittrick, 2013.

McGuckian, Medbh. *Selected Poems*. Loughcrew: Gallery Books, 1997. Kindle Edition

McKee, Lyra. 'Suicide of the Ceasefire Babies'. *Mosaic*. 2016. Accessed 26 July 2019. https://mosaicscience.com/story/conflict-suicide-northern-ireland/.

McKittrick, David, Seamus Kelters, Brian Feeney, Chris Thornton and David McVea. *Lost Lives: The Stories of the Men, Women and Children Who Died as a Result of the Northern Ireland Troubles*. London: Random House, 2001.

McLaughlin, Greg, and Stephen Baker. 'The media, the peace dividend and "bread and butter" politics'. *Political Quarterly* 83, no. 2 (2012): 292–8.

McNamee, Eoin. 'Country by Michael Hughes: A hard, rigorous and necessary book'. *Irish Times*. 2018. Accessed 26 July 2019. https://www.irishtimes.com/culture/books/country-by-michael-hughes-a-hard-rigorous-and-necessary-book-1.3580957.

McVeigh, Paul. 'Anna Burns: The Booker winner on why she is unable to write'. *Irish Times*. 2018. Accessed 14 September 2019. https://www.irishtimes.com/culture/books/anna-burns-the-booker-winner-on-why-she-is-unable-to-write-1.3726472.

Media Mole, 'Will self knocks "simple" Sally Rooney – in interview plugging his promotional macarons'. *New Statesman*. 2019. Accessed 14 September 2019. https://www.newstatesman.com/politics/media/2019/02/will-self-knocks-simple-sally-rooney-interview-plugging-his-promotional.

Miller, Laura. 'A novel about coming of age amid the Troubles'. *New Yorker*. 2018. Accessed 14 September 2019. https://www.newyorker.com/magazine/2018/12/10/a-novel-about-coming-of-age-amid-the-troubles.

Mitchell, Kaye. 'Cleaving to the scene of shame: Stigmatized childhoods in The End of Alice and Two Girls, Fat and Thin'. *Contemporary Women's Writing* 7, no. 3 (2012): 309–27.

Morales-Ladrón, Marisol. '*Milkman* by Anna Burns: Silence as an architectural form of containment'. *Irish Times*. 2019. Accessed 14 September 2019. https://www.

irishtimes.com/culture/books/milkman-by-anna-burns-silence-as-an-architectural-form-of-containment-1.3988554.

Morrissey, Sinéad. *Between Here and There*. Manchester: Carcanet, 2002.

Mulhall, Anne. 'The ends of Irish studies? On whiteness, academia, and activism'. *Irish University Review* 50, no. 1 (2020): 94–111.

Napier, Susan J. *The Fantastic in Modern Japanese Literature*. London: Routledge, 2006.

National Gallery Online. 'Tenebrism'. Accessed 16 July 2019. https://www.nationalgallery.org.uk/paintings/glossary/tenebrism.

Neville, Stuart. *So Say the Fallen*. London: Vintage, 2016.

Nikolopoulou, Kalliopi. 'Deserting Achilles reflections on intimacy and disinheritance'. *European Journal of English Studies* 9, no. 3 (2005): 229–50. doi:10.1080/13825570500363484.

Nuttall, Deirdre, and Críostóir MacCarthaigh. 'A "Protestant folk?" – history Ireland'. *History Ireland*. 2017. Accessed 26 July 2019, https://www.historyireland.com/volume-25/a-protestant-folk/.

O'Connell, Sean. 'Violence and social memory in twentieth-century Belfast: Stories of Buck Alec Robinson'. *Journal of British Studies* 53, no. 3 (2014): 734–56. doi:10.1017/jbr.2014.76.

O'Donnell, Roisín. *Wild Quiet*. Dublin: New Island Books, 2016.

Park, David. *Gods and Angels*. London: Bloomsbury, 2016. Kindle Edition.

Patterson, Glenn. *Backstop Land*. London: Head of Zeus, 2019.

Patterson, Glenn. *The Rest Just Follows*. London: Faber, 2014.

Pelaschiar, Laura. 'Transforming Belfast: The evolving role of the city in Northern Irish fiction'. *Irish University Review* 30, no. 1 (2000): 117–31.

Penna, Dominic. 'Britons switched from "pleasure-seeking" to "pain-avoiding" mentality during coronavirus pandemic'. *The Telegraph*. 2020. Accessed 1 June 2020. https://www.telegraph.co.uk/news/2020/05/09/britons-switched-pleasure-seeking-pain-avoiding-mentality-coronavirus/.

Prosser, Jay. 'Skin memories'. In *Thinking through the Skin*. Ed. Sara Ahmed and Jackie Stacey. London: Routledge, 2001: 52–68.

Pryce, Alex. 'Selective traditions: Feminism and the poetry of Colette Bryce, Leontia Flynn and Sinéad Morrissey'. PhD diss., Oxford University, UK, 2014.

Quigley, Geraldine. *Music Love Drugs War*. London: Penguin, 2019.

Richtarik, Marilynn J. *Stewart Parker: A Life*. Oxford: Oxford University Press, 2012.

Ripatrazone, Nick. 'Why do so many writers love to run?' *The Atlantic*, 2015. https://www.theatlantic.com/entertainment/archive/2015/11/why-writers-run/415146/.

Rolston, Bill. 'Dealing with the past in Northern Ireland: The current state of play'. *Estudios Irlandeses* 8 (2013): 143–9.

Roy, David. 'Co Armagh author Michael Hughes on new Troubles novel *Country*'. *Irish News*. 2018. Accessed 26 July 2019. https://www.irishnews.com/arts/2018/08/16/news/co-armagh-author-michael-hughes-on-new-troubles-novel-country-1407922/.

RTÉ, 'Inquiry finds widespread abuse of children in care'. *RTÉ*. 2017. Accessed 14 September 2019. https://www.rte.ie/ news/2017/0120/846364-inquiry-into-alleged-child-abuse-to-publish-report/.

Runciman, David. 'I could fix that: Clinton'. *London Review of Books* 31, no. 24 (2009). Accessed 16 July 2019. https://www.lrb.co.uk/v31/n24/ david-runciman/i-could-fix-that.

Ruprecht Fadem, Maureen E. *The Literature of Northern Ireland: Spectral Borderlands*. New York: Palgrave Macmillan, 2015.

Scarry, Elaine. *The Body in Pain: The Making and Unmaking of the World*. USA: Oxford University Press, 1987.

Sedgwick, Eve. *Touching, Feeling: Affect, Pedagogy, Performativity*. Durham, NC: Duke University Press, 2003.

Sedgwick, Eve Kosofsky, Adam Frank and Irving E. Alexander, eds. *Shame and Its Sisters: A Silvan Tomkins Reader*. Durham, NC: Duke University Press, 1995.

Seltzer, Mark. *Serial Killers: Death and Life in America's Wound Culture*. London: Routledge, 2013.

Sherratt-Bado, Dawn Miranda. 'Keep her country: An interview with Michael Hughes'. *Honest Ulsterman*. 2019. Accessed 26 July 2019. https://humag.co/features/ keep-her-country.

Sherratt-Bado, Dawn Miranda. '"Things we'd rather forget": Trauma, the Troubles, and magical realism in post-Agreement Northern Irish women's short stories'. *Open Library of Humanities* 4, no. 2 (2018). doi:10.16995/olh.247.

Smallwood, Kathie Beckman, and Dorothy C. VanDyck. 'Menopause counseling: Coping with realities and myths'. *Journal of Sex Education and Therapy* 5, no. 2 (1979): 72–6.

Smyth, Lisa. 'The cultural politics of sexuality and reproduction in Northern Ireland'. *Sociology* 40, no. 4 (2006): 663–80.

Sneddon, Andrew, and John Privilege, eds. 'The supernatural in Ulster Scots literature and folklore reader'. Centre for Ulster Scots Studies, University of Ulster. Accessed 7 May 2019. https://www.ulster.ac.uk/__data/assets/pdf_file/0011/226595/ MAGUS.pdf.

Stacey, Jackie. *Teratologies: A Cultural Study of Cancer*. London: Routledge, 2013.

Steel, Jayne. *Demons, Hamlets and Femme Fatales: Representations of Irish Republicanism in Popular Fiction*. Bern: Peter Lang, 2007.

Steel, Jayne. 'Vampira: Representations of the Irish female terrorist', *Irish Studies Review* 6, no. 3 (1998): 273–84.

Studemann, Frederick. 'Man Booker winner Anna Burns on lessons from the "Powder Keg"'. *Financial Times*. 2018. Accessed 14 September 2019. https://www.ft.com/ content/67502218-d2b5-11e8-a9f2-7574db66bcd5.

Sweeney, Joanne. 'David Park: I wanted to try to delve as deeply as I could into a man's heart and soul'. *Irish News*. 2018. Accessed 2 March 2019. http://www.irishnews.

com/arts/2018/03/31/news/david-park-i-wanted-to-try-to-delve-as-deeply-as-i-could-into-a-man-s-heart-and-soul-1288709/.

Taylor, Julie. *Modernism and Affect*. Edinburgh: Edinburgh University Press, 2015.

Thomson, Alex. 'Lyra McKee's partner: Theresa May "derelict in her duties to Northern Ireland"'. *Channel 4 News*. 2019. Accessed 26 July 2019. https://www.channel4.com/news/lyra-mckees-partner-theresa-may-derelict-in-her-duties-to-northern-ireland.

Uys, Joachim D. K., and Raymond J. M. Niesink. 'Pharmacological aspects of the combined use of 3, 4 methylenedioxymethamphetamine (MDMA, ecstasy) and gamma-hydroxybutyric acid (GHB): A review of the literature'. *Drug and Alcohol Review* 24, no. 4 (2005): 359–68.

Van der Kolk, Bessel A. *The Body Keeps the Score: Brain, Mind, and Body in the Healing of Trauma*. London: Penguin Books, 2015.

Vardy, Christopher. 'Happier days for all of us? Childhood and abuse in *Death of a Murderer*'. In *Rupert Thomson: Critical Essays*. Ed. Rebecca Pohl and Christopher Vardy. London: Gylphi, 2016: 65–87.

Walker, Michael. 'Northern Ireland's increasing problem with racism'. *Amnesty International*. 2018. Accessed 13 August 2019. https://www.amnesty.org.uk/blogs/belfast-and-beyond/northern-irelands-increasing-problem-racism.

Walsh, Fintan. 'Saving Ulster from sodomy and hysteria: Sex, politics and performance', *Contemporary Theatre Review* 23, no. 3 (2013): 291–301.

Ward, Margaret. *The Missing Sex: Putting Women into History*. Dublin: Attic Press, 1991.

Wiegman, Robyn. 'The times we're in: Queer feminist criticism and the reparative "Turn"'. *Feminist Theory* 15 (2014): 4–25.

Wills, Clair. *Improprieties: Politics and Sexuality in Northern Irish Poetry*. Oxford: Clarendon Press, 1993.

Wilson, Robert McLiam. *Eureka Street*. London: Vintage, 1997.

Woolf, Virginia. *Mrs Dalloway*. Oxford: Oxford World's Classics, 2000.

Wulfhart, Nell. 'Running the world: Belfast'. *Runner's World*. 2017. Accessed 14 September 2019. https://www.runnersworld.com/races-places/g20848842/running-the-world-belfast/.

Yee, Shannon. 'The brightening up side'. In *Belfast Stories*. Ed. Lisa Frank and Paul McVeigh. Galway: Doire Press, 2019: 147–58.

Index

Lightning Source UK Ltd.
Milton Keynes UK
UKHW020721120921
390370UK00002B/89

9 781350 074729